Undergraduate Topics in Computer Science

Undergraduate Topics in Computer Science (UTiCS) delivers high-quality instructional content for under-graduates studying in all areas of computing and information science. From core foundational and theoretical material to final-year topics and applications, UTiCS books take a fresh, concise, and modern approach and are ideal for self-study or for a one- or two-semester course. The texts are all authored by established experts in their fields, reviewed by an international advisory board, and contain numerous examples and problems. Many include fully worked solutions.

For other titles published in this series, go to
http://www.springer.com/series/7592

Pankaj Jalote

A Concise Introduction to
Software Engineering

 Springer

Pankaj Jalote, Btech, MS, PhD
Department of Computer Science and Engineering
IIT Delhi, India

Undergraduate Topics in Computer Science ISSN: 1863-7310
ISBN: 978-1-84800-301-9   e-ISBN: 978-1-84800-302-6
DOI: 10.1007/978-1-84800-302-6

British Library Cataloguing in Publication Data
A catalogue record for this book is available from the British Library

Library of Congress Control Number: 2008933221

Springer Science+Business Media
springer.com

Preface

An introductory course on Software Engineering remains one of the hardest subjects to teach largely because of the wide range of topics the area encompasses. I have believed for some time that we often tend to teach too many concepts and topics in an introductory course resulting in shallow knowledge and little insight on application of these concepts. And Software Engineering is finally about application of concepts to efficiently engineer good software solutions.

Goals

I believe that an introductory course on Software Engineering should focus on imparting to students the knowledge and skills that are needed to successfully execute a commercial project of a few person-months effort while employing proper practices and techniques. It is worth pointing out that a vast majority of the projects executed in the industry today fall in this scope—executed by a small team over a few months. I also believe that by carefully selecting the concepts and topics, we can, in the course of a semester, achieve this. This is the motivation of this book.

The goal of this book is to introduce to the students a limited number of concepts and practices which will achieve the following two objectives:

– Teach the student the skills needed to execute a smallish commercial project.

– Provide the students necessary conceptual background for undertaking advanced studies in software engineering, through courses or on their own.

Organization

I have included in this book only those concepts that I believe are foundational and through which the two objectives mentioned above can be met. Advanced topics have been consciously left out. As executing a software project requires skills in two dimensions—engineering and project management—this book focuses on key tasks in these two dimensions, and discusses concepts and techniques that can be applied to effectively execute these tasks.

The book is organized in a simple manner, with one chapter for each of the key tasks in a project. For engineering, these tasks are requirements analysis and specification, architecture design, module level design, coding and unit testing, and testing. For project management, the key tasks are project planning and project monitoring and control, but both are discussed together in one chapter on project planning as even monitoring has to be planned. In addition, the book contains one chapter that clearly defines the problem domain of Software Engineering, and another chapter that discusses the central concept of software process which integrates the different tasks executed in a project.

Each chapter opens with some introduction and then clearly lists the chapter goals, or what the reader can expect to learn from the chapter. For the task covered in the chapter, the important concepts are first discussed, followed by a discussion of the output of the task, the desired quality properties of the output, and some practical methods and notations for performing the task. The explanations are supported by examples, and the key learnings are summarized in the end for the reader. The chapter ends with some self-assessment exercises.

Target Audience

The book is primarily intented for an introductory course on Software Engineering in any undergraduate or graduate program. It is targeted for students who know programming but have not had a formal exposure to software engineering.

The book can also be used by professionals who are in a similar state—know some programming but want to be introduced to the systematic approach of software engineering.

Teaching Support and Supplemental Resources

Though the book is self-contained, some teaching support and supplemental resources are available through a website. The URL is:

http://www.cse.iitd.ac.in/ConciseIntroToSE

The resources available on the site include:

- The powerpoint presentations for each chapter in ppt format so instructors can change them to suit their style.

- Various templates for different outputs in a project, that can be used for the student project in the course.

- A case study with most of the major outputs of the project.

- Some practice exercises for unit testing and inspections.

Acknowledgments

I would like to express my gratitude to my editor, Wayne Wheeler, who conceived this idea of a concise introductory book and created this opportunity.

I would also like to express my thanks to my wife, Shikha, and my daughters Sumedha and Sunanda for once again bearing with my moods and odd hours.

Pankaj Jalote
New Delhi, May 2008

Contents

1
The Software Problem

Ask any student who has had some programming experience the following question: You are given a problem for which you have to build a software system that most students feel will be approximately 10,000 lines of (say C or Java) code. If you are working full time on it, how long will it take you to build this system?

The answer of students is generally 1 to 3 months. And, given the programming expertise of the students, there is a good chance that they will be able to build the software and demo it to the professor within 2 months. With 2 months as the completion time, the productivity of the student will be 5000 lines of code (LOC) per person-month.

Now let us take an alternative scenario—we act as clients and pose the same problem to a company that is in the business of developing software for clients. Though there is no standard productivity figure and it varies a lot, it is fair to say a productivity figure of 1000 LOC per person-month is quite respectable (though it can be as low as 100 LOC per person-month for embedded systems). With this productivity, a team of professionals in a software organization will take 10 person-months to build this software system.

Why this difference in productivity in the two scenarios? Why is it that the same students who can produce software at a productivity of a few thousand LOC per month while in college end up producing only about a thousand LOC per month when working in a company?

The answer, of course, is that two different things are being built in the two scenarios. In the first, a *student system* is being built which is primarily meant for demonstration purposes, and is not expected to be used later. Because it is

P. Jalote, *A Concise Introduction to Software Engineering*,
DOI: 10.1007/978-1-84800-302-6_1, © Springer-Verlag London Limited 2008

not to be used, nothing of significance depends on the software and the presence of bugs and lack of quality is not a major concern. Neither are the other quality issues like usability, maintainability, portability etc.

On the other hand, an *industrial-strength software system* is built to solve some problem of a client and is used by the client's organization for operating some part of business, and a malfunction of such a system can have huge impact in terms of financial or business loss, inconvenience to users, or loss of property and life. Consequently, the software system needs to be of high quality with respect to properties like reliability, usability, portability, etc.

This need for high quality and to satisfy the the end users has a major impact on the way software is developed and its cost. The rule of thumb Brooks gives suggests that the industrial-strength software may cost about 10 times the student software [16].

The software industry is largely interested in developing industrial-strength software, and the area of software engineering focuses on how to build such systems. That is, the problem domain for software engineering is industrial-strength software. In the rest of the book, when we use the term *software*, we mean industrial-strength software. In the remainder of this chapter, we will learn

– That quality, cost, and schedule are the main forces that drive a (industrial-strength) software project.

– How cost and productivity are defined and measured for such a project, and how quality of software is characterized and measured.

– That large scale and change are important attributes of the problem domain and solution approaches have to handle them.

1.1 Cost, Schedule, and Quality

Though the need for high quality distinguishes industrial strength software from others, cost and schedule are other major driving forces for such software. In the industrial-strength software domain, there are three basic forces at play—cost, schedule, and quality. The software should be produced at reasonable cost, in a reasonable time, and should be of good quality. These three parameters often drive and define a software project.

Industrial-strength software is very expensive primarily due to the fact that software development is extremely labor-intensive. To get an idea of the costs involved, let us consider the current state of practice in the industry. Lines of code (LOC) or thousands of lines of code (KLOC) delivered is by far the most commonly used measure of software size in the industry. As the main cost of producing software is the manpower employed, the cost of developing software is generally measured in terms of person-months of effort spent in development. And productivity is frequently measured in the industry in terms of LOC (or KLOC) per person-month.

The productivity in the software industry for writing fresh code generally ranges from few hundred to about 1000+ LOC per person-month. This productivity is over the entire development cycle, not just the coding task. Software companies often charge the client for whom they are developing the software between $3000 - $15,000 per person-month. With a productivity of 1000 LOC per person-month, it means that each line of delivered code costs between $3 and $15! And even small projects can easily end up with software of 50,000 LOC. With this productivity, such a software project will cost between $150,000 and $750,000!

Schedule is another important factor in many projects. Business trends are dictating that the time to market of a product should be reduced; that is, the cycle time from concept to delivery should be small. For software this means that it needs to be developed faster, and within the specified time. Unfortunately, the history of software is full of cases where projects have been substantially late.

Clearly, therefore, reducing the cost and the cycle time for software development are central goals of software engineering. Productivity in terms of output (KLOC) per person-month can adequately capture both cost and schedule concerns. If productivity is higher, it should be clear that the cost in terms of person-months will be lower (the same work can now be done with fewer person-months). Similarly, if productivity is higher, the potential of developing the software in less time improves—a team of higher productivity will finish a job in less time than a same-size team with lower productivity. (The actual time the project will take, of course, depends also on the number of people allocated to the project.) Hence, pursuit of higher productivity is a basic driving force behind software engineering and a major reason for using the different tools and techniques.

Besides cost and schedule, the other major factor driving software engineering is quality. Today, quality is one of the main mantras, and business strategies are designed around it. Unfortunately, a large number of instances have occurred regarding the unreliability of software—the software often does not do what it is supposed to do or does something it is not supposed to do. Clearly, developing high-quality software is another fundamental goal of software engineering. However, while cost is generally well understood, the concept of quality in the context of software needs further elaboration.

The international standard on software product quality [55] suggests that

Figure 1.1: Software quality attributes.

software quality comprises six main attributes, as shown in Figure 1.1. These attributes can be defined as follows:

- **Functionality.** The capability to provide functions which meet stated and implied needs when the software is used.

- **Reliability.** The capability to provide failure-free service.

- **Usability.** The capability to be understood, learned, and used.

- **Efficiency.** The capability to provide appropriate performance relative to the amount of resources used.

- **Maintainability.** The capability to be modified for purposes of making corrections, improvements, or adaptation.

- **Portability.** The capability to be adapted for different specified environments without applying actions or means other than those provided for this purpose in the product.

With multiple dimensions to quality, different projects may emphasize different attributes, and a global single number for quality is not possible. However, despite the fact that there are many quality attributes, reliability is generally accepted to be the main quality criterion. As unreliability of software is due to the presence of defects in the software, one measure of quality is the number of defects in the delivered software per unit size (generally taken to be thousands of lines of code, or KLOC). With this as the major quality criterion, the quality objective is to reduce the number of defects per KLOC as much as possible. Current best practices in software engineering have been able to reduce the defect density to less than 1 defect per KLOC.

To determine the quality of a software product, we need to determine the number of defects in the software that was delivered. This number is clearly not known at delivery time and may never be known. One approach to measure quality is to log the defects found in 6 months (or 1 year) after delivery and define quality with respect to these defects. This means that quality of delivered software can only be determined 6 months after its delivery. The defect density can, however, also be estimated from past data of similar projects—if similar approaches are being used, then it is expected that the current project will have similar defect density as the past projects.

It should be pointed out that to use this definition of quality, what a defect is must be clearly defined. A defect could be some problem in the software that causes the software to crash or a problem that causes an output to be not properly aligned or one that misspells some word, etc. The exact definition of what is considered a defect will clearly depend on the project or the standards the organization developing the project uses (typically it is the latter).

Besides reliability, another quality attribute of great interest is maintainability. Once the software is delivered and deployed, it enters the *maintenance* phase. Why is maintenance needed for software, when software has no physical components that can degrade with age? Software needs to be maintained because of the residual defects remaining in the system. It is commonly believed that the state of the art today is limited and developing software with zero defect density is not possible. These defects, once discovered, need to be removed, leading to what is called *corrective maintenance*. Maintenance is also needed to change the delivered software to satisfy the enhanced needs of the users and the environment, leading to *adaptive maintenance*. Over the life of a software system, maintenance cost can far exceed the cost of original development. The maintenance-to-development-cost ratio has been variously suggested as 80:20, 70:30, or 60:40. Due to this high cost, maintainability attribute of delivered software is of high interest—it is clearly desirable to have software systems that are easier to maintain.

1.2 Scale and Change

Though cost, schedule, and quality are the main driving forces for a project in our problem domain (of industry strength software), there are some other characteristics of the problem domain that also influence the solution approaches employed. We focus on two such characteristics—scale and change.

Most industrial-strength software systems tend to be large and complex, requiring tens of thousands of lines of code. Sizes of some of the well-known software products are given in Table 1.1.

As can be expected, development of a large system requires a different set of methods compared to developing a small system, as the methods that are used for developing small systems often do not scale up to large systems. An example will illustrate this point. Consider the problem of counting people in a room versus taking a census of a country. Both are essentially counting problems. But the methods used for counting people in a room will just not work when

Table 1.1: Size in KLOC of some well-known products.

Size (KLOC)	Software	Languages
980	gcc	ansic, cpp, yacc
320	perl	perl, ansic, sh
200	openssl	ansic, cpp, perl
100	apache	ansic, sh
65	sendmail	ansic
30,000	Red Hat Linux	ansic, cpp
40,000	Windows XP	ansic, cpp

taking a census. A different set of methods will have to be used for conducting a census, and the census problem will require considerably more management, organization, and validation, in addition to counting.

Similarly, methods that one can use to develop programs of a few hundred lines cannot be expected to work when software of a few hundred thousand lines needs to be developed. A different set of methods must be used for developing large software.

Any software project involves the use of engineering and project management. In small projects, informal methods for development and management can be used. However, for large projects, both have to be much more rigorous, as illustrated in Figure 1.2. In other words, to successfully execute a project, a proper method for engineering the system has to be employed and the project has to be tightly managed to make sure that cost, schedule, and quality are under control. Large scale is a key characteristic of the problem domain and the solution approaches should employ tools and techniques that have the ability to build large software systems.

Change is another characteristic of the problem domain which the approaches for development must handle. As the complete set of requirements for the system is generally not known (often cannot be known at the start of the project) or stated, as development proceeds and time passes, additional requirements are identified, which need to be incorporated in the software being developed. This need for changes requires that methods for development embrace change and accommodate it efficiently. Change requests can be quite disruptive to a project, and if not handled properly, can consume up to 30 to 40% of the development cost [14].

As discussed above, software has to be changed even after it has been deployed. Though traditionally changes in software during maintenance have been distinguished from changes that occur while the development is taking place, these lines are blurring, as fundamentally the changes in both of these scenarios

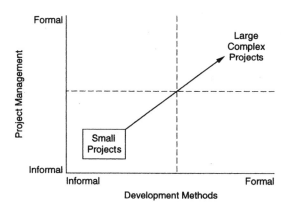

Figure 1.2: The problem of scale.

are similar—existing source code needs to be changed due to some changes in the requirements or due to some defects that need to be removed.

Overall, as the world changes faster, software has to change faster, even while under development. Changes in requirements are therefore a characteristic of the problem domain. In today's world, approaches that cannot accept and accommodate change are of little use—they can solve only those few problems that are change resistant.

1.3 Summary

– The problem domain for software engineering is industrial-strength software. This software is meant to solve some problem of some set of users, and is expected to be of high quality.

– In this problem domain, cost, schedule, and quality are basic driving forces. Hence, methods and tools that will be used for solving problems in this domain must ensure high productivity and high quality.

– Productivity is measured as amount of output per unit of input resource. In software, output can be measured in terms of lines of code delivered, and as human time is the main resource, input can be measured as person-months. Productivity can therefore be measured as lines of code delivered per person-month.

– Software quality has many attributes which include functionality, reliability, usability, efficiency, maintainability, and portability. Reliability is often

considered as the main quality attribute, and as unreliability in software is
due to defects in the software, quality can be characterized by number of
defects per thousand lines of code.

– The problems in this domain often tend to be very large and where the
needs of the customers change fast. Hence the techniques used for developing
industrial-strength software should be such that they are capable of building
large software systems, and have the capability to handle changes.

Self-Assessment Exercises

1. What are the main differences between a student software and industrial-strength
software?
2. If developing a program for solving a problem requires effort E, it is estimated
that an industrial-strength software for solving that problem will require 10E
effort. Where do you think this extra effort cost is spent?
3. What measurements will you take in a project to measure the productivity, and
how will you determine the productivity from these measures?
4. What are the different attributes of software quality? If for an accounting software we are most interested in ensuring that the software does not make any
computation mistakes, then which of the quality attributes should we be most
concerned about?
5. What are some of the project management tasks that you will do differently for
a large project as compared to a small project? How will your execution of these
tasks change?
6. Suppose changes are to be made to a software system that is in operation. Why
will changes to such a system cost a lot more than just making changes to the
source code files?

2

Software Processes

Now that we have a better understanding of the problem domain that software engineering deals with, let us orient our discussion to software engineering itself. *Software engineering* is defined as the systematic approach to the development, operation, maintenance, and retirement of software [52].

We have seen that besides delivering software, high quality, low cost, and low cycle time are also goals which software engineering must achieve. In other words, the systematic approach must help achieve a high quality and productivity (Q&P). In software, the three main factors that influence Q&P are people, processes, and technology. That is, the final quality delivered and productivity achieved depends on the skills of the people involved in the software project, the processes people use to perform the different tasks in the project, and the tools they use.

As it is people who ultimately develop and deliver (and productivity is measured with respect to people's effort as the basic input), the main job of processes is to help people achieve higher Q&P by specifying what tasks to do and how to do them. Tools are aids that help people perform some of the tasks more efficiently and with fewer errors. It should therefore be clear that to satisfy the objective of delivering software with high Q&P, processes form the core. Consequently, in software engineering, the focus is primarily on processes, which are referred to as the systematic approach in the definition given above. It is this focus on process that distinguishes software engineering from most other computing disciplines. Many other computing disciplines focus on some type of product—operating systems, databases, etc.—while software engineering focuses on the process for producing the products.

P. Jalote, *A Concise Introduction to Software Engineering*,
DOI: 10.1007/978-1-84800-302-6_2, © Springer-Verlag London Limited 2008

As processes form the heart of software engineering, with tools and technology providing support to efficiently execute the processes, this book focuses primarily on processes. In this chapter we will discuss:

– Role of a process and a process model in a project.

– Various component processes in the software process and the key role of the development process and the project management process.

– Various models for the development process—waterfall, prototyping, iterative, RUP, timeboxing, and XP.

– The overall structure of the project management process and its key phases.

2.1 Process and Project

A process is a sequence of steps performed for a given purpose [52]. As mentioned earlier, while developing (industrial strength) software, the purpose is to develop software to satisfy the needs of some users or clients, as shown in Figure 2.1. A *software project* is one instance of this problem, and the development process is what is used to achieve this purpose.

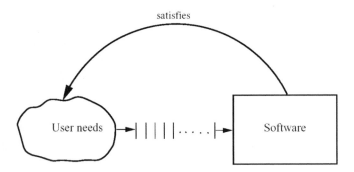

Figure 2.1: Basic problem.

So, for a project its development process plays a key role—it is by following the process the desired end goal of delivering the software is achieved. However, as discussed earlier, it is not sufficient to just reach the final goal of having the desired software, but we want that the project be done at low cost and in low cycle time, and deliver high-quality software. The role of process increases due to these additional goals, and though many processes can achieve the basic goal of developing software in Figure 2.1, to achieve high Q&P we need some "optimum" process. It is this goal that makes designing a process a challenge.

We must distinguish process specification or description from the process itself. A process is a dynamic entity which captures the actions performed. Process specification, on the other hand, is a description of process which presumably can be followed in some project to achieve the goal for which the process is designed.

In a project, a process specification may be used as the process the project plans to follow. The actual process is what is actually done in the project. Note that the actual process can be different from the planned process, and ensuring that the specified process is being followed is a nontrivial problem. However, in this book, we will assume that the planned and actual processes are the same and will not distinguish between the two and will use the term *process* to refer to both.

A *process model* specifies a general process, which is "optimum" for a class of projects. That is, in the situations for which the model is applicable, using the process model as the project's process will lead to the goal of developing software with high Q&P. A process model is essentially a compilation of best practices into a "recipe" for success in the project. In other words, a process is a means to reach the goals of high quality, low cost, and low cycle time, and a process model provides a process structure that is well suited for a class of projects.

A process is often specified at a high level as a sequence of stages. The sequence of steps for a stage is the process for that stage, and is often referred to as a subprocess of the process.

2.2 Component Software Processes

As defined above, a process is the sequence of steps executed to achieve a goal. Since many different goals may have to be satisfied while developing software, multiple processes are needed. Many of these do not concern software engineering, though they do impact software development. These could be considered nonsoftware process. Business processes, social processes, and training processes are all examples of processes that come under this. These processes also affect the software development activity but are beyond the purview of software engineering.

The processes that deal with the technical and management issues of software development are collectively called the *software process*. As a software project will have to engineer a solution and properly manage the project, there are clearly two major components in a software process—a *development process* and a *project management process*. The development process specifies all the engineering activities that need to be performed, whereas the management process specifies how to plan and control these activities so that cost, schedule, quality, and other objectives are met. Effective development and project management processes are the key to achieving the objectives of delivering the desired software satisfying the user needs, while ensuring high productivity and quality.

During the project many products are produced which are typically composed of many items (for example, the final source code may be composed of many source files). These items keep evolving as the project proceeds, creating many versions on the way. As development processes generally do not focus on evolution and changes, to handle them another process called *software configuration control process* is often used. The objective of this component process is to primarily deal with managing change, so that the integrity of the products is not violated despite changes.

These three constituent processes focus on the projects and the products and can be considered as comprising the *product engineering processes*, as their main objective is to produce the desired product. If the software process can be viewed as a static entity, then these three component processes will suffice. However, a software process itself is a dynamic entity, as it must change to adapt to our increased understanding about software development and availability of newer technologies and tools. Due to this, a process to manage the software process is needed.

The basic objective of the process management process is to improve the software process. By *improvement*, we mean that the capability of the process to produce quality goods at low cost is improved. For this, the current software process is studied, frequently by studying the projects that have been done using the process. The whole process of understanding the current process, analyzing its properties, determining how to improve, and then affecting the improvement is dealt with by the *process management process*.

The relationship between these major component processes is shown in Figure 2.2. These component processes are distinct not only in the type of activities performed in them, but typically also in the people who perform the activities specified by the process. In a typical project, development activities are performed by programmers, designers, testers, etc.; the project management process activities are performed by the project management; configuration control process activities are performed by a group generally called the *configuration controller*; and the process management process activities are performed by the *software engineering process group* (SEPG).

In this book, we will focus primarily on processes relating to product

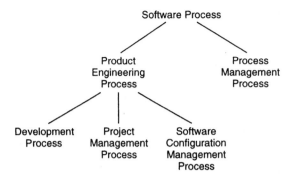

Figure 2.2: Software processes.

engineering, particularly the development and project management processes. Much of the book discusses the different phases of a development process and the subprocesses or *methodologies* used for executing these phases. For the rest of the book, we will use the term *software process* to mean product engineering processes, unless specified otherwise.

2.3 Software Development Process Models

For the software development process, the goal is to produce a high-quality software product. It therefore focuses on activities directly related to production of the software, for example, design, coding, and testing. As the development process specifies the major development and quality control activities that need to be performed in the project, it forms the core of the software process. The management process is often decided based on the development process.

A project's development process defines the tasks the project should perform, and the order in which they should be done. A process limits the degrees of freedom for a project by specifying what types of activities must be undertaken and in what order, such that the "shortest" (or the most efficient) path is obtained from the user needs to the software satisfying these needs. The process drives a project and heavily influences the outcome.

As discussed earlier, a process model specifies a general process, usually as a set of stages in which a project should be divided, the order in which the stages should be executed, and any other constraints and conditions on the execution of stages. The basic premise behind a process model is that, in the situations for which the model is applicable, using the process model as the project's process will lead to low cost, high quality, reduced cycle time, or provide other benefits. In other words, the process model provides generic guidelines for developing a suitable process for a project.

Due to the importance of the development process, various models have been proposed. In this section we will discuss some of the major models.

2.3.1 Waterfall Model

The simplest process model is the *waterfall model*, which states that the phases are organized in a linear order. The model was originally proposed by Royce [74], though variations of the model have evolved depending on the nature of activities and the flow of control between them. In this model, a project begins with feasibility analysis. Upon successfully demonstrating the feasibility of a project, the requirements analysis and project planning begins. The design starts after the requirements analysis is complete, and coding begins after the design is complete. Once the programming is completed, the code is integrated and testing is done. Upon successful completion of testing, the system is installed. After this, the regular operation and maintenance of the system takes place. The model is shown in Figure 2.3.

The basic idea behind the phases is *separation of concerns*—each phase deals with a distinct and separate set of concerns. By doing this, the large and complex task of building the software is broken into smaller tasks (which, by themselves, are still quite complex) of specifying requirements, doing design, etc. Separating the concerns and focusing on a select few in a phase gives a better handle to the engineers and managers in dealing with the complexity of the problem.

The requirements analysis phase is mentioned as "analysis and planning." *Planning* is a critical activity in software development. A good plan is based on the requirements of the system and should be done before later phases begin. However, in practice, detailed requirements are not necessary for planning. Consequently, planning usually overlaps with the requirements analysis, and a plan is ready before the later phases begin. This plan is an additional input to all the later phases.

Linear ordering of activities has some important consequences. First, to clearly identify the end of a phase and the beginning of the next, some certification mechanism has to be employed at the end of each phase. This is usually done by some verification and validation means that will ensure that the output of a phase is consistent with its input (which is the output of the previous phase), and that the output of the phase is consistent with the overall requirements of the system.

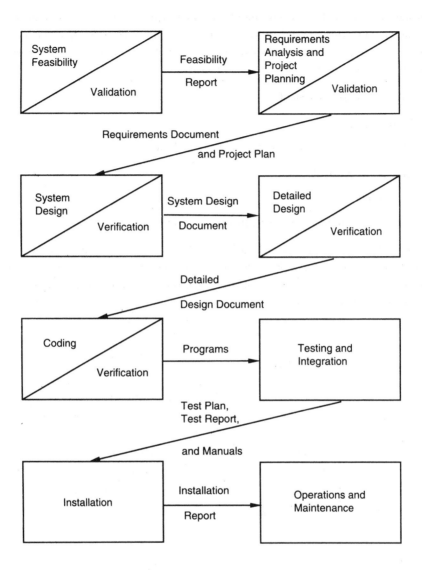

Figure 2.3: The waterfall model.

The consequence of the need for certification is that each phase must have some defined output that can be evaluated and certified. That is, when the activities of a phase are completed, there should be some product that is produced by that phase. The outputs of the earlier phases are often called *work products* and are usually in the form of documents like the requirements document or design document. For the coding phase, the output is the code. Though the set of documents that should be produced in a project is dependent on how the process is implemented, the following documents generally form a reasonable set that should be produced in each project:

- Requirements document

- Project plan

- Design documents (architecture, system, detailed)

- Test plan and test reports

- Final code

- Software manuals (e.g., user, installation, etc.)

One of the main advantages of the waterfall model is its simplicity. It is conceptually straightforward and divides the large task of building a software system into a series of cleanly divided phases, each phase dealing with a separate logical concern. It is also easy to administer in a contractual setup—as each phase is completed and its work product produced, some amount of money is given by the customer to the developing organization.

The waterfall model, although widely used, has some strong limitations. Some of the key limitations are:

1. It assumes that the requirements of a system can be frozen (i.e., baselined) before the design begins. This is possible for systems designed to automate an existing manual system. But for new systems, determining the requirements is difficult as the user does not even know the requirements. Hence, having unchanging requirements is unrealistic for such projects.

2. Freezing the requirements usually requires choosing the hardware (because it forms a part of the requirements specification). A large project might take a few years to complete. If the hardware is selected early, then due to the speed at which hardware technology is changing, it is likely that the final software will use a hardware technology on the verge of becoming obsolete. This is clearly not desirable for such expensive software systems.

3. It follows the "big bang" approach—the entire software is delivered in one shot at the end. This entails heavy risks, as the user does not know until the very end what they are getting. Furthermore, if the project runs out of money in the middle, then there will be no software. That is, it has the "all or nothing" value proposition.

4. It encourages "requirements bloating". Since all requirements must be specified at the start and only what is specified will be delivered, it encourages

the users and other stakeholders to add even those features which they think might be needed (which finally may not get used).

5. It is a document-driven process that requires formal documents at the end of each phase.

Despite these limitations, the waterfall model has been the most widely used process model. It is well suited for routine types of projects where the requirements are well understood. That is, if the developing organization is quite familiar with the problem domain and the requirements for the software are quite clear, the waterfall model works well, and may be the most efficient process.

2.3.2 Prototyping

The goal of a prototyping-based development process is to counter the first limitation of the waterfall model. The basic idea here is that instead of freezing the requirements before any design or coding can proceed, a throwaway prototype is built to help understand the requirements. This prototype is developed based on the currently known requirements. Development of the prototype obviously undergoes design, coding, and testing, but each of these phases is not done very formally or thoroughly. By using this prototype, the client can get an actual feel of the system, which can enable the client to better understand the requirements of the desired system. This results in more stable requirements that change less frequently.

Prototyping is an attractive idea for complicated and large systems for which there is no manual process or existing system to help determine the requirements. In such situations, letting the client "play" with the prototype provides invaluable and intangible inputs that help determine the requirements for the system. It is also an effective method of demonstrating the feasibility of a certain approach. This might be needed for novel systems, where it is not clear that constraints can be met or that algorithms can be developed to implement the requirements. In both situations, the risks associated with the projects are being reduced through the use of prototyping. The process model of the prototyping approach is shown in Figure 2.4.

A development process using throwaway prototyping typically proceeds as follows [40]. The development of the prototype typically starts when the preliminary version of the requirements specification document has been developed. At this stage, there is a reasonable understanding of the system and its needs and which needs are unclear or likely to change. After the prototype has been developed, the end users and clients are given an opportunity to use and explore the prototype. Based on their experience, they provide feedback to the

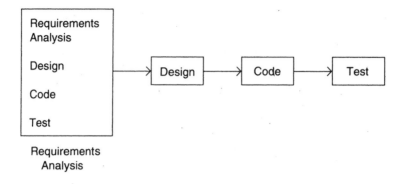

Figure 2.4: The prototyping model.

developers regarding the prototype: what is correct, what needs to be modified, what is missing, what is not needed, etc. Based on the feedback, the prototype is modified to incorporate some of the suggested changes that can be done easily, and then the users and the clients are again allowed to use the system. This cycle repeats until, in the judgment of the prototype developers and analysts, the benefit from further changing the system and obtaining feedback is outweighed by the cost and time involved in making the changes and obtaining the feedback. Based on the feedback, the initial requirements are modified to produce the final requirements specification, which is then used to develop the production quality system.

For prototyping for the purposes of requirement analysis to be feasible, its cost must be kept low. Consequently, only those features are included in the prototype that will have a valuable return from the user experience. Exception handling, recovery, and conformance to some standards and formats are typically not included in prototypes. In prototyping, as the prototype is to be discarded, there is no point in implementing those parts of the requirements that are already well understood. Hence, the focus of the development is to include those features that are not properly understood. And the development approach is "quick and dirty" with the focus on quick development rather than quality. Because the prototype is to be thrown away, only minimal documentation needs to be produced during prototyping. For example, design documents, a test plan, and a test case specification are not needed during the development of the prototype. Another important cost-cutting measure is to reduce testing. Because testing consumes a major part of development expenditure during regular software development, this has a considerable impact in reducing costs. By using these types of cost-cutting methods, it is possible to keep the cost of the prototype to less than a few percent of the total development cost.

And the returns from this extra cost can be substantial. First, the experience of developing the prototype will reduce the cost of the actual software development. Second, as requirements will be more stable now due to the feedback from the prototype, there will be fewer changes in the requirements. Consequently the costs incurred due to changes in the requirements will be substantially reduced. Third, the quality of final software is likely to be far superior, as the experience engineers have obtained while developing the prototype will enable them to create a better design, write better code, and do better testing. And finally, developing a prototype mitigates many risks that exist in a project where requirements are not well known.

Overall, prototyping is well suited for projects where requirements are hard to determine and the confidence in the stated requirements is low. In such projects where requirements are not properly understood in the beginning, using the prototyping process model can be the most effective method for developing the software. It is also an excellent technique for reducing some types of risks associated with a project.

2.3.3 Iterative Development

The iterative development process model counters the third and fourth limitations of the waterfall model and tries to combine the benefits of both prototyping and the waterfall model. The basic idea is that the software should be developed in increments, each increment adding some functional capability to the system until the full system is implemented.

The iterative enhancement model [4] is an example of this approach. In the first step of this model, a simple initial implementation is done for a subset of the overall problem. This subset is one that contains some of the key aspects of the problem that are easy to understand and implement and which form a useful and usable system. A *project control list* is created that contains, in order, all the tasks that must be performed to obtain the final implementation. This project control list gives an idea of how far along the project is at any given step from the final system.

Each step consists of removing the next task from the list, designing the implementation for the selected task, coding and testing the implementation, performing an analysis of the partial system obtained after this step, and updating the list as a result of the analysis. These three phases are called *the design phase, implementation phase*, and *analysis phase*. The process is iterated until the project control list is empty, at which time the final implementation of the system will be available. The iterative enhancement model is shown in Figure 2.5.

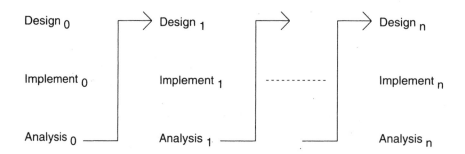

Figure 2.5: The iterative enhancement model.

The project control list guides the iteration steps and keeps track of all tasks that must be done. Based on the analysis, one of the tasks in the list can include redesign of defective components or redesign of the entire system. However, redesign of the system will generally occur only in the initial steps. In the later steps, the design would have stabilized and there is less chance of redesign. Each entry in the list is a task that should be performed in one step of the iterative enhancement process and should be simple enough to be completely understood. Selecting tasks in this manner will minimize the chances of error and reduce the redesign work. The design and implementation phases of each step can be performed in a top-down manner or by using some other technique.

Though there are clear benefits of iterative development, particularly in allowing changing requirements, not having the all-or-nothing risk, etc., there are some costs associated with iterative development also. For example, as the requirements for future iterations are not known, the design of a system may not be too robust. Also, changes may have to be made to the existing system to accommodate requirements of the future iterations, leading to extra rework and/or discarding of work done earlier. Overall, it may not offer the best technical solution, but the benefits may outweigh the costs in many projects.

Another common approach for iterative development is to do the requirements and the architecture design in a standard waterfall or prototyping approach, but deliver the software iteratively. That is, the building of the system, which is the most time and effort-consuming task, is done iteratively, though most of the requirements are specified upfront. We can view this approach as having one iteration delivering the requirements and the architecture plan, and then further iterations delivering the software in increments. At the start of each delivery iteration, which requirements will be implemented in this release are decided, and then the design is enhanced and code developed to implement the requirements. The iteration ends with delivery of a working software system providing some value to the end user. Selecting of requirements for an iteration is done primarily based on the value the requirement provides to the end users and how critical they are for supporting other requirements. This approach is shown in Figure 2.6.

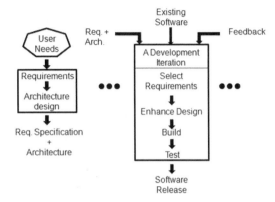

Figure 2.6: Iterative delivery approach.

The advantage of this approach is that as the requirements are mostly known upfront, an overall view of the system is available and a proper architecture can be designed which can remain relatively stable. With this, hopefully rework in development iterations will diminish. At the same time, the value to the end customer is delivered iteratively so it does not have the all-or-nothing risk. Also, since the delivery is being done incrementally, and planning and execution of each iteration is done separately, feedback from an iteration can be incorporated in the next iteration. Even new requirements that may get uncovered can also be incorporated. Hence, this model of iterative development also provides some of the benefits of the model discussed above.

The iterative approach is becoming extremely popular, despite some difficulties in using it in this context. There are a few key reasons for its increasing popularity. First and foremost, in today's world clients do not want to invest too much without seeing returns. In the current business scenario, it is preferable to see returns continuously of the investment made. The iterative model permits this—after each iteration some working software is delivered, and the risk to the client is therefore limited. Second, as businesses are changing rapidly today, they never really know the "complete" requirements for the software, and there is a need to constantly add new capabilities to the software to adapt the business to changing situations. Iterative process allows this. Third, each iteration provides a working system for feedback, which helps in developing stable requirements for the next iteration. Below we will describe some other process models, all of them using some iterative approach.

2.3.4 Rational Unified Process

Rational Unified Process (RUP) [51, 63] is another iterative process model
that was designed by Rational, now part of IBM. Though it is a general process model, it was designed for object-oriented development using the Unified
Modeling Language (UML). (We will discuss these topics in a later chapter).

RUP proposes that development of software be divided into *cycles*, each
cycle delivering a fully working system. Generally, each cycle is executed as a
separate project whose goal is to deliver some additional capability to an existing system (built by the previous cycle). Hence, for a project, the process for a
cycle forms the overall process. Each cycle itself is broken into four consecutive
phases:

- Inception phase

- Elaboration phase

- Construction phase

- Transition phase

Each phase has a distinct purpose, and completion of each phase is a well-
defined milestone in the project with some clearly defined outputs. The purpose
of the inception phase is to establish the goals and scope of the project, and
completion of this phase is the *lifecycle objectives* milestone. This milestone
should specify the vision and high-level capability of the eventual system, what
business benefits it is expected to provide, some key illustrative use cases of the
system, key risks of the project, and a basic plan of the project regarding the
cost and schedule. Based on the output of this phase, a go/no-go decision may
be taken. And if the project is to proceed, then this milestone represents that
there is a shared vision among the stakeholders and they agree to the project,
its vision, benefits, cost, usage, etc.

In the elaboration phase, the architecture of the system is designed, based
on the detailed requirements analysis. The completion of this phase is the *lifecycle architecture* milestone. At the end of this phase, it is expected that most
of the requirements have been identified and specified, and the architecture of
the system has been designed (and specified) in a manner that it addresses the
technical risks identified in the earlier phase. In addition, a high-level project
plan for the project has been prepared showing the remaining phases and iterations in those, and the current perception of risks. By the end of this phase,

the critical engineering decisions regarding the choice of technologies, architecture, etc. have been taken, and a detailed understanding of the project exists. Outputs of this milestone allow technical evaluation of the proposed solution, as well as a better informed decision about cost-benefit analysis of the project.

In the construction phase, the software is built and tested. This phase results in the software product to be delivered, along with associated user and other manuals, and successfully completing this phase results in the *initial operational capability* milestone being achieved.

The purpose of the transition phase is to move the software from the development environment to the client's environment, where it is to be hosted. This is a complex task which can require additional testing, conversion of old data for this software to work, training of personnel, etc. The successful execution of this phase results in achieving the milestone *product release*. The different phases and milestones in RUP are shown in Figure 2.7.

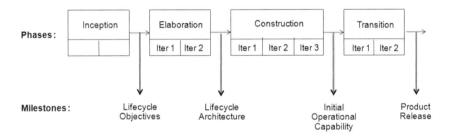

Figure 2.7: The RUP model.

Though these phases are consecutive, each phase itself may have multiple iterations, with each iteration delivering to an internal or external customer some well-defined output which is often a part of the final deliverable of that phase's milestone. Generally, it is expected that the construction phase will be broken into multiple iterations, each iteration producing a working system which can be used for feedback, evaluation, beta-testing, etc. Though iterations in construction are done often and it is clear what an iteration in this phase delivers, iterations may be done meaningfully in other phases as well. For example, in the elaboration phase, the first iteration may just specify the overall architecture and high-level requirements, while the second iteration may be done to thrash out the details. As another example, there may be multiple iterations to transition the developed software, with each iteration "making live" some part or some feature of the developed software.

RUP has carefully chosen the phase names so as not to confuse them with the engineering tasks that are to be done in the project, as in RUP the engineering tasks and phases are separate. Different engineering activities may be performed in a phase to achieve its milestones. RUP groups the activities into different subprocesses which it calls *core process workflows*. These subprocesses correspond to the tasks of performing requirements analysis, doing design, implementing the design, testing, project management, etc. Some of the subprocesses are shown in Table 2.1.

One key difference of RUP from other models is that it has separated the phases from the tasks and allows multiple of these subprocesses to function within a phase. In waterfall (or waterfall-based iterative model), a phase within a process was linked to a particular task performed by some process like requirements, design, etc. In RUP these tasks are separated from the stages, and it allows, for example, during construction, execution of the requirements process. That is, it allows some part of the requirement activity be done even in construction, something the waterfall did not allow. So, a project, if it so wishes, may do detailed requirements only for some features during the elaboration phase, and may do detailing of other requirements while the construction is going on (maybe the first iteration of it). This not only allows a project a greater degree of flexibility in planning when the different tasks should be done, it also captures the reality of the situation—it is often not possible to specify all requirements at the start and it is best to start the project with some requirements and work out the details later.

Though a subprocess may be active in many phases, as can be expected, the volume of work or the effort being spent on the subprocess will vary with phases. For example, it is expected that a lot more effort will be spent in the requirement subprocess during elaboration, and less will be spent in construction, and still less, if any, will be spent in transition. Similarly, the model has the development process active in elaboration, which allows a project to build a prototype during the elaboration phase to help its requirements activity, if needed. However, most of the implementation does happen in the construction phase. The effort spent in a subprocess in different phases will, of course, depend on the project. However, a general pattern is indicated in Table 2.1 by specifying if the level of effort for the phase is high, medium, low, etc.

Table 2.1: Activity level of subprocesses in different phases of RUP.

	Inception	Elaboration	Construction	Transition
Requirements	High	High	Low	Nil
Anal. and Design	Low	High	Medium	Nil
Implementation	Nil	Low	High	Low
Test	Nil	Low	High	Medium
Deployment	Nil	Nil	Medium	High
Proj. Mgmt.	Medium	Medium	Medium	Medium
Config. Mgmt	Low	Low	High	High

Overall, RUP provides a flexible process model, which follows an iterative approach not only at a top level (through cycles), but also encourages iterative approach during each of the phases in a cycle. And in phases, it allows the different tasks to be done as per the needs of the project.

2.3.5 Timeboxing Model

To speed up development, parallelism between the different iterations can be employed. That is, a new iteration commences before the system produced by the current iteration is released, and hence development of a new release happens in parallel with the development of the current release. By starting an iteration before the previous iteration has completed, it is possible to reduce the average delivery time for iterations. However, to support parallel execution, each iteration has to be structured properly and teams have to be organized suitably. The timeboxing model proposes an approach for these [60, 59].

In the timeboxing model, the basic unit of development is a time box, which is of fixed duration. Since the duration is fixed, a key factor in selecting the requirements or features to be built in a time box is what can be fit into the time box. This is in contrast to regular iterative approaches where the functionality is selected and then the time to deliver is determined. Timeboxing changes the perspective of development and makes the schedule a nonnegotiable and a high-priority commitment.

Each time box is divided into a sequence of stages, like in the waterfall model. Each stage performs some clearly defined task for the iteration and produces a clearly defined output. The model also requires that the duration of each stage, that is, the time it takes to complete the task of that stage, is approximately the same. Furthermore, the model requires that there be a dedicated team for each stage. That is, the team for a stage performs only tasks of that stage—tasks for other stages are performed by their respective teams. This is quite different from other iterative models where the implicit assumption is that the same team performs all the different tasks of the project or the iteration.

Having time-boxed iterations with stages of equal duration and having dedicated teams renders itself to pipelining of different iterations. (Pipelining is a concept from hardware in which different instructions are executed in parallel, with the execution of a new instruction starting once the first stage of the previous instruction is finished.)

To illustrate the use of this model, consider a time box consisting of three stages: requirement specification, build, and deployment. The requirement stage is executed by its team of analysts and ends with a prioritized list of requirements to be built in this iteration along with a high-level design. The build team develops the code for implementing the requirements, and performs the testing. The tested code is then handed over to the deployment team, which performs predeployment tests, and then installs the system for production use. These three stages are such that they can be done in approximately equal time in an iteration.

With a time box of three stages, the project proceeds as follows. When the requirements team has finished requirements for timebox-1, the requirements are given to the build team for building the software. The requirements team then goes on and starts preparing the requirements for timebox-2. When the build for timebox-1 is completed, the code is handed over to the deployment team, and the build team moves on to build code for requirements for timebox-2, and the requirements team moves on to doing requirements for timebox-3. This pipelined execution of the timeboxing process is shown in Figure 2.8 [59].

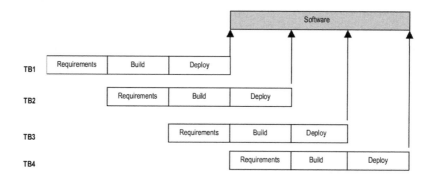

Figure 2.8: Executing the timeboxing process model.

With a three-stage time box, at most three iterations can be concurrently in progress. If the time box is of size T days, then the first software delivery will occur after T days. The subsequent deliveries, however, will take place after every T/3 days. For example, if the time box duration T is 9 weeks (and each stage duration is 3 weeks), the first delivery is made 9 weeks after the start of the project. The second delivery is made after 12 weeks, the third after 15 weeks, and so on. Contrast this with a linear execution of iterations, in which the first delivery will be made after 9 weeks, the second after 18 weeks, the third after 27 weeks, and so on.

There are three teams working on the project—the requirements team, the build team, and the deployment team. The teamwise activity for the 3-stage pipeline discussed above is shown in Figure 2.9 [59].

It should be clear that the duration of each iteration has not been reduced.

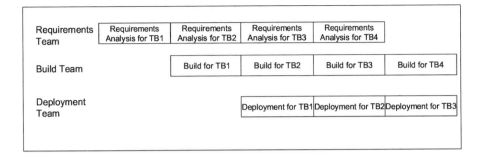

Figure 2.9: Tasks of different teams.

The total work done in a time box and the effort spent in it also remains the same—the same amount of software is delivered at the end of each iteration as the time box undergoes the same stages. If the effort and time spent in each iteration also remains the same, then what is the cost of reducing the delivery time? The real cost of this reduced time is in the resources used in this model. With timeboxing, there are dedicated teams for different stages and the total team size for the project is the sum of teams of different stages. This is the main difference from the situation where there is a single team which performs all the stages and the entire team works on the same iteration.

Hence, the timeboxing provides an approach for utilizing additional manpower to reduce the delivery time. It is well known that with standard methods of executing projects, we cannot compress the cycle time of a project substantially by adding more manpower. However, through the timeboxing model, we can use more manpower in a manner such that by parallel execution of different stages we are able to deliver software quicker. In other words, it provides a way of shortening delivery times through the use of additional manpower.

Timeboxing is well suited for projects that require a large number of features to be developed in a short time around a stable architecture using stable technologies. These features should be such that there is some flexibility in grouping them for building a meaningful system in an iteration that provides value to the users. The main cost of this model is the increased complexity of project management (and managing the products being developed) as multiple developments are concurrently active. Also, the impact of unusual situations in an iteration can be quite disruptive. Further details about the model, as well as a detailed example of applying the model on a real commercial project, are given in [60, 59].

2.3.6 Extreme Programming and Agile Processes

Agile development approaches evolved in the 1990s as a reaction to documentation and bureaucracy-based processes, particularly the waterfall approach.
Agile approaches are based on some common principles, some of which are
[www.extremeprogramming.org]:

- Working software is the key measure of progress in a project.

- For progress in a project, therefore, software should be developed and delivered rapidly in small increments.

- Even late changes in the requirements should be entertained (small-increment
  model of development helps in accommodating them).

- Face-to-face communication is preferred over documentation.

- Continuous feedback and involvement of customer is necessary for developing
  good-quality software.

- Simple design which evolves and improves with time is a better approach
  than doing an elaborate design up front for handling all possible scenarios.

- The delivery dates are decided by empowered teams of talented individuals
  (and are not dictated).

Many detailed agile methodologies have been proposed, some of which are
widely used now. Extreme programming (XP) is one of the most popular and
well-known approaches in the family of agile methods. Like all agile approaches,
it believes that changes are inevitable and rather than treating changes as undesirable, development should embrace change. And to accommodate change,
the development process has to be lightweight and quick to respond. For this,
it develops software iteratively, and avoids reliance on detailed and multiple
documents which are hard to maintain. Instead it relies on face-to-face communication, simplicity, and feedback to ensure that the desired changes are
quickly and correctly reflected in the programs. Here we briefly discuss the
development process of XP, as a representative of an agile process.

An extreme programming project starts with *user stories* which are short
(a few sentences) descriptions of what scenarios the customers and users would
like the system to support. They are different from traditional requirements
specification primarily in details—user stories do not contain detailed requirements which are to be uncovered only when the story is to be implemented,
therefore allowing the details to be decided as late as possible. Each story is
written on a separate card, so they can be flexibly grouped.

The empowered development team estimates how long it will take to implement a user story. The estimates are rough, generally stated in weeks. Using

these estimates and the stories, *release planning* is done which defines which stories are to be built in which system release, and the dates of these releases. Frequent and small releases are encouraged, and for a release, iterations are employed. Acceptance tests are also built from the stories, which are used to test the software before the release. Bugs found during the acceptance testing for an iteration can form work items for the next iteration. This overall process is shown in Figure 2.10.

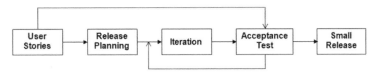

Figure 2.10: Overall process in XP.

Development is done in iterations, each iteration lasting no more than a few weeks. An iteration starts with *iteration planning* in which the stories to be implemented in this iteration are selected—high-value and high-risk stories are considered as higher priority and implemented in early iterations. Failed acceptance tests in previous iteration also have to be handled. Details of the stories are obtained in the iteration for doing the development.

The development approach used in an iteration has some unique practices. First, it envisages that development is done by pairs of programmers (called pair programming and which we will discuss further in Chapter 7), instead of individual programmers. Second, it suggests that for building a code unit, automated unit tests be written first before the actual code is written, and then the code should be written to pass the tests. This approach is referred to as test-driven development, in contrast to regular code-first development in which programmers first write code and then think of how to test it. (We will discuss test-driven development further in Chapter 7.) As functionality of the unit increases, the unit tests are enhanced first, and then the code is enhanced to pass the new set of unit tests. Third, as it encourages simple solutions as well as change, it is expected that the design of the solution devised earlier may at some point become unsuitable for further development. To handle this situation, it suggests that *refactoring* be done to improve the design, and then use the refactored code for further development. During refactoring, no new functionality is added, only the design of the existing programs is improved. (Refactoring will be discussed further in Chapter 7.) Fourth, it encourages frequent integration of different units. To avoid too many changes in the base code happening together, only one pair at a time can release their changes and integrate into the common code base. The process within an iteration is shown in Figure 2.11.

Figure 2.11: An iteration in XP.

This is a very simplified description of XP. There are many other rules in XP relating to issues like rights of programmers and customers, communication between the team members and use of metaphors, trust and visibility to all stakeholders, collective ownership of code in which any pair can change any code, team management, building quick *spike solutions* to resolve difficult technical and architectural issues or to explore some approach, how bugs are to be handled, how what can be done within an iteration is to be estimated from the progress made in the previous iteration, how meetings are to be conducted, how a day in the development should start, etc. The website www.extremeprogramming.org is a good source on these, as well as other aspects of XP.

XP, and other agile methods, are suitable for situations where the volume and pace of requirements change is high, and where requirement risks are considerable. Because of its reliance on strong communication between all the team members, it is effective when teams are collocated and of modest size, of up to about 20 members. And as it envisages strong involvement of the customer in the development, as well as in planning the delivery dates, it works well when the customer is willing to be heavily involved during the entire development, working as a team member.

2.3.7 Using Process Models in a Project

We have seen many different development process models. What is the need for the different models? As mentioned earlier, while developing (industrial strength) software, the purpose is not only to develop software to satisfy the needs of some users or clients, but we want that the project be done in low cost and cycle time, and deliver high-quality software. In addition, there could be other constraints in a project that the project may need to satisfy. Hence, given the constraints of the project, we would like to employ the process model that is likely to maximize the chances of delivering the software, and achieve the highest Q&P. Hence, selecting a suitable development process model for a project is a key decision that a project manager has to take. Let us illustrate this by a few examples.

Suppose a small team of developers has been entrusted with the task of building a small auction site for a local university. The university administration is willing to spend some time at the start to help develop the requirements, but it is expected that their availability will be limited later. The team has been given 4 months to finish the project, and an extension of the deadline seems very improbable. It also seems that the auction site will have some features that are essential, but will also have some features that are desirable but without which the system can function reasonably well.

With these constraints, it is clear that a waterfall model is not suitable for this project, as the "all or nothing" risk that it entails is unacceptable due to the inflexible deadline. The iterative enhancement model where each iteration does a complete waterfall is also not right as it requires requirements analysis for each iteration, and the users and clients are not available later. However, the iterative delivery approach in which the complete requirements are done in the first iteration but delivery is done in iterations seems well suited, with delivery being done in two (or three) iterations (as time is short). From the requirements, the project team can decide what functionality is essential to have in a working system and include it in the first iteration. The other desirable features can be planned for the second iteration. With this approach, the chances of completing the first iteration before the final deadline increase. That is, with this model, the chances of delivering a working system increase. RUP, as it allows iterations in each phase, is also a suitable model.

Consider another example where the customers are in a highly competitive environment where requirements depend on what the competition is doing, and delivering functionality regularly is highly desirable. Furthermore, to reduce cost, the customer wants to outsource as much project work as possible to another team in another country.

For this project, clearly waterfall is not suitable as requirements are not even known at the start. Iterative enhancement also may not work as it may not be able to deliver rapidly. XP will be hard to apply as it requires that the entire team, including the customer, be collocated. For this project, the timeboxing model seems to fit the best. The whole project can employ three teams—one of analysts who will work with the customer to determine the requirements, one to do the development (which could be in some low-cost destination), and the third to do the deployment, which will be where the site is hosted. By suitably staffing the teams, the duration of each of the three phases—analysis and design, build, and deployment—can be made approximately equal. Then the timeboxing model can be applied.

Consider another project, where a university wants to automate the registration process. It already has a database of courses and pre-requisites, and a database of student records. In this project, as the requirements are well understood (since registrations have been happening manually), the waterfall model seems to be the optimum.

2.4 Project Management Process

While the selection of the development process decides the phases and tasks to be done, it does not specify things like how long each phase should last, or how many resources should be assigned to a phase, or how a phase should be monitored. And quality and productivity in the project will also depend critically on these decisions. To meet the cost, quality, and schedule objectives, resources have to be properly allocated to each activity for the project, and progress of different activities has to be monitored and corrective actions taken when needed. All these activities are part of the project management process. Hence, a project management process is necessary to ensure that the engineering process ends up meeting the real-world objectives of cost, schedule, and quality.

The project management process specifies all activities that need to be done by the project management to ensure that cost and quality objectives are met. Its basic task is to ensure that, once a development process is chosen, it is implemented optimally. That is, the basic task is to plan the detailed implementation of the process for the particular project and then ensure that the plan is properly executed. For a large project, a proper management process is essential for success.

The activities in the management process for a project can be grouped broadly into three phases: planning, monitoring and control, and termination analysis. Project management begins with planning, which is perhaps the most critical project management activity. The goal of this phase is to develop a *plan* for software development following which the objectives of the project can be met successfully and efficiently. A software plan is usually produced before the development activity begins and is updated as development proceeds and data about progress of the project becomes available. During planning, the major activities are cost estimation, schedule and milestone determination, project staffing, quality control plans, and controlling and monitoring plans. Project planning is undoubtedly the single most important management activity, and it forms the basis for monitoring and control. We will devote one full chapter later in the book to project planning.

Project monitoring and control phase of the management process is the longest in terms of duration; it encompasses most of the development process. It includes all activities the project management has to perform while the development is going on to ensure that project objectives are met and the development proceeds according to the developed plan (and update the plan, if needed). As cost, schedule, and quality are the major driving forces, most of the activity of this phase revolves around monitoring factors that affect these. Monitoring potential risks for the project, which might prevent the project from meeting its objectives, is another important activity during this phase. And if the information obtained by monitoring suggests that objectives may not be met, necessary actions are taken in this phase by exerting suitable control on the development activities.

Monitoring a development process requires proper information about the project. Such information is typically obtained by the management process from the development process. Consequently, the implementation of a development process model should ensure that each step in the development process produces information that the management process needs for that step. That is, the development process provides the information the management process needs. However, interpretation of the information is part of monitoring and control.

Whereas monitoring and control last the entire duration of the project, the last phase of the management process—termination analysis—is performed when the development process is over. The basic reason for performing termination analysis is to provide information about the development process and learn from the project in order to improve the process. This phase is also often called *postmortem analysis*. In iterative development, this analysis can be done after each iteration to provide feedback to improve the execution of further iterations. We will not discuss it further in the book; for an example of a postmortem report the reader is referred to [57].

The temporal relationship between the management process and the development process is shown in Figure 2.12. This is an idealized relationship showing that planning is done before development begins, and termination analysis is done after development is over. As the figure shows, during the development, from the various phases of the development process, quantitative information flows to the monitoring and control phase of the management process, which uses the information to exert control on the development process.

We will in a later chapter discuss in detail the project planning phase. As a plan also includes planning for monitoring, we will not discuss the monitoring separately but discuss it as part of the planning activity.

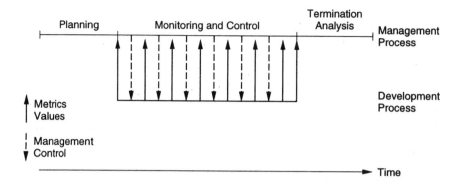

Figure 2.12: Temporal relationship between development and management process.

2.5 Summary

– The quality and productivity achieved in a software project depends on the process used for executing the project. Due to this, processes form the heart of software engineering.

– A process is the set of activities that are performed in some order so that the desired results will be achieved. A process model is a general process specification which has been found to be best suited for some situations.

– A software process consists of many different component processes, most important being the development process and the project management process.

– Development process focuses on how the software is to be engineered. There are many different process models, each being well suited for some type of problems.

  – The waterfall model is conceptually the simplest model of software development, where the requirement, design, coding, and testing phases are performed in linear progression. It has been very widely used, and is suitable for well-understood problems.

  – In the prototyping model, a prototype is built before building the final system, which is used to further develop the requirements leading to more stable requirements. This is useful for projects where requirements are not clear.

  – In the iterative development model, software is developed in iterations, each iteration resulting in a working software system. This model does not require all requirements to be known at the start, allows feedback from earlier iterations for next ones, and reduces risk as it delivers value as the project proceeds.

- In RUP, a project is executed in a sequence of four phases—inception, elaboration, construction, and transition, each ending in a defined milestone. A phase may itself be done iteratively. The subprocesses of requirements, design, coding, testing, etc. are considered as active throughout the project, though their intensity varies from phase to phase. RUP is a flexible framework which can allow a project to follow a traditional waterfall if it wants to, or allow prototyping, if it so wishes.

- In the timeboxing model, the different iterations are of equal time duration, and are divided into equal length stages. There is a committed team for each stage of an iteration. The different iterations are then executed in a pipelined manner, with each dedicated team working on its stage but for different iterations. As multiple iterations are concurrently active, this model reduces the average completion time of each iteration and hence is useful in situations where short cycle time is highly desirable.

- Agile approaches to development are based on some key principles like developing software in small iterations, working system as the measure of progress, and allowing change at any time. In extreme programming (XP) approach, a project starts with short user stories, details of which are obtained in the iteration in which they are implemented. In an iteration, development is done by programmer-pairs, following the practices of test-driven development, frequent integration, and having simple designs which are refactored when needed.

- The project management process focuses on planning and controlling the development process and consists of three major phases—planning, monitoring and control, and termination analysis. Much of project management revolves around the project plan, which is produced during the planning phase.

Self-Assessment Exercises

1. What is the relationship between a process model, process specification, and process for a project?
2. What are the key outputs during an iteration in a project following an iterative development model?
3. Which of the development process models discussed in this chapter would you employ for the following projects?

a) A simple data processing project.
b) A data entry system for office staff who have never used computers before. The user interface and user-friendliness are extremely important.
c) A spreadsheet system that has some basic features and many other desirable features that use these basic features.
d) A web-based system for a new business where requirements are changing fast and where an in-house development team is available for all aspects of the project.
e) A Web-site for an on-line store which has a long list of desired features it wants to add, and it wants a new release with new features to be done very frequently.

4. A project uses the timeboxing process model with three stages in each time box (as discussed in the chapter), but with unequal length. Suppose the requirement specification stage takes 2 weeks with a team of 2 people, the build stage takes 3 weeks with a team of 4 people, and deployment takes 1 week with a team of 2 people. Design the process for this project that maximizes resource utilization. Assume that each resource can do any task. (Hint: Exploit the fact that the sum of durations of the first and the third stage is equal to the duration of the second stage.)

5. What effect is the project monitoring activity likely to have on the development process?

3

Software Requirements Analysis and Specification

IEEE defines a requirement as "(1) A condition of capability needed by a user to solve a problem or achieve an objective; (2) A condition or a capability that must be met or possessed by a system ... to satisfy a contract, standard, specification, or other formally imposed document" [53]. Note that in software requirements we are dealing with the requirements of the proposed system, that is, the capabilities that the system, which is yet to be developed, should have.

As we have seen, all development models require requirements to be specified. Approaches like agile require only high-level requirements to be specified in written form—detailed requirements are elicited through interaction with the customer in the iteration the requirement is to be implemented and directly reflected in software. Other approaches prefer that the requirements are specified precisely. In such situations, the goal of the requirements activity is to produce the Software Requirements Specification (SRS) that describes *what* the proposed software should do without describing *how* the software will do it.

In this chapter we will discuss:

- The role of the SRS in a project and the value a good SRS brings to it.

- The different activities in the process for producing the desired SRS.

- The desired characteristics of an SRS, the structure of an SRS document, and its key components.

P. Jalote, *A Concise Introduction to Software Engineering*,
DOI: 10.1007/978-1-84800-302-6_3, © Springer-Verlag London Limited 2008

– The use case approach for analyzing and specifying functional requirements, and how use cases can be developed.

– Some other approaches for analyzing requirements like the data flow diagram.

– How requirements are validated.

3.1 Value of a Good SRS

The origin of most software systems is in the needs of some clients. The software system itself is created by some developers. Finally, the completed system will be used by the end users. Thus, there are three major parties interested in a new system: the client, the developer, and the users. Somehow the requirements for the system that will satisfy the needs of the clients and the concerns of the users have to be communicated to the developer. The problem is that the client usually does not understand software or the software development process, and the developer often does not understand the client's problem and application area. This causes a communication gap between the parties involved in the development project. A basic purpose of the SRS is to bridge this communication gap so they have a shared vision of the software being built. Hence, one of the main advantages of a good SRS is:

– An SRS establishes the basis for agreement between the client and the supplier on what the software product will do.

This basis for agreement is frequently formalized into a legal contract between the client (or the customer) and the developer (the supplier). So, through SRS, the client clearly describes what it expects from the supplier, and the developer clearly understands what capabilities to build in the software. A related, but important, advantage is:

– An SRS provides a reference for validation of the final product.

That is, the SRS helps the client determine if the software meets the requirements. Without a proper SRS, there is no way a client can determine if the software being delivered is what was ordered, and there is no way the developer can convince the client that all the requirements have been fulfilled.

Providing the basis of agreement and validation should be strong enough reasons for both the client and the developer to do a thorough and rigorous job of requirement understanding and specification, but there are other very practical and pressing reasons for having a good SRS.

Studies have shown that many errors are made during the requirements phase. And an error in the SRS will manifest itself as an error in the final system implementing the SRS. Clearly, if we want a high-quality end product that has few errors, we must begin with a high-quality SRS. In other words, we can conclude that:

– A high-quality SRS is a prerequisite to high-quality software.

Finally, the quality of SRS has an impact on cost (and schedule) of the project. We know that errors can exist in the SRS. It is also known that the cost of fixing an error increases almost exponentially as time progresses [10, 12]. Hence, by improving the quality of requirements, we can have a huge savings in the future by having fewer expensive defect removals. In other words,

– A high-quality SRS reduces the development cost.

3.2 Requirement Process

The requirement process is the sequence of activities that need to be performed in the requirements phase and that culminate in producing a high-quality document containing the SRS. The requirements process typically consists of three basic tasks: problem or requirement analysis, requirements specification, and requirements validation.

Problem analysis often starts with a high-level "problem statement." During analysis the problem domain and the environment are modeled in an effort to understand the system behavior, constraints on the system, its inputs and outputs, etc. The basic purpose of this activity is to obtain a thorough understanding of what the software needs to provide. Frequently, during analysis, the analyst will have a series of meetings with the clients and end users. In the early meetings, the clients and end users will explain to the analyst about their work, their environment, and their needs as they perceive them. Any documents describing the work or the organization may be given, along with outputs of the existing methods of performing the tasks. In these early meetings, the analyst is basically the listener, absorbing the information provided. Once the analyst understands the system to some extent, he uses the next few meetings to seek clarifications of the parts he does not understand. He may document the information or build some models, and he may do some brainstorming or thinking about what the system should do. In the final few meetings, the analyst essentially explains to the client what he understands the system should do and uses the meetings as a means of verifying if what he proposes the system should do is indeed consistent with the objectives of the clients.

The understanding obtained by problem analysis forms the basis of *requirements specification*, in which the focus is on clearly specifying the requirements in a document. Issues such as representation, specification languages, and tools are addressed during this activity. As analysis produces large amounts of information and knowledge with possible redundancies, properly organizing and describing the requirements is an important goal of this activity.

Requirements validation focuses on ensuring that what have been specified in the SRS are indeed all the requirements of the software and making sure that the SRS is of good quality. The requirements process terminates with the production of the validated SRS. We will discuss this more later in the chapter.

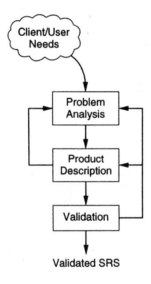

Figure 3.1: The requirement process.

It should be pointed out that the requirements process is not a linear sequence of these three activities and there is considerable overlap and feedback between these activities. The overall requirement process is shown in Figure 3.1. As shown in the figure, from the specification activity we may go back to the analysis activity. This happens as frequently some parts of the problem are analyzed and then specified before other parts are analyzed and specified. Furthermore, the process of specification frequently shows shortcomings in the knowledge of the problem, thereby necessitating further analysis. Once the specification is done, it goes through the validation activity. This activity may reveal problems in the specification itself, which requires going back to the specification step, or may reveal shortcomings in the understanding of the problem, which requires going back to the analysis activity.

3.3 Requirements Specification

The final output is the SRS document. As analysis precedes specification, the first question that arises is: If formal modeling is done during analysis, why are the outputs of modeling not treated as an SRS? The main reason is that modeling generally focuses on the problem structure, not its external behavior. Consequently, things like user interfaces are rarely modeled, whereas they frequently form a major component of the SRS. Similarly, for ease of modeling, frequently "minor issues" like erroneous situations (e.g., error in output) are rarely modeled properly, whereas in an SRS, behavior under such situations also has to be specified. Similarly, performance constraints, design constraints, standards compliance, recovery, etc., are not included in the model, but must be specified clearly in the SRS because the designer must know about these to properly design the system. It should therefore be clear that the outputs of a model cannot form a desirable SRS.

The transition from analysis to specification should also not be expected to be straightforward, even if some formal modeling is used during analysis. A good SRS needs to specify many things, some of which are not satisfactorily handled during analysis. Essentially, what passes from requirements analysis activity to the specification activity is the knowledge acquired about the system. The modeling is essentially a tool to help obtain a thorough and complete knowledge about the proposed system. The SRS is written based on the knowledge acquired during analysis. As converting knowledge into a structured document is not straightforward, specification itself is a major task, which is relatively independent.

3.3.1 Desirable Characteristics of an SRS

To properly satisfy the basic goals, an SRS should have certain properties and should contain different types of requirements. Some of the desirable characteristics of an SRS are [53]:

1. Correct

2. Complete

3. Unambiguous

4. Verifiable

5. Consistent

6. Ranked for importance and/or stability

An SRS is *correct* if every requirement included in the SRS represents something required in the final system. It is *complete* if everything the software is supposed to do and the responses of the software to all classes of input data are specified in the SRS. It is *unambiguous* if and only if every requirement stated has one and only one interpretation. Requirements are often written in natural language, which is inherently ambiguous. If the requirements are specified in a natural language, the SRS writer has to be especially careful to ensure that there are no ambiguities.

An SRS is *verifiable* if and only if every stated requirement is verifiable. A requirement is verifiable if there exists some cost-effective process that can check whether the final software meets that requirement. It is *consistent* if there is no requirement that conflicts with another. Terminology can cause inconsistencies; for example, different requirements may use different terms to refer to the same object. There may be logical or temporal conflict between requirements that causes inconsistencies. This occurs if the SRS contains two or more requirements whose logical or temporal characteristics cannot be satisfied together by any software system. For example, suppose a requirement states that an event e is to occur before another event f. But then another set of requirements states (directly or indirectly by transitivity) that event f should occur before event e. Inconsistencies in an SRS can reflect some major problems.

Generally, all the requirements for software are not of equal importance. Some are critical, others are important but not critical, and there are some which are desirable but not very important. Similarly, some requirements are "core" requirements which are not likely to change as time passes, while others are more dependent on time. Some provide more value to the users than others. An SRS is ranked for importance and/or stability if for each requirement the importance and the stability of the requirement are indicated. Stability of a requirement reflects the chances of it changing in the future. It can be reflected in terms of the expected change volume. This understanding of value each requirement provides is essential for iterative development—selection of requirements for an iteration is based on this evaluation.

Of all these characteristics, completeness is perhaps the most important and also the most difficult property to establish. One of the most common defects in requirements specification is incompleteness. Missing requirements necessitate additions and modifications to the requirements later in the development cycle, which are often expensive to incorporate. Incompleteness is also a major source of disagreement between the client and the supplier.

Some, however, believe that completeness in all details may not be desirable. The pursuit of completeness can lead to specifying details and assumptions that may be commonly understood. (For example, specifying in detail what a common operation like add a record means.) And specifying these details can result in a large requirements document, which has its own problems including making validation harder. On the other hand, if too few details are given, the chances of developer's understanding being different from others' increases, which can lead to defects in the software.

For completeness, a reasonable goal is to have "sufficient detail" for the project at hand. For example, if the waterfall model is to be followed in the project, it is better to have detailed specifications so the need for changes is minimized. On the other hand, for iterative development, as feedback is possible and opportunity for change is also there, the specification can be less detailed. And if an agile approach is being followed, then completeness should be sought only for top-level requirements, as details may not be required in written form, and are elicited when the requirement is being implemented. Together the performance and interface requirements and design constraints can be called *nonfunctional requirements*.

3.3.2 Components of an SRS

Completeness of specifications is difficult to achieve and even more difficult to verify. Having guidelines about what different things an SRS should specify will help in completely specifying the requirements. The basic issues an SRS must address are:

- Functionality

- Performance

- Design constraints imposed on an implementation

- External interfaces

Functional requirements specify the expected behavior of the system—which outputs should be produced from the given inputs. They describe the relationship between the input and output of the system. For each functional requirement, a detailed description of all the data inputs and their source, the units of measure, and the range of valid inputs must be specified.

All the operations to be performed on the input data to obtain the output should be specified. This includes specifying the validity checks on the input and output data, parameters affected by the operation, and equations or other logical operations that must be used to transform the inputs into corresponding outputs. For example, if there is a formula for computing the output, it should be specified.

An important part of the specification is the system behavior in abnormal situations, like invalid input (which can occur in many ways) or error during computation. The functional requirement must clearly state what the system should do if such situations occur. Specifically, it should specify the behavior of the system for invalid inputs and invalid outputs. Furthermore, behavior for situations where the input is valid but the normal operation cannot be performed should also be specified. An example of this situation is a reservation system, where a reservation cannot be made even for a valid request if there is no availability. In short, the system behavior for all foreseen inputs and all foreseen system states should be specified.

The *performance requirements* part of an SRS specifies the performance constraints on the software system. All the requirements relating to the performance characteristics of the system must be clearly specified. There are two types of performance requirements: static and dynamic.

Static requirements are those that do not impose constraint on the execution characteristics of the system. These include requirements like the number of terminals to be supported, the number of simultaneous users to be supported, and the number of files that the system has to process and their sizes. These are also called *capacity* requirements of the system.

Dynamic requirements specify constraints on the execution behavior of the system. These typically include response time and throughput constraints on the system. Response time is the expected time for the completion of an operation under specified circumstances. Throughput is the expected number of operations that can be performed in a unit time. For example, the SRS may specify the number of transactions that must be processed per unit time, or what the response time for a particular command should be. Acceptable ranges of the different performance parameters should be specified, as well as acceptable performance for both normal and peak workload conditions.

All of these requirements should be stated in measurable terms. Requirements such as "response time should be good" or the system must be able to "process all the transactions quickly" are not desirable because they are imprecise and not verifiable. Instead, statements like "the response time of command x should be less than one second 90% of the times" or "a transaction should be processed in less than one second 98% of the times" should be used to declare performance specifications.

There are a number of factors in the client's environment that may restrict the choices of a designer leading to *design constraints*. Such factors include standards that must be followed, resource limits, operating environment, reliability and security requirements, and policies that may have an impact on the design of the system. An SRS should identify and specify all such constraints. Some examples of these are:

Standards Compliance: This specifies the requirements for the standards the system must follow. The standards may include the report format and accounting procedures. There may be audit requirements which may require logging of operations.

Hardware Limitations: The software may have to operate on some existing or predetermined hardware, thus imposing restrictions on the design. Hardware limitations can include the type of machines to be used, operating system available on the system, languages supported, and limits on primary and secondary storage.

Reliability and Fault Tolerance: Fault tolerance requirements can place a major constraint on how the system is to be designed, as they make the system more complex and expensive. Recovery requirements are often an integral part here, detailing what the system should do if some failure occurs to ensure certain properties.

Security: Security requirements are becoming increasingly important. These requirements place restrictions on the use of certain commands, control access to data, provide different kinds of access requirements for different people, require the use of passwords and cryptography techniques, and maintain a log of activities in the system. They may also require proper assessment of security threats, proper programming techniques, and use of tools to detect flaws like buffer overflow.

In the *external interface* specification part, all the interactions of the software with people, hardware, and other software should be clearly specified. For the user interface, the characteristics of each user interface of the software product should be specified. User interface is becoming increasingly important and must be given proper attention. A preliminary user manual should be created with all user commands, screen formats, an explanation of how the system will appear to the user, and feedback and error messages. Like other specifications, these requirements should be precise and verifiable. So, a statement like "the system should be user friendly" should be avoided and statements like "commands should be no longer than six characters" or "command names should reflect the function they perform" used.

For hardware interface requirements, the SRS should specify the logical characteristics of each interface between the software product and the hardware components. If the software is to execute on existing hardware or on predetermined hardware, all the characteristics of the hardware, including memory restrictions, should be specified. In addition, the current use and load characteristics of the hardware should be given.

The interface requirement should specify the interface with other software the system will use or that will use the system. This includes the interface with the operating system and other applications. The message content and format of each interface should be specified.

3.3.3 Structure of a Requirements Document

Requirements have to be specified using some specification language. Though formal notations exist for specifying specific properties of the system, natural languages are now most often used for specifying requirements. When formal languages are employed, they are often used to specify particular properties or for specific parts of the system, as part of the overall SRS.

All the requirements for a system, stated using a formal notation or natural language, have to be included in a document that is clear and concise. For this, it is necessary to properly organize the requirements document. Here we discuss the organization based on the IEEE guide to software requirements specifications [53].

The IEEE standards recognize the fact that different projects may require their requirements to be organized differently, that is, there is no one method that is suitable for all projects. It provides different ways of structuring the SRS. The first two sections of the SRS are the same in all of them. The general structure of an SRS is given in Figure 3.2.

```
1. Introduction
        1.1 Purpose
        1.2 Scope
        1.3 Definitions, Acronyms, and Abbreviations
        1.4 References
        1.5 Overview
2. Overall Description
        2.1 Product Perspective
        2.2 Product Functions
        2.3 User Characteristics
        2.4 General Constraints
        2.5 Assumptions and Dependencies
3. Specific Requirements
```

Figure 3.2: General structure of an SRS.

The introduction section contains the purpose, scope, overview, etc., of the requirements document. The key aspect here is to clarify the motivation and business objectives that are driving this project, and the scope of the project. The next section gives an overall perspective of the system—how it fits into the larger system, and an overview of all the requirements of this system. Detailed requirements are not mentioned. Product perspective is essentially the relationship of the product to other products; defining if the product is independent or is a part of a larger product, and what the principal interfaces of the product are. A general abstract description of the functions to be performed by the product is given. Schematic diagrams showing a general view of different functions and their relationships with each other can often be useful. Similarly, typical characteristics of the eventual end user and general constraints are also specified.

If agile methods are being used, this may be sufficient for the initial requirements phase, as these approaches prefer to do the detailed requirements when the requirement is to be implemented.

The detailed requirements section describes the details of the requirements that a developer needs to know for designing and developing the system. This is typically the largest and most important part of the document. For this section, different organizations have been suggested in the standard. These requirements can be organized by the modes of operation, user class, object, feature, stimulus, or functional hierarchy [53]. One method to organize the specific requirements is to first specify the external interfaces, followed by functional requirements, performance requirements, design constraints, and system attributes. This structure is shown in Figure 3.3 [53].

The external interface requirements section specifies all the interfaces of the software: to people, other software, hardware, and other systems. User interfaces are clearly a very important component; they specify each human interface the system plans to have, including screen formats, contents of menus, and command structure. In hardware interfaces, the logical characteristics of each interface between the software and hardware on which the software can run are specified. Essentially, any assumptions the software is making about the hardware are listed here. In software interfaces, all other software that is needed for this software to run is specified, along with the interfaces. Communication interfaces need to be specified if the software communicates with other entities in other machines.

In the functional requirements section, the functional capabilities of the system are described. In this organization, the functional capabilities for all the modes of operation of the software are given. For each functional requirement, the required inputs, desired outputs, and processing requirements will have to be specified. For the inputs, the source of the inputs, the units of measure, valid

```
3. Detailed Requirements
    3.1 External Interface Requirements
        3.1.1 User Interfaces
        3.1.2 Hardware Interfaces
        3.1.3 Software Interfaces
        3.1.4 Communication Interfaces
    3.2. Functional Requirements
        3.2.1 Mode 1
                3.2.1.1 Functional Requirement 1.1
                :
                3.2.1.n Functional Requirement 1.n
        :
        3.2.m Mode m
                3.2.m.1 Functional Requirement m.1
                :
                3.2.m.n Functional Requirement m.n
    3.3 Performance Requirements
    3.4 Design Constraints
    3.5 Attributes
    3.6 Other Requirements
```

Figure 3.3: One organization for specific requirements.

ranges, accuracies, etc., have to be specified. For specifying the processing, all operations that need to be performed on the input data and any intermediate data produced should be specified. This includes validity checks on inputs, sequence of operations, responses to abnormal situations, and methods that must be used in processing to transform the inputs into corresponding outputs.

The performance section should specify both static and dynamic performance requirements. All factors that constrain the system design are described in the performance constraints section. The attributes section specifies some of the overall attributes that the system should have. Any requirement not covered under these is listed under other requirements. Design constraints specify all the constraints imposed on design (e.g., security, fault tolerance, and standards compliance).

When use cases are employed, then the functional requirements section of the SRS is replaced by use case descriptions. And the product perspective part of the SRS may provide an overview or summary of the use cases.

3.4 Functional Specification with Use Cases

Functional requirements often form the core of a requirements document. The traditional approach for specifying functionality is to specify each function that the system should provide. Use cases specify the functionality of a system by specifying the behavior of the system, captured as interactions of the users with the system. Use cases can be used to describe the business processes of the larger business or organization that deploys the software, or it could just describe the behavior of the software system. We will focus on describing the behavior of software systems that are to be built.

Though use cases are primarily for specifying behavior, they can also be used effectively for analysis. Later when we discuss how to develop use cases, we will discuss how they can help in eliciting requirements also.

Use cases drew attention after they were used as part of the object-oriented modeling approach proposed by Jacobson [56]. Due to this connection with an object-oriented approach, use cases are sometimes viewed as part of an object-oriented approach to software development. However, they are a general method for describing the interaction of a system (even non-IT systems). The discussion of use cases here is based on the concepts and processes discussed in [24].

3.4.1 Basics

A software system (in our case whose requirements are being uncovered) may be used by many users, or by other systems. In use case terminology, an *actor* is a person or a system which uses the system for achieving some goal. Note that as an actor interacts for achieving some goal, it is a logical entity that represents a group of users (people or system) who behave in a similar manner. Different actors represent groups with different goals. So, it is better to have a "receiver" and a "sender" actor rather than having a generic "user" actor for a system in which some messages are sent by users and received by some other users.

A *primary actor* is the main actor that initiates a use case (UC) for achieving a goal, and whose goal satisfaction is the main objective of the use case. The primary actor is a logical concept and though we assume that the primary actor executes the use case, some agent may actually execute it on behalf of the primary actor. For example, a VP may be the primary actor for *get sales growth report by region* use case, though it may actually be executed by an assistant. We consider the primary actor as the person who actually uses the outcome of the use case and who is the main consumer of the goal. Time-driven trigger is another example of how a use case may be executed on behalf of the primary actor (in this situation the report is generated automatically at some time).

Note, however, that although the goal of the primary actor is the driving force behind a use case, the use case must also fulfill goals that other stakeholders might have for this use case. That is, the main goal of a use case is to describe behavior of the system that results in satisfaction of the goals of all the stakeholders, although the use case may be driven by the goals of the primary actor. For example, a use case "Withdraw money from the ATM" has a customer as its primary actor and will normally describe the entire interaction of the customer with the ATM. However, the bank is also a stakeholder of the ATM system and its goals may include that all steps are logged, money is given only if there are sufficient funds in the account, and no more than some amount is given at a time, etc. Satisfaction of these goals should also be shown by the use case "Withdraw money from the ATM."

For describing interaction, use cases use scenarios. A *scenario* describes a set of actions that are performed to achieve a goal under some specified conditions. The set of actions is generally specified as a sequence (as that is the most convenient way to express it in text), though in actual execution the actions specified may be executed in parallel or in some different order. Each step in a scenario is a logically complete action performed either by the actor or the system. Generally, a step is some action by the actor (e.g., enter information), some logical step that the system performs to progress toward achieving its goals (e.g., validate information, deliver information), or an internal state change by the system to satisfy some goals (e.g., log the transaction, update the record).

A use case always has a *main success scenario*, which describes the interaction if nothing fails and all steps in the scenario succeed. There may be many success scenarios. Though the use case aims to achieve its goals, different situations can arise while the system and the actor are interacting which may not permit the system to achieve the goal fully. For these situations, a use case has *extension scenarios* which describe the system behavior if some of the steps in the main scenario do not complete successfully. Sometimes they are also called *exception scenarios*. A use case is a collection of all the success and extension scenarios related to the goal. The terminology of use cases is summarized in Table 3.1.

To achieve the desired goal, a system can divide it into subgoals. Some of these subgoals may be achieved by the system itself, but they may also be treated as separate use cases executed by supporting actors, which may be another system. For example, suppose for verifying a user in "Withdraw money from the ATM" an authentication service is used. The interaction with

Table 3.1: Use case terms.

Term	Definition
Actor	A person or a system which uses the system being built for achieving some goal.
Primary actor	The main actor for whom a use case is initiated and whose goal satisfaction is the main objective of the use case.
Scenario	A set of actions that are performed to achieve a goal under some specified conditions.
Main success scenario	Describes the interaction if nothing fails and all steps in the scenario succeed.
Extension scenario	Describes the system behavior if some of the steps in the main scenario do not complete successfully.

this service can be treated as a separate use case. A scenario in a use case may therefore employ another use case for performing some of the tasks. In other words, use cases permit a hierarchic organization.

It should be evident that the basic system model that use cases assume is that a system primarily responds to requests from actors who use the system. By describing the interaction between actors and the system, the system behavior can be specified, and through the behavior its functionality is specified. A key advantage of this approach is that use cases focus on external behavior, thereby cleanly avoiding doing internal design during requirements, something that is desired but not easy to do with many modeling approaches.

Use cases are naturally textual descriptions, and represent the behavioral requirements of the system. This behavior specification can capture most of the functional requirements of the system. Therefore, use cases do not form the complete SRS, but can form a part of it. The complete SRS, as we have seen, will need to capture other requirements like performance and design constraints.

Though the detailed use cases are textual, diagrams can be used to supplement the textual description. For example, the use case diagram of UML provides an overview of the use cases and actors in the system and their dependency. A UML use case diagram generally shows each use case in the system as an ellipse, shows the primary actor for the use case as a stick figure connected to the use case with a line, and shows dependency between use cases by arcs between use cases. Some other relationships between use cases can also be represented. However, as use cases are basically textual in nature, diagrams play a limited role in either developing or specifying use cases. We will not discuss use case diagrams further.

3.4.2 Examples

Let us illustrate these concepts with a few use cases, which we will also use to explain other concepts related to use cases. Let us consider that a small on-line auction system is to be built for a university community, called the University Auction System (UAS), through which different members of the university can sell and buy goods. We will assume that there is a separate financial subsystem through which the payments are made and that each buyer and seller has an account in it.

In this system, though we have the same people who might be buying and selling, we have "buyers" and "sellers" as separate logical actors, as both have different goals to achieve. Besides these, the auction system itself is a stakeholder and an actor. The financial system is another. Let us first consider the main use cases of this system—"put an item for auction," "make a bid," and "complete an auction." These use cases are given in Figure 3.4.

The use cases are self-explanatory. This is the great value of use cases—they are natural and story-like which makes them easy to understand by both an analyst and a layman. This helps considerably in minimizing the communication gap between the developers and other stakeholders.

Some points about the use case are worth discussing. The use cases are generally numbered for reference purposes. The name of the use case specifies the goal of the primary actor (hence there is no separate line specifying the goal). The primary actor can be a person or a system—for UC1 and UC2, they are persons but for UC3, it is a system. The primary actor can also be another software which might request a service. The *precondition* of a use case specifies what the system will ensure before allowing the use case to be initiated. Common preconditions are "user is logged in," "input data exists in files or other data structures," etc. For an operation like delete it may be that "item exists," or for a tracking use case it may be that the "tracking number is valid."

It is worth noting that the use case description list contains some actions that are not necessarily tied to the goals of the primary actor. For example, the last step in UC2 is to update the bid price of other bidders. This action is clearly not needed by the current bidder for his goal. However, as the system and other bidders are also stakeholders for this use case, the use case has to ensure that their goals are also satisfied. Similar is the case with the last item of UC1.

The exception situations are also fairly clear. We have listed only the most obvious ones. There can be many more, depending on the goals of the organization. For example, there could be one "user does not complete the transaction," which is a failure condition that can occur anywhere. What should be done in

– *UC1*: **Put an item for auction**
Primary Actor: Seller
Precondition: Seller has logged in
Main Success Scenario:

1. Seller posts an item (its category, description, picture, etc.) for auction
2. System shows past prices of similar items to seller
3. Seller specifies the starting bid price and a date when auction will close
4. System accepts the item and posts it

Exception Scenarios:
– 2 a) There are no past items of this category

  • System tells the seller this situation

– *UC2*: **Make a bid**
Primary Actor: Buyer
Precondition: The buyer has logged in
Main Success Scenario:

1. Buyer <u>searches</u> or <u>browses</u> and selects some item
2. System shows the rating of the seller, the starting bid, the current bids, and the highest bid; asks buyer to make a bid
3. Buyer specifies a bid price
4. System accepts the bid; Blocks funds in bidders account
5. System updates the max bid price, informs other users, and updates the records for the item

Exception Scenarios:
– 3 a) The bid price is lower than the current highest

  • System informs the bidder and asks to rebid
– 4 a) The bidder does not have enough funds in his account

  • System cancels the bid, asks the user to get more funds

– *UC3*: **Complete auction of an item**
Primary Actor: Auction System
Precondition: The last date for bidding has been reached
Main Success Scenario:

1. Select highest bidder; send email to selected bidder and seller informing final bid price; send email to other bidders also
2. <u>Debit bidder's account and credit seller's</u>
3. Unblock all other bidders funds
4. <u>Transfer from seller's acct. commission amt. to organization's acct.</u>
5. Remove item from the site; update records

Exception Scenarios: None

Figure 3.4: Main use cases in an auction system.

this case has to then be specified (e.g., all the records are cleaned).

A use case can employ other use cases to perform some of its work. For example, in UC2 actions like "block the necessary funds" or "debit bidder's account and credit seller's" are actions that need to be performed for the use case to succeed. However, they are not performed in this use case, but are treated as use cases themselves whose behavior has to be described elsewhere. If these use cases are also part of the system being built, then there must be descriptions of these in the requirements document. If they belong to some other system, then proper specifications about them will have to be obtained. The financial actions may easily be outside the scope of the auction system, so will not be described in the SRS. However, actions like "search" and "browse" are most likely part of this system and will have to be described in the SRS.

This allows use cases to be hierarchically organized and refinement approach can be used to define a higher-level use case in terms of lower services and then defining the lower services. However, these lower-level use cases are proper use cases with a primary actor, main scenario, etc. The primary actor will often be the primary actor of the higher-level use case. For example, the primary actor for the use case "find an item" is the buyer. It also implies that while listing the scenarios, new use cases and new actors might emerge. In the requirements document, all the use cases that are mentioned in this one will need to be specified if they are a part of the system being built.

3.4.3 Extensions

Besides specifying the primary actor, its goal, and the success and exceptional scenarios, a use case can also specify a scope. If the system being built has many subsystems, as is often the case, sometimes system use cases may actually be capturing the behavior of some subsystem. In such a situation it is better to specify the scope of that use case as the subsystem. For example, a use case for a system may be log in. Even though this is a part of the system, the interaction of the user with the system described in this use case is limited to the interaction with the "login and authentication" subsystem. If "login and authentication" has been identified as a subsystem or a component, then it is better to specify it as the scope. Generally, a business use case has the enterprise or the organization as the scope; a system use case has the system being built as the scope; and a component use case is where the scope is a subsystem.

UCs where the scope is the enterprise can often run over a long period of time (e.g., process an application of a prospective candidate). These use cases may require many different systems to perform different tasks before the UC can be completed. (Example: for processing an application the HR department has to do some things, the travel department has to arrange the travel and lodging, and the technical department has to conduct the interview.) The system and subsystem use cases are generally of the type that can be completed in one relatively short sitting. All the three use cases above are system use cases. As mentioned before, we will focus on describing the behavior of the software system we are interested in building. However, the enterprise-level UCs provide the context in which the systems operate. Hence, sometimes it may be useful to describe some of the key business processes as *summary-level* use cases to provide the context for the system being designed and built.

For example, let us describe the overall use case of performing an auction. A possible use case is given in Figure 3.5. This use case is not a one-sitting use case and is really a business process, which provides the context for the earlier use cases. Though this use case is also largely done by the system and is probably part of the system being built, frequently such use cases may not be completely part of the software system and may involve manual steps as well. For example, in the "auction an item" use case, if the delivery of the item being auctioned was to be ensured by the auctioning site, then that will be a step in this use case and it will be a manual step.

- *Use Case 0*: **Auction an item**
  Primary Actor: Auction system
  Scope : Auction conducting organization
  Precondition: None
  Main Success Scenario:
  1. Seller performs *Put an item for auction*
  2. Various bidders perform *make a bid*
  3. On final date perform *Complete the auction of the item*
  4. Get feedback from seller; get feedback from buyer; update records

---

Figure 3.5: A summary-level use case.

Use cases may also specify post conditions for the main success scenario, or some minimal guarantees they provide in all conditions. For example, in some use cases, atomicity may be a minimal guarantee. That is, no matter what exceptions occur, either the entire transaction will be completed and the goal achieved, or the system state will be as if nothing was done. With atomicity, there will be no partial results and any partial changes will be rolled back.

3.4.4 Developing Use Cases

UCs not only document requirements, as their form is like storytelling and uses text, both of which are easy and natural with different stakeholders, they also are a good medium for discussion and brainstorming. Hence, UCs can also be used for requirements elicitation and problem analysis. While developing use cases, informal or formal models may also be built, though they are not required.

UCs can be evolved in a stepwise refinement manner with each step adding more details. This approach allows UCs to be presented at different levels of abstraction. Though any number of levels of abstraction are possible, four natural levels emerge:

- **Actors and goals.** The actor-goal list enumerates the use cases and specifies the actors for each goal. (The name of the use case is generally the goal.) This table may be extended by giving a brief description of each of the use cases. At this level, the use cases together specify the scope of the system and give an overall view of what it does. Completeness of functionality can be assessed fairly well by reviewing these.

- **Main success scenarios.** For each of the use cases, the main success scenarios are provided at this level. With the main scenarios, the system behavior for each use case is specified. This description can be reviewed to ensure that interests of all the stakeholders are met and that the use case is delivering the desired behavior.

- **Failure conditions.** Once the success scenario is listed, all the possible failure conditions can be identified. At this level, for each step in the main success scenario, the different ways in which a step can fail form the failure conditions. Before deciding what should be done in these failure conditions (which is done at the next level), it is better to enumerate the failure conditions and review for completeness.

- **Failure handling.** This is perhaps the most tricky and difficult part of writing a use case. Often the focus is so much on the main functionality that people do not pay attention to how failures should be handled. Determining what should be the behavior under different failure conditions will often identify new business rules or new actors.

The different levels can be used for different purposes. For discussion on overall functionality or capabilities of the system, actors and goal-level description is very useful. Failure conditions, on the other hand, are very useful for understanding and extracting detailed requirements and business rules under special cases.

These four levels can also guide the analysis activity. A step-by-step approach for analysis when employing use cases is:

Step 1. Identify the actors and their goals and get an agreement with the concerned stakeholders as to the goals. The actor-goal list will clearly define the scope of the system and will provide an overall view of what the system capabilities are.

Step 2. Understand and specify the main success scenario for each UC, giving more details about the main functions of the system. Interaction and discussion are the primary means to uncover these scenarios though models may be built, if required. During this step, the analyst may uncover that to complete some use case some other use cases are needed, which have not been identified. In this case, the list of use cases will be expanded.

Step 3. When the main success scenario for a use case is agreed upon and the main steps in its execution are specified, then the failure conditions can be examined. Enumerating failure conditions is an excellent method of uncovering special situations that can occur and which must be handled by the system.

Step 4. Finally, specify what should be done for these failure conditions. As details of handling failure scenarios can require a lot of effort and discussion, it is better to first enumerate the different failure conditions and then get the details of these scenarios. Very often, when deciding the failure scenarios, many new business rules of how to deal with these scenarios are uncovered.

Though we have explained the basic steps in developing use cases, at any step an analyst may have to go back to earlier steps as during some detailed analysis new actors may emerge or new goals and new use cases may be uncovered. That is, using use cases for analysis is also an interactive task.

What should be the level of detail in a use case? There is no one answer to a question like this; the actual answer always depends on the project and the situation. So it is with use cases. Generally it is good to have sufficient details which are not overwhelming but are sufficient to build the system and meet its quality goals. For example, if there is a small collocated team building the system, it is quite likely that use cases which list the main exception conditions and give a few key steps for the scenarios will suffice. On the other hand, for a project whose development is to be subcontracted to some other organization, it is better to have more detailed use cases.

For writing use cases, general technical writing rules apply. Use simple grammar, clearly specify who is performing the step, and keep the overall scenario as simple as possible. Also, when writing steps, for simplicity, it is better to combine some steps into one logical step, if it makes sense. For example, steps "user enters his name," "user enters his SSN," and "user enters his address" can be easily combined into one step "user enters personal information."

3.5 Other Approaches for Analysis

The basic aim of problem analysis is to obtain a clear understanding of the needs of the clients and the users, what exactly is desired from the software, and what the constraints on the solution are. Frequently the client and the users do not understand or know all their needs, because the potential of the new system is often not fully appreciated. The analysts have to ensure that the real needs of the clients and the users are uncovered, even if they don't know them clearly. That is, the analysts are not just collecting and organizing information about the client's organization and its processes, but they also act as *consultants* who play an *active* role of helping the clients and users identify their needs.

The basic principle used in analysis is the same as in any complex task: divide and conquer. That is, *partition* the problem into subproblems and then try to understand each subproblem and its relationship to other subproblems in an effort to understand the total problem.

The concepts of *state* and *projection* can sometimes also be used effectively in the partitioning process. A state of a system represents some conditions about the system. Frequently, when using state, a system is first viewed as operating in one of the several possible states, and then a detailed analysis is performed for each state. This approach is sometimes used in real-time software or process-control software.

In *projection*, a system is defined from multiple points of view [86]. While using projection, different viewpoints of the system are defined and the system is then analyzed from these different perspectives. The different "projections" obtained are combined to form the analysis for the complete system. Analyzing the system from the different perspectives is often easier, as it limits and focuses the scope of the study.

In the remainder of this section we will discuss two other methods for problem analysis. As the goal of analysis is to understand the problem domain, an analyst must be familiar with different methods of analysis and pick the approach that he feels is best suited to the problem at hand.

3.5.1 Data Flow Diagrams

Data flow diagrams (also called *data flow graphs*) are commonly used during problem analysis. Data flow diagrams (DFDs) are quite general and are not limited to problem analysis for software requirements specification. They were in use long before the software engineering discipline began. DFDs are very useful in understanding a system and can be effectively used during analysis.

A DFD shows the flow of data through a system. It views a system as a function that transforms the inputs into desired outputs. Any complex system will not perform this transformation in a "single step," and data will typically undergo a series of transformations before it becomes the output. The DFD aims to capture the transformations that take place within a system to the input data so that eventually the output data is produced. The agent that performs the transformation of data from one state to another is called a *process* (or a *bubble*). Thus, a DFD shows the movement of data through the different transformations or processes in the system. The processes are shown by named circles and data flows are represented by named arrows entering or leaving the bubbles. A rectangle represents a source or sink and is a net originator or consumer of data. A source or a sink is typically outside the main system of study. An example of a DFD for a system that pays workers is shown in Figure 3.6.

In this DFD there is one basic input data flow, the weekly timesheet, which originates from the source *worker*. The basic output is the paycheck, the sink for which is also the worker. In this system, first the employee's record is retrieved, using the employee ID, which is contained in the timesheet. From the employee record, the rate of payment and overtime are obtained. These rates and the regular and overtime hours (from the timesheet) are used to compute the pay. After the total pay is determined, taxes are deducted. To compute the tax deduction, information from the tax-rate file is used. The amount of tax deducted is recorded in the employee and company records. Finally, the paycheck is issued for the net pay. The amount paid is also recorded in company records.

Some conventions used in drawing this DFD should be explained. All external files such as employee record, company record, and tax rates are shown as a labeled straight line. The need for multiple data flows by a process is represented by a "*" between the data flows. This symbol represents the AND relationship. For example, if there is a "*" between the two input data flows A and B for a process, it means that A AND B are needed for the process. In the DFD, for the process "weekly pay" the data flow "hours" and "pay rate" both are needed, as shown in the DFD. Similarly, the OR relationship is represented by a "+" between the data flows.

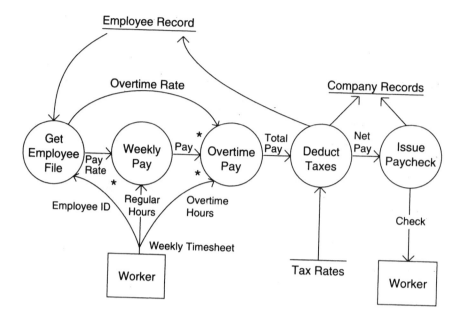

Figure 3.6: DFD of a system that pays workers.

This DFD is an abstract description of the system for handling payment. It does not matter if the system is automated or manual. This diagram could very well be for a manual system where the computations are all done with calculators, and the records are physical folders and ledgers. The details and minor data paths are not represented in this DFD. For example, what happens if there are errors in the weekly timesheet is not shown in this DFD. This is done to avoid getting bogged down with details while constructing a DFD for the overall system. If more details are desired, the DFD can be further refined.

It should be pointed out that a DFD is *not* a flowchart. A DFD represents the flow of data, while a flowchart shows the flow of control. A DFD does not represent procedural information. So, while drawing a DFD, one *must not* get involved in procedural details, and procedural thinking must be consciously avoided. For example, considerations of loops and decisions must be ignored. In drawing the DFD, the designer has to specify the major transforms in the path of the data flowing from the input to output. *How* those transforms are performed is *not* an issue while drawing the data flow graph.

Many systems are too large for a single DFD to describe the data processing clearly. It is necessary that some decomposition and abstraction mechanism be used for such systems. DFDs can be hierarchically organized, which helps in progressively partitioning and analyzing large systems. Such DFDs together are called a *leveled DFD set* [28].

A leveled DFD set has a starting DFD, which is a very abstract representation of the system, identifying the major inputs and outputs and the major processes in the system. Often, before the initial DFD, a *context diagram* may be drawn in which the entire system is shown as a single process with all its inputs, outputs, sinks, and sources. Then each process is refined and a DFD is drawn for the process. In other words, a bubble in a DFD is expanded into a DFD during refinement. For the hierarchy to be consistent, it is important that the net inputs and outputs of a DFD for a process are the same as the inputs and outputs of the process in the higher-level DFD. This refinement stops if each bubble is considered to be "atomic," in that each bubble can be easily specified or understood. It should be pointed out that during refinement, though the net input and output are preserved, a refinement of the data might also occur. That is, a unit of data may be broken into its components for processing when the detailed DFD for a process is being drawn. So, as the processes are decomposed, data decomposition also occurs.

In a DFD, data flows are identified by unique names. These names are chosen so that they convey some meaning about what the data is. However, for specifying the precise structure of data flows, a *data dictionary* is often used. The associated data dictionary states precisely the structure of each data flow in the DFD. To define the data structure, a regular expression type notation is used. While specifying the structure of a data item, sequence or composition is represented by "+", selection by vertical bar "|" (means one OR the other), and repetition by "*".

3.5.2 ER Diagrams

Entity relationship diagrams (ERDs) have been used for years for modeling the data aspects of a system. An ERD can be used to model the data in the system and how the data items relate to each other, but does not cover how the data is to be processed or how the data is actually manipulated and changed in the system. It is used often by database designers to represent the structure of the database and is a useful tool for analyzing software systems which employ databases. ER models form the logical database design and can be easily converted into initial table structure for a relational database.

ER diagrams have two main concepts and notations to representing them. These are entities and relationships. Entities are the main information holders or concepts in a system. Entities can be viewed as types which describe all elements of some type which have common properties. Entities are represented as boxes in an ER diagram, with a box representing all instances of the concept or type the entity is representing. An entity is essentially equivalent to a table in a database or a sheet in a spreadsheet, with each row representing an instance of this entity. Entities may have attributes, which are properties of the concept being represented. Attributes can be viewed as the columns of the database table and are represented as ellipses attached to the entity. To avoid cluttering, attributes are sometimes not shown in an ER diagram.

If all identities are identified and represented, we will have a set of labeled boxes in the diagram, each box representing some entity. Entities, of course, do not exist in isolation. They have relationships between them and that is the reason why they exist together in the same system.

Relationships between two entities are represented by a line connecting the boxes representing the entities. Having a line between two boxes means that each element of one entity is related to elements of the other entity, and vice versa. This relationship can also be given a name by labeling the line. In some notations, the name of the relationship is mentioned inside a diamond. Some examples of relationships are: studies-in (between students and college), works-for (between employees and companies), and owner (between people and cars). Note that the relationships need not be between two distinct entities. There can be a relationship between elements of the same entity. For example, for an entity type Employee, there can be a relationship Supervisor, which is between elements of the entity Employee.

An ER diagram specifies some properties of the relationship also. In particular, it can specify if the relationship is optional (or necessary), and with how many elements an element of an entity is related to. This leads to many forms of relationships. The common ones are one-to-one (that one element of an entity is related to exactly one element of the other entity), one-to-many or many-to-one (that one element is related to many elements of the other entity), and many-to-many (that one element of entity A is related to many elements of entity B and one element of entity B is related to many elements of entity A). There are various notations to express the nature of relationships; a common one is to put "0", "1", or "M" on the two sides of the relationship line to represent the cardinality of the relationship. Thus, for a one-to-many relationship, a "1" will be put on one end and "N" will be put on the other end of the line.

Relationships reflect some properties of the problem domain. For example, a course has many students and a student is taking many courses, leading to many-to-many relationship between courses and students. But a student studies in exactly one college though the college has many students, leading to many-to-one relationship between students and college. A department in a college has exactly one head, and one person can be Head of only one department, leading to one-to-one relationship.

Let us draw the ER diagram for the university auction system, some use cases of which were discussed earlier. From the use cases described, we can easily identify some entities—users, categories, items, and bids. The relationships between them are also clear. A user can sell many items, but each item has only one seller, so there is a one-to-many relationship "Sell" between the user and items. Similarly, there is a one-to-many relationship between items and bids, between users and bids, and between categories and items. The ER diagram of this is shown in Figure 3.7.

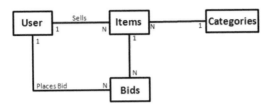

Figure 3.7: ER diagram for an auction system.

From the ER diagram, it is easy to determine the initial logical structure of the tables. Each entity represents a table, and relationships determine what fields a table must have to support the relationship, in addition to having fields for each of the attributes. For example, from the ER diagram for the auction system, we can say that there will be four tables for users, categories, items, and bids. As user is related to item by one-to-many, the item table should have a user-ID field to uniquely identify the user who is selling the item. Similarly, the bid table must have a user-ID to identify the user who placed the bid, and an item-ID to identify the item for which the bid has been made.

As we can see, an ER diagram is complementary to methods like use cases. Whereas use cases focus on the nature of interaction and functionality, ER diagrams focus on the structure of the entities being used in the use cases. Due to their complementary nature, both use cases and ER diagrams can be used while analyzing the requirements of a system and both may be contained in an SRS.

3.6 Validation

The development of software starts with a requirements document, which is also used to determine eventually whether or not the delivered software system is acceptable. It is therefore important that the requirements specification contains no errors and specifies the client's requirements correctly. Furthermore, as the longer an error remains undetected, the greater the cost of correcting it, it is extremely desirable to detect errors in the requirements before the design and development of the software begin.

Due to the nature of the requirements specification phase, there is a lot of room for misunderstanding and committing errors, and it is quite possible that the requirements specification does not accurately represent the client's needs. The basic objective of the requirements validation activity is to ensure that the SRS reflects the actual requirements accurately and clearly. A related objective is to check that the SRS document is itself of good quality.

Before we discuss validation, let us consider the type of errors that typically occur in an SRS. Many different types of errors are possible, but the most common errors that occur can be classified in four types: omission, inconsistency, incorrect fact, and ambiguity. *Omission* is a common error in requirements. In this type of error, some user requirement is simply not included in the SRS; the omitted requirement may be related to the behavior of the system, its performance, constraints, or any other factor. Omission directly affects the external completeness of the SRS. Another common form of error in requirements is *inconsistency*. Inconsistency can be due to contradictions within the requirements themselves or to incompatibility of the stated requirements with the actual requirements of the client or with the environment in which the system will operate. The third common requirement error is *incorrect fact*. Errors of this type occur when some fact recorded in the SRS is not correct. The fourth common error type is *ambiguity*. Errors of this type occur when there are some requirements that have multiple meanings, that is, their interpretation is not unique.

Some projects have collected data about requirement errors. In [27] the effectiveness of different methods and tools in detecting requirement errors in specifications for a data processing application is reported. On average, a total of more than 250 errors were detected, and the percentage of different types of errors was:

Omission	Incorrect Fact	Inconsistency	Ambiguity
26%	10%	38%	26%

In [5] the errors detected in the requirements specification of the A-7 project (which deals with a real-time flight control software) were reported. A total of about 80 errors were detected, out of which about 23% were clerical in nature. Of the remaining, the distribution with error type was:

Omission	Incorrect Fact	Inconsistency	Ambiguity
32%	49%	13%	5%

Though the distribution of errors is different in these two cases, reflecting the difference in application domains and the error detection methods used, they do suggest that the major problems (besides clerical errors) are omission, incorrect fact, inconsistency, and ambiguity. If we take the average of the two data tables, it shows that all four classes of errors are very significant, and a good fraction of errors belong to each of these types. This implies that besides improving the quality of the SRS itself (e.g., no clerical errors), the validation should focus on uncovering these types of errors.

As requirements are generally textual documents that cannot be executed, inspections and reviews are eminently suitable for requirements validation. Consequently, inspections of the SRS, frequently called requirements review, are the most common method of validation. Because requirements specification formally specifies something that originally existed informally in people's minds, requirements validation must involve the clients and the users. Due to this, the requirements review team generally consists of client as well as user representatives.

Requirements review is a review by a group of people to find errors and point out other matters of concern in the requirements specifications of a system. The review group should include the author of the requirements document, someone who understands the needs of the client, a person of the design team, and the person(s) responsible for maintaining the requirements document. It is also good practice to include some people not directly involved with product development, like a software quality engineer.

Although the primary goal of the review process is to reveal any errors in the requirements, such as those discussed earlier, the review process is also used to consider factors affecting quality, such as testability and readability. During the review, one of the jobs of the reviewers is to uncover the requirements that are too subjective and too difficult to define criteria for testing that requirement. During the review, the review team must go through each requirement and if any errors are there, then they discuss and agree on the nature of the error. A detailed inspection process may be used (we will discuss one such process later in Chapter 7 in the context of coding).

Requirements reviews are probably the most effective means for detecting requirement errors. The data in [5] about the A-7 project shows that about 33% of the total requirement errors detected were detected by review processes, and about 45% of the requirement errors were detected during the design phase when the requirement document is used as a reference for design. This clearly suggests that if requirements are reviewed then, not only a substantial fraction of the errors are detected by them, but a vast majority of the remaining errors are detected soon afterward in the design activity.

Though requirements reviews remain the most commonly used and viable means for requirement validation, other possibilities arise if some special-purpose tools for modeling and analysis are used. For example, if the requirements are written in a formal specification language or a language specifically designed for machine processing, then it is possible to have tools to verify some properties of requirements. These tools will focus on checks for internal consistency and completeness, which sometimes lead to checking of external completeness. However, these tools cannot directly check for external completeness (after all, how will a tool know that some requirement has been completely omitted?). For this reason, requirements reviews are needed even if the requirements are specified through a tool or are in a formal notation.

3.7 Summary

– The main goal of the requirements process is to produce the software requirements specification (SRS) which accurately captures the client's requirements and which forms the basis of software development and validation.

– There are three basic activities in the requirements process—problem analysis, specification, and validation. The goal of analysis is to understand the different aspects of the problem, its context, and how it fits within the client's organization. In requirements specification the understood problem is specified or written, producing the SRS. Requirements validation is done to ensure that the requirements specified in the SRS are indeed what are desired.

– The key desirable characteristics of an SRS are: correctness, completeness, consistency, unambiguousness, verifiability, and ranked for importance.

– A good SRS should specify all the functions the software needs to support, performance requirements of the system, the design constraints that exist, and all the external interfaces.

– Use cases are a popular approach for specifying functional requirements.

  – Each use case specifies the interaction of the system with the primary actor, who initiates the use case for achieving some goal.

  – A use case has a precondition, a normal scenario, as well as many exceptional scenarios, thereby providing the complete behavior of the system.

  – For developing use cases, first the actors and goal should be identified, then the main success scenarios, then the failure conditions, and finally the failure handling.

– With data flow diagrams, a system is analyzed from the point of view of how data flows through the system. A DFD consists of processes and data flows through the processes.

– Omission, incorrect fact, inconsistency, and ambiguity are the most common errors in an SRS. For validation, the most commonly used method is doing a structured group review of the requirements.

Self-Assessment Exercises

1. The basic goal of the requirements activity is to get an SRS that has some desirable properties. What is the role of modeling in developing such an SRS?
2. What are the main components of an SRS? And what are the main criteria for evaluating the quality of an SRS?
3. What are the main error types for requirements?
4. Take an on-line social networking site of your choice. List the major use cases for this system, along with the goals, preconditions, and exception scenarios.
5. Do the same exercise for a conference management site which allows authors to submit papers, program chairs to assign reviewers and do the final paper selection based on reviews, and reviewers to enter the review.
6. Who do you think should be included in the requirements review team?

4

Planning a Software Project

Planning is the most important project management activity. It has two basic objectives—establish reasonable cost, schedule, and quality goals for the project, and to draw out a plan to deliver the project goals. A project succeeds if it meets its cost, schedule, and quality goals. Without the project goals being defined, it is not possible to even declare if a project has succeeded. And without detailed planning, no real monitoring or controlling of the project is possible. Often projects are rushed toward implementation with not enough effort spent on planning. No amount of technical effort later can compensate for lack of careful planning. Lack of proper planning is a sure ticket to failure for a large software project. For this reason, we treat project planning as an independent chapter. Note that we also cover the monitoring phase of the project management process as part of planning, as how the project is to be monitored is also a part of the planning phase.

The inputs to the planning activity are the requirements specification and maybe the architecture description. A very detailed requirements document is not essential for planning, but for a good plan all the important requirements must be known, and it is highly desirable that key architecture decisions have been taken.

There are generally two main outputs of the planning activity: the overall *project management plan* document that establishes the project goals on the cost, schedule, and quality fronts, and defines the plans for managing risk, monitoring the project, etc.; and the detailed plan, often referred to as the *detailed project schedule*, specifying the tasks that need to be performed to meet the goals, the resources who will perform them, and their schedule. The

P. Jalote, *A Concise Introduction to Software Engineering*,
DOI: 10.1007/978-1-84800-302-6_4, © Springer-Verlag London Limited 2008

overall plan guides the development of the detailed plan, which then becomes the main guiding document during project execution for project monitoring.

In this chapter, we will discuss

— How to estimate effort and schedule for the project to establish project goals and milestones and determine the team size needed for executing the project.

— How to establish quality goals for the project and prepare a quality plan.

— How to identify high-priority risks that can threaten the success of the project, and plan for their mitigation.

— How to plan for monitoring a project using measurements to check if a project is progressing as per the plan.

— How to develop a detailed task schedule from the overall estimates and other planning tasks done such that, if followed, the overall goals of the project will be met.

4.1 Effort Estimation

For a software development project, overall effort and schedule estimates are essential prerequisites for planning the project. These estimates are needed before development is initiated, as they establish the cost and schedule goals of the project. Without these, even simple questions like "is the project late?" "are there cost overruns?" and "when is the project likely to complete?" cannot be answered. A more practical use of these estimates is in bidding for software projects, where cost and schedule estimates must be given to a potential client for the development contract. (As the bulk of the cost of software development is due to the human effort, cost can easily be determined from effort by using a suitable person-month cost value.) Effort and schedule estimates are also required for determining the staffing level for a project during different phases, for the detailed plan, and for project monitoring.

The accuracy with which effort can be estimated clearly depends on the level of information available about the project. The more detailed the information, the more accurate the estimation can be. Of course, even with all the information available, the accuracy of the estimates will depend on the effectiveness and accuracy of the estimation procedures or models employed and the process. If from the requirements specifications, the estimation approach can produce estimates that are within 20% of the actual effort about two-thirds of the time, then the approach can be considered good. Here we discuss two commonly used approaches.

4.1.1 Top-Down Estimation Approach

Although the effort for a project is a function of many parameters, it is generally
agreed that the primary factor that controls the effort is the size of the project.
That is, the larger the project, the greater is the effort requirement. The top-
down approach utilizes this and considers effort as a function of *project size*.
Note that to use this approach, we need to first determine the nature of the
function, and then to apply the function, we need to estimate the size of the
project for which effort is to be estimated.

If past productivity on similar projects is known, then it can be used as
the estimation function to determine effort from the size. If productivity is P
KLOC/PM, then the effort estimate for the project will be SIZE/P person-
months. Note that as productivity itself depends on the size of the project
(larger projects often have lower productivity), this approach can work only if
the size and type of the project are similar to the set of projects from which the
productivity P was obtained (and that in the new project a similar productivity
can be obtained by following a process similar to what was used in earlier
projects).

A more general function for determining effort from size that is commonly
used is of the form:

$$EFFORT = a * SIZE^b,$$

where a and b are constants [2], and project size is generally in KLOC (size
could also be in another size measure called *function points* which can be determined from requirements). Values for these constants for an organization
are determined through regression analysis, which is applied to data about
the projects that have been performed in the past. For example, Watson and
Felix [81] analyzed the data of more than 60 projects done at IBM Federal
Systems Division, ranging from 4000 to 467,000 lines of delivered source code,
and found that if the SIZE estimate is in thousands of delivered lines of code
(KLOC), the total effort, E, in person-months (PM) can be given by the equation $E = 5.2(SIZE)^{.91}$. In the COnstructive COst MOdel (COCOMO) [12, 13],
for the initial estimate (also called *nominal estimate*) the equation for an organic project is $E = 3.9(SIZE)^{.91}$.

Though size is the primary factor affecting cost, other factors also have
some effect. In the COCOMO model, after determining the initial estimate,
some other factors are incorporated for obtaining the final estimate. To do this,
COCOMO uses a set of 15 different attributes of a project called *cost driver
attributes*. Examples of the attributes are required software reliability, product
complexity, analyst capability, application experience, use of modern tools, and
required development schedule. Each cost driver has a rating scale, and for
each rating, a multiplying factor is provided. For example, for the reliability,

the rating scale is very low, low, nominal, high, and very high; the multiplying factors for these ratings are .75, .88, 1.00, 1.15, and 1.40, respectively. So, if the reliability requirement for the project is judged to be low, then the multiplying factor is .75, while if it is judged to be very high, the factor is 1.40. The attributes and their multiplying factors for different ratings are shown in Table 4.1 [12, 13].

Table 4.1: Effort multipliers for different cost drivers.

Cost Drivers	Rating				
	Very Low	Low	Nom-inal	High	Very High
Product Attributes					
RELY, required reliability	.75	.88	1.00	1.15	1.40
DATA, database size		.94	1.00	1.08	1.16
CPLX, product complexity	.70	.85	1.00	1.15	1.30
Computer Attributes					
TIME, execution time constraint			1.00	1.11	1.30
STOR, main storage constraint			1.00	1.06	1.21
VITR, virtual machine volatility		.87	1.00	1.15	1.30
TURN, computer turnaround time		.87	1.00	1.07	1.15
Personnel Attributes					
ACAP, analyst capability	1.46	1.19	1.00	.86	.71
AEXP, application exp.	1.29	1.13	1.00	.91	.82
PCAP, programmer capability	1.42	1.17	1.00	.86	.70
VEXP, virtual machine exp.	1.21	1.10	1.00	.90	
LEXP, prog. language exp.	1.14	1.07	1.00	.95	
Project Attributes					
MODP, modern prog. practices	1.24	1.10	1.00	.91	.82
TOOL, use of SW tools	1.24	1.10	1.00	.91	.83
SCHED, development schedule	1.23	1.08	1.00	1.04	1.10

The multiplying factors for all 15 cost drivers are multiplied to get the effort adjustment factor (EAF). The final effort estimate, E, is obtained by multiplying the initial estimate by the EAF. In other words, adjustment is made to the size-based estimate using the rating for these 15 different factors.

As an example, consider a system being built for supporting auctions in a university (some of the use cases of this were discussed in the previous chapter). From the use cases and other requirements, it is decided that the system will comprise a few different modules. The modules and their expected sizes are:

Login	200 LOC
Payment	200 LOC
Administrator interface	600 LOC
Seller functions	200 LOC
Buyer functions	500 LOC
View and bookkeeping	300 LOC
TOTAL	2000 LOC

The total size of this software is estimated to be 2 KLOC. If we want to use COCOMO for estimation, we should estimate the value of the different cost drivers. Suppose we expect that the complexity of the system is high, the programmer capability is low, and the application experience of the team is low. All other factors have a nominal rating. From these, the effort adjustment factor (EAF) is

$$EAF = 1.15 * 1.17 * 1.13 = 1.52.$$

The initial effort estimate for the project is obtained from the relevant equations. We have

$$E_i = 3.9 * 2^{.91} = 7.3 \text{ PM}.$$

Using the EAF, the adjusted effort estimate is

$$E = 1.52 * 7.3 = 11.1 \text{ PM}.$$

From the overall estimate, estimates of the effort required for the different phases in the projects can also be determined. This is generally done by using an effort distribution among phases. The percentage of total effort spent in a phase varies with the type and size of the project, and can be obtained from data of similar projects in the past. A general distribution of effort among different phases was discussed in the previous chapter. The effort distribution suggested by COCOMO for one type of software systems is given in Table 4.2.

Table 4.2: Phasewise distribution of effort.

Phase	Size			
	Small 2 KLOC	Intermediate 8 KLOC	Medium 32 KLOC	Large 128 KLOC
Product design	16	16	16	16
Detailed design	26	25	24	23
Code and unit test	42	40	38	36
Integration and test	16	19	22	25

It should be noted that to use the top-down approach for estimation, even if we have a suitable function, we need to have an estimate of the project size. In other words, we have replaced the problem of effort estimation by size estimation. One may then ask, why not directly do effort estimation rather than size estimation? The answer is that size estimation is often easier than direct effort estimation. This is mainly due to the fact that the system size can be estimated from the sizes of its components (which is often easier to do) by adding the size estimates of all the components. Similar property does not hold for effort estimation, as effort for developing a system is *not* the sum of effort for developing the components (as additional effort is needed for integration and other such activities when building a system from developed components).

Clearly for top-down estimation to work well, it is important that good estimates for the size of the software be obtained. There is no known "simple" method for estimating the size accurately. When estimating software size, the best way may be to get as much detail as possible about the software to be developed and to be aware of our biases when estimating the size of the various components. By obtaining details and using them for size estimation, the estimates are likely to be closer to the actual size of the final software.

4.1.2 Bottom-Up Estimation Approach

A somewhat different approach for effort estimation is the *bottom-up approach*. In this approach, the project is first divided into tasks and then estimates for the different tasks of the project are obtained. From the estimates of the different tasks, the overall estimate is determined. That is, the overall estimate of the project is derived from the estimates of its parts. This type of approach is also called *activity-based estimation*. Essentially, in this approach the size and complexity of the project is captured in the set of tasks the project has to perform.

The bottom-up approach lends itself to direct estimation of effort; once the project is partitioned into smaller tasks, it is possible to directly estimate the effort required for them, especially if tasks are relatively small. One difficulty in this approach is that to get the overall estimate, all the tasks have to be enumerated. A risk of bottom-up methods is that one may omit some activities. Also, directly estimating the effort for some overhead tasks, such as project management, that span the project can be difficult.

If architecture of the system to be built has been developed and if past information about how effort is distributed over different phases is known, then the bottom-up approach need not completely list all the tasks, and a less tedious approach is possible. Here we describe one such approach used in a commercial organization [58].

In this approach, the major programs (or units or modules) in the software being built are first determined. Each program unit is then classified as simple, medium, or complex based on certain criteria. For each classification unit, an average effort for coding (and unit testing) is decided. This average coding effort can be based on past data from a similar project, from some guidelines, or on experience of people.

Once the number of units in the three categories of complexity is known and the estimated coding effort for each program is selected, the total coding effort for the project is known. From the total coding effort, the effort required for the other phases and activities in the project is determined as a percentage of coding effort. For this, from information about the past performance of the process, the likely distribution of effort in different phases of this project is determined. This distribution is then used to determine the effort for other phases and activities from the effort estimate of coding. From these estimates, the total effort for the project is obtained.

This approach lends itself to a judicious mixture of experience and data. If suitable past data are not available (for example, if launching a new type of project), one can estimate the coding effort using experience once the nature of the different types of units is specified. With this estimate, we can obtain the estimate for other activities by working with some reasonable or standard effort distribution. This strategy can easily account for activities that are sometimes difficult to enumerate early but do consume effort by budgeting effort for an "other" or "miscellaneous" category.

The procedure for estimation can be summarized as the following sequence of steps:

1. Identify modules in the system and classify them as simple, medium, or complex.

2. Determine the average coding effort for simple/medium/complex modules.

3. Get the total coding effort using the coding effort of different types of modules and the counts for them.

4. Using the effort distribution for similar projects, estimate the effort for other tasks and the total effort.

5. Refine the estimates based on project-specific factors.

This procedure uses a judicious mixture of past data (in the form of distribution of effort) and experience of the programmers. This approach is also simple and similar to how many of us plan any project. For this reason, for small projects, many people find this approach natural and comfortable.

Note that this method of classifying programs into a few categories and using an average coding effort for each category is used only for effort estimation. In detailed scheduling, when a project manager assigns each unit to a member

of the team for coding and budgets time for the activity, characteristics of the
unit are taken into account to give more or less time than the average.

4.2 Project Schedule and Staffing

After establishing a goal on the effort front, we need to establish the goal
for delivery schedule. With the effort estimate (in person-months), it may be
tempting to pick any project duration based on convenience and then fix a
suitable team size to ensure that the total effort matches the estimate. However,
as is well known now, person and months are not fully interchangeable in a
software project. Person and months can be interchanged arbitrarily only if
all the tasks in the project can be done in parallel, and no communication
is needed between people performing the tasks. This is not true for software
projects—there are dependencies between tasks (e.g., testing can only be done
after coding is done), and a person performing some task in a project needs to
communicate with others performing other tasks. As Brooks has pointed out
[16], "... man and months are interchangeable only for activities that require
no communication among men, like sowing wheat or reaping cotton. This is
not even approximately true of software ...."

However, for a project with some estimated effort, multiple schedules (or
project duration) are indeed possible. For example, for a project whose effort
estimate is 56 person-months, a total schedule of 8 months is possible with 7
people. A schedule of 7 months with 8 people is also possible, as is a schedule
of approximately 9 months with 6 people. (But a schedule of 1 month with 56
people is not possible. Similarly, no one would execute the project in 28 months
with 2 people.) In other words, once the effort is fixed, there is some flexibility
in setting the schedule by appropriately staffing the project, but this flexibility
is not unlimited. Empirical data also suggests that no simple equation between
effort and schedule fits well [72].

The objective is to fix a reasonable schedule that can be achieved (if suitable number of resources are assigned). One method to determine the overall
schedule is to determine it as a function of effort. Such function can be determined from data from completed projects using statistical techniques like
fitting a regression curve through the scatter plot obtained by plotting the effort and schedule of past projects. This curve is generally nonlinear because the
schedule does not grow linearly with effort. Many models follow this approach
[2, 12]. The IBM Federal Systems Division found that the total duration, M, in
calendar months can be estimated by $M = 4.1E^{.36}$. In COCOMO, the equation
for schedule for an organic type of software is $M = 2.5E^{.38}$. As schedule is not

a function solely of effort, the schedule determined in this manner is essentially a guideline.

Another method for checking a schedule for medium-sized projects is the rule of thumb called the *square root check* [58]. This check suggests that the proposed schedule can be around the square root of the total effort in person-months. This schedule can be met if suitable resources are assigned to the project. For example, if the effort estimate is 50 person-months, a schedule of about 7 to 8 months will be suitable.

From this macro estimate of schedule, we can determine the schedule for the major milestones in the project. To determine the milestones, we must first understand the manpower ramp-up that usually takes place in a project. The number of people that can be gainfully utilized in a software project tends to follow the Rayleigh curve [71, 72]. That is, in the beginning and the end, few people are needed on the project; the peak team size (PTS) is needed somewhere near the middle of the project; and again fewer people are needed after that. This occurs because only a few people are needed and can be used in the initial phases of requirements analysis and design. The human resources requirement peaks during coding and unit testing, and during system testing and integration, again fewer people are required.

Often, the staffing level is not changed continuously in a project and approximations of the Rayleigh curve are used: assigning a few people at the start, having the peak team during the coding phase, and then leaving a few people for integration and system testing. If we consider design and analysis, build, and test as three major phases, the manpower ramp-up in projects typically resembles the function shown in Figure 4.1 [58].

For ease of scheduling, particularly for smaller projects, often the required people are assigned together around the start of the project. This approach can lead to some people being unoccupied at the start and toward the end. This slack time is often used for supporting project activities like training and documentation.

Given the effort estimate for a phase, we can determine the duration of the phase if we know the manpower ramp-up. For these three major phases, the percentage of the schedule consumed in the build phase is smaller than the percentage of the effort consumed because this phase involves more people. Similarly, the percentage of the schedule consumed in the design and testing phases exceeds their effort percentages. The exact schedule depends on the planned manpower ramp-up, and how many resources can be used effectively in a phase on that project. Generally speaking, design requires about a quarter of the schedule, build consumes about half, and integration and system testing consume the remaining quarter. COCOMO gives 19% for design, 62% for programming, and 18% for integration.

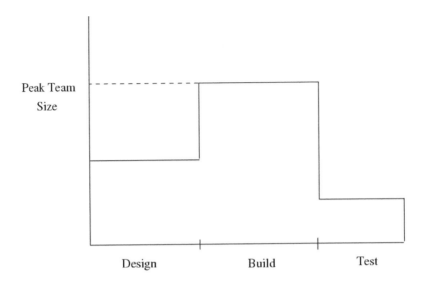

Figure 4.1: Manpower ramp-up in a typical project.

4.3 Quality Planning

Having set the goals for effort and schedule, the goal for the third key dimension of a project—quality—needs to be defined. However, unlike schedule and effort, quantified quality goal setting for a project and then planning to meet it is much harder. For effort and schedule goals, we can easily check if a detailed plan meets these goals (e.g., by seeing if the last task ends before the target date and if the sum total of effort of all tasks is less than the overall effort goal). For quality, even if we set the goal in terms of expected delivered defect density, it is not easy to plan for achieving this goal or for checking if a plan can meet these goals. Hence, often, quality goals are specified in terms of acceptance criteria—the delivered software should finally work for all the situations and test cases in the acceptance criteria. Further, there may even be an acceptance criterion on the number of defects that can be found during the acceptance testing. For example, no more than n defects are uncovered by acceptance testing.

The quality plan is the set of quality-related activities that a project plans to do to achieve the quality goal. To plan for quality, let us first understand the defect injection and removal cycle, as it is defects that determine the quality of the final delivered software.

Software development is a highly people-oriented activity and hence it is error-prone. In a software project, we start with no defects (there is no software to contain defects). Defects are injected into the software being built during the different phases in the project. That is, during the transformation from user needs to software to satisfy those needs, defects are injected in the transformation activities undertaken. These injection stages are primarily the requirements specification, the high-level design, the detailed design, and coding. To ensure that high-quality software is delivered, these defects are removed through the quality control (QC) activities. The QC activities for defect removal include requirements reviews, design reviews, code reviews, unit testing, integration testing, system testing, acceptance testing, etc. Figure 4.2 shows the process of defect injection and removal.

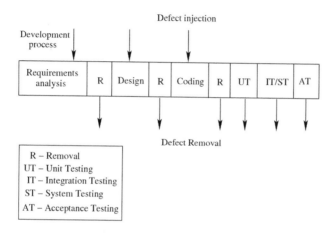

Figure 4.2: Defect injection and removal cycle.

As the final goal is to deliver software with low defect density, ensuring quality revolves around two main themes: reduce the defects being injected, and increase the defects being removed. The first is often done through standards, methodologies, following of good processes, etc., which help reduce the chances of errors by the project personnel. (There are specific techniques for defect prevention also.) The quality plan therefore focuses mostly on planning suitable quality control tasks for removing defects.

Reviews and testing are two most common QC activities utilized in a project. Whereas reviews are structured, human-oriented processes, testing is the process of executing software (or parts of it) in an attempt to identify defects. The most common approach for quality planning in a project is to specify the QC activities to be performed in the project, and have suitable guidelines for performing each of the QC tasks, such that the chances of meeting the quality goals are high. During project execution, these activities are carried out in accordance with the defined procedures.

When this approach is used for ensuring quality, making quantitative claims can be quite hard. For quantitative assessment of the quality processes, metrics-based analysis is necessary. That, however, is an advanced topic, beyond the scope of this book (and indeed many organizations). Hence, for ensuring quality, the reliance is primarily on applying suitable QC techniques at the right places in the process, and using experience to ensure that sufficient QC tasks are done in the project.

Hence, the quality plan for the project is largely a specification of which QC task is to be done and when, and what process and guidelines are to be used for performing the QC task. The choice depends on the nature and goals and constraints of the project. Typically, the QC tasks will be schedulable tasks in the detailed schedule of the project. For example, it will specify what documents will be inspected, what parts of the code will be inspected, and what levels of testing will be performed. The plan can be considerably enhanced if some expectations of defect levels that are expected to be found for the different quality control tasks are also mentioned—these can then aid the monitoring of quality as the project proceeds.

4.4 Risk Management Planning

A software project is a complex undertaking. Unforeseen events may have an adverse impact on a project's ability to meet the cost, schedule, or quality goals. Risk management is an attempt to minimize the chances of failure caused by unplanned events. The aim of risk management is not to avoid getting into projects that have risks but to minimize the impact of risks in the projects that are undertaken.

A risk is a probabilistic event—it may or may not occur. For this reason, we frequently have an optimistic tendency to simply not see risks or to hope that they will not occur. Social and organizational factors also may stigmatize risks and discourage clear identification of them [19]. This kind of attitude gets the project in trouble if the risk events materialize, something that is likely to happen in a large project. Not surprisingly, then, risk management is considered first among the best practices for managing large software projects [17]. It first came to the forefront with Boehm's tutorial on risk management [11]. Since then, several books have targeted risk management for software [18, 45].

4.4.1 Risk Management Concepts

Risk is defined as an exposure to the chance of injury or loss. That is, risk implies that there is a possibility that something negative may happen. In the context of software projects, negative implies that there is an adverse effect on cost, quality, or schedule. *Risk management* is the area that tries to ensure that the impact of risks on cost, quality, and schedule is minimal.

Risk management can be considered as dealing with the possibility and actual occurrence of those events that are not "regular" or commonly expected, that is, they are probabilistic. The commonly expected events, such as people going on leave or some requirements changing, are handled by normal project management. So, in a sense, risk management begins where normal project management ends. It deals with events that are infrequent, somewhat out of the control of the project management, and which can have a major impact on the project.

Most projects have risk. The idea of risk management is to minimize the possibility of risks materializing, if possible, or to minimize the effects if risks actually materialize. For example, when constructing a building, there is a risk that the building may later collapse due to an earthquake. That is, the possibility of an earthquake is a risk. If the building is a large residential complex, then the potential cost in case the earthquake risk materializes can be enormous. This risk can be reduced by shifting to a zone that is not earthquake-prone. Alternatively, if this is not acceptable, then the effects of this risk materializing are minimized by suitably constructing the building (the approach taken in Japan and California). At the same time, if a small dumping ground is to be constructed, no such approach might be followed, as the financial and other impact of an actual earthquake on such a building is so low that it does not warrant special measures.

It should be clear that risk management has to deal with identifying the undesirable events that can occur, the probability of their occurring, and the loss if an undesirable event does occur. Once this is known, strategies can be formulated for either reducing the probability of the risk materializing or reducing the effect of risk materializing. So the risk management revolves around *risk assessment* and *risk control*.

4.4.2 Risk Assessment

The goal of risk assessment is to prioritize the risks so that attention and resources can be focused on the more risky items. *Risk identification* is the first step in risk assessment, which identifies all the different risks for a particular project. These risks are project-dependent and identifying them is an exercise in envisioning what can go wrong. Methods that can aid risk identification include checklists of possible risks, surveys, meetings and brainstorming, and reviews of plans, processes, and work products [45].

Checklists of frequently occurring risks are probably the most common tool
for risk identification—most organizations prepare a list of commonly occurring
risks for projects, prepared from a survey of previous projects. Such a list can
form the starting point for identifying risks for the current project.

Based on surveys of experienced project managers, Boehm [11] has produced
a list of the top 10 risk items likely to compromise the success of a software
project. Figure 4.3 shows some of these risks along with the techniques preferred
by management for managing these risks. Top risks in a commercial software
organization can be found in [58].

	Risk Item	Risk Management Techniques
1	Personnel Shortfalls	Staffing with top talent; Job matching; Team building; Key personnel agreements; Training; Prescheduling key people
2	Unrealistic Schedules and Budgets	Detailed cost and schedule estimation; Design to cost; Incremental development; Software reuse; Requirements scrubbing
3	Developing the Wrong Software Functions	Organization analysis; Machine analysis; User surveys; Prototyping; Early user's manuals
4	Developing the Wrong User Interface	Prototyping; Scenarios; Task analysis; User characterization
5	Gold Plating	Requirements scrubbing; Prototyping; Cost benefit analysis; Design to cost

Figure 4.3: Top risk items and techniques for managing them.

The top-ranked risk item is personnel shortfalls. This involves just having
fewer people than necessary or not having people with specific skills that a
project might require. Some of the ways to manage this risk are to get the
top talent possible and to match the needs of the project with the skills of the
available personnel. Adequate training, along with having some key personnel
for critical areas of the project, will also reduce this risk.

The second item, unrealistic schedules and budgets, happens very frequently
due to business and other reasons. It is very common that high-level management imposes a schedule for a software project that is not based on the characteristics of the project and is unrealistic. Underestimation may also happen
due to inexperience or optimism.

The next few items are related to requirements. Projects run the risk of
developing the wrong software if the requirements analysis is not done properly

and if development begins too early. Similarly, often improper user interface may be developed. This requires extensive rework of the user interface later or the software benefits are not obtained because users are reluctant to use it. Gold plating refers to adding features in the software that are only marginally useful. This adds unnecessary risk to the project because gold plating consumes resources and time with little return.

Risk identification merely identifies the undesirable events that might take place during the project, i.e., enumerates the "unforeseen" events that might occur. It does not specify the probabilities of these risks materializing nor the impact on the project if the risks indeed materialize. Hence, the next tasks are *risk analysis* and *prioritization*.

In risk analysis, the probability of occurrence of a risk has to be estimated, along with the loss that will occur if the risk does materialize. This is often done through discussion, using experience and understanding of the situation, though structured approaches also exist.

Once the probabilities of risks materializing and losses due to materialization of different risks have been analyzed, they can be prioritized. One approach for prioritization is through the concept of *risk exposure* (RE) [11], which is sometimes called *risk impact*. RE is defined by the relationship

$$RE = Prob(UO) * Loss(UO),$$

where $Prob(UO)$ is the probability of the risk materializing (i.e., undesirable outcome) and $Loss(UO)$ is the total loss incurred due to the unsatisfactory outcome. The loss is not only the direct financial loss that might be incurred but also any loss in terms of credibility, future business, and loss of property or life. The RE is the expected value of the loss due to a particular risk. For risk prioritization using RE is, the higher the RE, the higher the priority of the risk item.

4.4.3 Risk Control

The main objective of risk management is to identify the top few risk items and then focus on them. Once a project manager has identified and prioritized the risks, the top risks can be easily identified. The question then becomes what to do about them. Knowing the risks is of value only if you can prepare a plan so that their consequences are minimal—that is the basic goal of risk management.

One obvious strategy is risk avoidance, which entails taking actions that will avoid the risk altogether, like the earlier example of shifting the building site to a zone that is not earthquake-prone. For some risks, avoidance might be possible.

For most risks, the strategy is to perform the actions that will either reduce the probability of the risk materializing or reduce the loss due to the risk materializing. These are called *risk mitigation steps*. To decide what mitigation steps to take, a list of commonly used risk mitigation steps for various risks is very useful here. For the risks mentioned in Figure 4.3, suitable risk mitigation steps are also given.

Note that unlike risk assessment, which is largely an analytical exercise, risk mitigation comprises active measures that have to be performed to minimize the impact of risks. In other words, selecting a risk mitigation step is not just an intellectual exercise. The risk mitigation step must be executed (and monitored). To ensure that the needed actions are executed properly, they must be incorporated into the detailed project schedule.

Risk prioritization and consequent planning are based on the risk perception at the time the risk analysis is performed. Because risks are probabilistic events that frequently depend on external factors, the threat due to risks may change with time as factors change. Clearly, then, the risk perception may also change with time. Furthermore, the risk mitigation steps undertaken may affect the risk perception.

This dynamism implies that risks in a project should not be treated as static and must be monitored and reevaluated periodically. Hence, in addition to monitoring the progress of the planned risk mitigation steps, a project must periodically revisit the risk perception and modify the risk mitigation plans, if needed. *Risk monitoring* is the activity of monitoring the status of various risks and their control activities. One simple approach for risk monitoring is to analyze the risks afresh at each major milestone, and change the plans as needed.

4.4.4 A Practical Risk Management Planning Approach

Though the concept of risk exposure is rich, a simple practical way of doing risk planning is to simply categorize risks and the impacts in a few levels and then use it for prioritization. This approach is used in many organizations. Here we discuss a simple approach used in an organization [58]. In this approach, the probability of a risk occurring is categorized as low, medium, or high. The risk impact can also be classified as low, medium, and high. With these ratings, the following simple method for risk prioritization can be specified:

1. For each risk, rate the probability of its happening as low, medium, or high.

Table 4.3: Risk management plan for a project.

	Risk	Prob.	Impact	Exp.	Mitigation Plan
1	Failure to meet the high performance	High	High	High	Study white papers and guidelines on perf. Train team on perf. tuning. Update review checklist to look for perf. pitfalls. Test application for perf. during system testing.
2	Lack of people with right skills	Med	Med	Med	Train resources. Review prototype with customer. Develop coding practices.
3	Complexity of application	Med	Med	Med	Ensure ongoing knowledge transfer. Deploy persons with prior experience with the domain.
4	Manpower attrition	Med	Med	Med	Train a core group of four people. Rotate assignments among people. Identify backups for key roles.
5	Unclear requirements	Med	Med	Med	Review a prototype. Conduct a midstage review.

2. For each risk, assess its impact on the project as low, medium, or high.

3. Rank the risks based on the probability and effects on the project; for example, a high-probability, high-impact item will have higher rank than a risk item with a medium probability and high impact. In case of conflict, use judgment.

4. Select the top few risk items for mitigation and tracking.

An example of this approach is given in Table 4.3, which shows the various ratings and the risk mitigation steps [58]. As we can see, the risk management plan, which is essentially this table, can be very brief and focused. For monitoring the risks, one way is to redo risk management planning at milestones, giving more attention to the risks listed in the project plan. During risk monitoring at milestones, reprioritization may occur and mitigation plans for the remainder of the project may change, depending on the current situation and the impact of mitigation steps taken earlier.

4.5 Project Monitoring Plan

A project management plan is merely a document that can be used to guide the execution of a project. Even a good plan is useless unless it is properly executed. And execution cannot be properly driven by the plan unless it is monitored carefully and the actual performance is tracked against the plan.

Monitoring requires measurements to be made to assess the situation of a project. If measurements are to be taken during project execution, we must plan carefully regarding what to measure, when to measure, and how to measure. Hence, measurement planning is a key element in project planning. In addition, how the measurement data will be analyzed and reported must also be planned in advance to avoid the situation of collecting data but not knowing what to do with it. Without careful planning for data collection and its analysis, neither is likely to happen. In this section we discuss the issues of measurements and project tracking.

4.5.1 Measurements

The basic purpose of measurements in a project is to provide data to project management about the project's current state, such that they can effectively monitor and control the project and ensure that the project goals are met. As project goals are established in terms of software to be delivered, cost, schedule, and quality, for monitoring the state of a project, size, effort, schedule, and defects are the basic measurements that are needed [43, 75]. Schedule is one of the most important metrics because most projects are driven by schedules and deadlines. Only by monitoring the actual schedule can we properly assess if the project is on time or if there is a delay. It is, however, easy to measure because calendar time is usually used in all plans.

Effort is the main resource consumed in a software project. Consequently, tracking of effort is a key activity during monitoring; it is essential for evaluating whether the project is executing within budget. For effort data some type of timesheet system is needed where each person working on the project enters the amount of time spent on the project. For better monitoring, the effort spent on various tasks should be logged separately. Generally effort is recorded through some on-line system (like the weekly activity report system in [57]), which allows a person to record the amount of time spent against a particular activity in a project. At any point, total effort on an activity can be aggregated.

Because defects have a direct relationship to software quality, tracking of defects is critical for ensuring quality. A large software project may include thousands of defects that are found by different people at different stages. Just to keep track of the defects found and their status, defects must be logged and their closure tracked. If defects found are being logged, monitoring can focus on how many defects have been found so far, what percentage of defects are still open, and other issues. Defect tracking is considered one of the best practices for managing a project [17].

Size is another fundamental metric because it represents progress toward delivering the desired functionality, and many data (for example, delivered defect density) are normalized with respect to size. The size of delivered software can be measured in terms of LOC (which can be determined through the use of regular editors and line counters) or function points. At a more gross level, just the number of modules or number of features might suffice.

For effective monitoring, a project must plan for collecting these measurements. Most often, organizations provide tools and policy support for recording this basic data, which is then available to project managers for tracking.

4.5.2 Project Monitoring and Tracking

The main goal of project managers for monitoring a project is to get visibility into the project execution so that they can determine whether any action needs to be taken to ensure that the project goals are met. As project goals are in terms of effort, schedule, and quality, the focus of monitoring is on these aspects. Different levels of monitoring might be done for a project. The three main levels of monitoring are activity level, status reporting, and milestone analysis. Measurements taken on the project are employed for monitoring.

Activity-level monitoring ensures that each activity in the detailed schedule has been done properly and within time. This type of monitoring may be done daily in project team meetings or by the project manager checking the status of all the tasks scheduled to be completed on that day. A completed task is often marked as 100% complete in detailed schedule—this is used by tools like the Microsoft Project to track the percentage completion of the overall project or a higher-level task. This monitoring is to ensure that the project continues to proceed as per the planned schedule.

Status reports are often prepared weekly to take stock of what has happened and what needs to be done. Status reports typically contain a summary of the activities successfully completed since the last status report, any activities that have been delayed, any issues in the project that need attention, and if everything is in place for the next week. Again, the purpose of this is to ensure that the project is proceeding as per the planned schedule.

The *milestone analysis* is done at each milestone or every few weeks, if milestones are too far apart, and is more elaborate. Analysis of actual versus estimated for effort and schedule is often included in the milestone analysis. If the deviation is significant, it may imply that the project may run into trouble and might not meet its objectives. This situation calls for project managers to understand the reasons for the variation and to apply corrective and preventive actions if necessary. Defects found by different quality control tasks, and the number of defects fixed may also be reported. This report monitors the progress of the project with respect to all the goals.

4.6 Detailed Scheduling

The activities discussed so far result in a *project management plan* document that establishes the project goals for effort, schedule, and quality; and defines the approach for risk management, ensuring quality, and project monitoring. Now this overall plan has to be translated into a detailed action plan which can then be followed in the project, and which, if followed, will lead to a successful project. That is, we need to develop a detailed plan or schedule of what to do when such that following this plan will lead to delivering the software with expected quality and within cost and schedule. Whereas the overall planning document is typically prepared at the start of the project and is relatively static, the detailed plan is a dynamic document that reflects the current plan of the project. The detailed plan is what assigns work items to individual members of the team.

For the detailed schedule, the major phases identified during effort and schedule estimation, are broken into small schedulable activities in a hierarchical manner. For example, the detailed design phase can be broken into tasks for developing the detailed design for each module, review of each detailed design, fixing of defects found, and so on. For each detailed task, the project manager estimates the time required to complete it and assigns a suitable resource so that the overall schedule is met, and the overall effort also matches. In addition to the engineering tasks that are the outcome of the development process, the QC tasks identified in the quality plan, the monitoring activities defined in the monitoring plan, and the risk mitigation activities should also be scheduled.

At each level of refinement, the project manager determines the effort for the overall task from the detailed schedule and checks it against the effort estimates. If this detailed schedule is not consistent with the overall schedule and effort estimates, the detailed schedule must be changed. If it is found that the best detailed schedule cannot match the milestone effort and schedule, then the earlier estimates must be revised. Thus, scheduling is an iterative process.

Generally, the project manager refines the tasks to a level so that the lowest-level activity can be scheduled to occupy no more than a few days from a single resource. Activities related to tasks such as project management, coordination, database management, and configuration management may also be listed in the schedule, even though these activities have less direct effect on determining the schedule because they are ongoing tasks rather than schedulable activities. Nevertheless, they consume resources and hence are often included in the project schedule.

Rarely will a project manager complete the detailed schedule of the entire project all at once. Once the overall schedule is fixed, detailing for a phase may only be done at the start of that phase.

For detailed scheduling, tools like Microsoft Project or a spreadsheet can be very useful. For each lowest-level activity, the project manager specifies the effort, duration, start date, end date, and resources. Dependencies between activities, due either to an inherent dependency (for example, you can conduct a unit test plan for a program only after it has been coded) or to a resource-related dependency (the same resource is assigned two tasks), may also be specified. From these tools the overall effort and schedule of higher-level tasks can be determined.

A detailed project schedule is never static. Changes may be needed because the actual progress in the project may be different from what was planned, because newer tasks are added in response to change requests, or because of other unforeseen situations. Changes are done as and when the need arises.

The final schedule, frequently maintained using some suitable tool, is often the most "live" project plan document. During the project, if plans must be changed and additional activities must be done, after the decision is made, the changes must be reflected in the detailed schedule, as this reflects the tasks actually planned to be performed. Hence, the detailed schedule becomes the main document that tracks the activities and schedule.

It should be noted that only the number of resources is decided during the overall project planning. However, detailed scheduling can be done effectively only after actual assignment of people has been done, as task assignment needs information about the capabilities of the team members. In our discussion above, we have implicitly assumed that the project's team is led by a project manager, who does the planning and task assignment. This form of hierarchical team organization is fairly common, and was earlier called the Chief Programmer Team.

As an example, consider the example of a project from [58]. The overall effort estimate for this project is 501 person-days, or about 24 person-months (this estimation was done using the bottom-up approach discussed earlier). The customer gave approximately 5.5 months to finish the project. Because this is more than the square root of effort in person-months, this schedule was accepted. Hence, these define the effort and schedule goals of the project.

The milestones are determined by using the effort estimates for the phases and an estimate of the number of resources available. Table 4.4 shows the high-level schedule of the project. This project uses the RUP process in which initial requirement and design is done in two iterations and the development is done in three iterations. The overall project duration with these milestones is 140 days.

Table 4.4: High-level schedule for the project.

Task	Duration (days)	Work (person -days)	Start date	End date
Project initiation	33.78	24.2	5/4/00	6/23/00
Regular activities	87.11	35.13	6/5/00	10/16/00
Training	95.11	49.37	5/8/00	9/29/00
Knowledge sharing tasks	78.22	19.56	6/2/00	9/30/00
Inception phase	26.67	22.67	4/3/00	5/12/00
Elaboration Iteration 1	27.56	55.16	5/15/00	6/23/00
Elaboration Iteration 2	8.89	35.88	6/26/00	7/7/00
Construction Iteration 1	8.89	24.63	7/10/00	7/21/00
Construction Iteration 2	6.22	28.22	7/20/00	7/28/00
Construction Iteration 3	6.22	27.03	7/31/00	8/8/00
Transition phase	56	179.62	8/9/00	11/3/00
Back-end work	4.44	6.44	8/14/00	8/18/00

This high-level schedule is an outcome of the overall project planning, and is not suitable for assigning resources and detailed planning.

For detailed scheduling, these tasks are broken into schedulable activities. In this way, the schedule also becomes a checklist of tasks for the project. As mentioned above, this exploding of top-level activities is not done fully at the start but rather takes place many times during the project.

Table 4.5 shows part of the detailed schedule of the construction-iteration 1 phase of the project. For each activity, the table specifies the activity by a short name, the module to which the activity is contributing, and the effort (the duration may also be specified). For each task, how much is completed is given in the % Complete column. This information is used for activity tracking. The detailed schedule also specifies the resource to which the task is assigned (specified by initials of the person). Sometimes, the predecessors of the activity (the activities upon which the task depends) are also specified. This information helps in determining the critical path and the critical resources. This project finally had a total of about 325 schedulable tasks.

Table 4.5: Portion of the detailed schedule.

Module	Task	Effort (days)	Start date	End date	% done	Resourse
-	Requirements	1.33	7/10	7/21	100	bb,bj
-	Design review	0.9	7/11	7/12	100	bb,bj,sb
-	Rework	0.8	7/12	7/13	100	bj, sb
History	Coding	1.87	7/10	7/12	100	hp
History	Review UC17	0.27	7/14	7/14	100	bj,dd
History	Review UC19	0.27	7/14	7/14	100	bj,dd
History	Rework	2.49	7/17	7/17	100	dd,sb,hp
History	Test UC17	0.62	7/18	7/18	100	sb
History	Test UC19	0.62	7/18	7/18	100	hp
History	Rework	0.71	7/18	7/18	100	bj,sb,hp
Config.	Reconciliation	2.49	7/19	7/19	100	bj,sb,hp
Mgmt.	Tracking	2.13	7/10	7/19	100	bb
Quality	Analysis	0.62	7/19	7/19	100	bb

4.7 Summary

– Project planning serves two purposes: to set the overall goals or expectations for the project and the overall approach for managing the project, and to schedule tasks to be done such that the goals are met. In overall planning, effort and schedule estimation are done to establish the cost and schedule goals for the project as well as key milestones. Project quality planning and risk management planning establish approaches for achieving quality goals and ensuring that the project does not fail in the face of risks. In the detailed schedule, tasks for achieving each milestone are identified and scheduled to be executed by specific team members such that the overall schedule and effort for different milestones is met.

– In a top-down approach for estimating effort for the project, the effort is estimated from the size estimate, which may be refined using other characteristics of the project. Effort for different phases is determined from the overall effort using effort distribution data. COCOMO is one model that uses this approach. In a bottom-up approach to estimation, the modules to be built are identified first, and then using an average effort for coding such modules, the overall coding effort is determined. From coding effort, effort for other phases and overall project are determined, using the effort distribution data.

– Some flexibility exists in setting the schedule goal for a project. An overall schedule can be determined as a function of effort, and then adjusted to meet the project needs and constraints. Once a reasonable schedule is chosen, the staffing requirements of the project are determined using the project's effort. Schedule for milestones are determined from effort estimates and the effective team size in different phases. With estimation and scheduling, the effort and schedule goals for the project are established.

– Setting measurable quality goals for a project is harder. The quality goal can be set in terms of performance during acceptance testing. A quality plan consists of quality control tasks that should be performed in the project to achieve the quality goal.

– A project can have risks, and to meet project goals under the presence of risks requires proper risk management. Risks are those events which may or may not occur, but if they do occur, they can have a negative impact on the project. Risks can be prioritized based on the expected loss from a risk, which is a combination of the probability of the risk and the total possible loss due to risk materializing. For high-priority risks, activities are planned during normal project execution such that if the risks do materialize, their effect is minimal.

– The progress of the project needs to be monitored using suitable measurements so corrective actions can be taken, when needed. The measurements commonly used for monitoring are actual schedule, effort consumed, defects found, and the size of the product. Status reports and milestone reports on actual vs. estimated on effort and schedule, activities that got missed, defects found so far, and risks, can suffice to effectively monitor the performance of a project with respect to its plan.

– The overall project management plan document containing the effort, schedule, and quality goals, and plans for quality, monitoring, and risk management, sets the overall context.

– For execution, the overall schedule is broken into a detailed schedule of tasks to be done so as to meet the goals and constraints. These tasks are assigned to specific team members, with identified start and end dates. The schedule has to be such that it is consistent with the overall schedule and effort estimates. Tasks planned for quality, monitoring, and risk management are also scheduled in the detailed schedule. This detailed schedule lays out the path the project should follow in order to achieve the project objectives. It is the most live project planning document and any changes in the project plan must be reflected suitably in the detailed schedule.

Self-Assessment Exercises

1. What is the role of effort estimation in a project, and why is it important to do this estimation early?
2. If an architecture of the proposed system has been designed specifying the major components in the system, and you have source code of similar components available in your organization's repository, which method will you use for estimation?
3. Suppose an organization plans to use COCOMO for effort estimation, but it wants to use only three cost drivers—product complexity, programmer capability, and development schedule. In this situation, from the initial estimate, by how much can the final estimate vary?
4. Why are all combinations of people and months that are consistent with the effort estimate not feasible?
5. A customer asks you to complete a project, whose effort estimate is E, in time T. How will you decide whether to accept this schedule or not?
6. For a group student project being done in a semester course, list the major risks that a typical project will face, and risk mitigation strategy for the high-priority risks.
7. Suppose you make a detailed schedule for your project whose effort and schedule estimates for various milestones have been done in the project plan. How will you check if the detailed schedule is consistent with the overall plan? What will you do if it is not?

5
Software Architecture

Any complex system is composed of subsystems that interact under the control of system design such that the system provides the expected behavior. When designing such a system, therefore, the logical approach is to identify the subsystems that should compose the system, the interfaces of these subsystems, and the rules for interaction between the subsystems. This is what software architecture aims to do.

Software architecture is a relatively recent area. As the software systems increasingly become distributed and more complex, architecture becomes an important step in building the system. Due to a wide range of options now available for how a system may be configured and connected, carefully designing the architecture becomes very important. It is during the architecture design where choices like using some type of middleware, or some type of back-end database, or some type of server, or some type of security component are made. Architecture is also the earliest place when properties like reliability and performance can be evaluated for the system, a capability that is increasingly becoming important.

In this chapter, we will discuss:

- The key roles an architecture description plays in a software project.

- The multiple architectural views that can be used to specify different structural aspects of the system being built.

- The component and connector architecture of a system, and how it can be expressed.

P. Jalote, *A Concise Introduction to Software Engineering*,
DOI: 10.1007/978-1-84800-302-6_5, © Springer-Verlag London Limited 2008

- Different styles that have been proposed for component and connector view that can be used to design the architecture of the proposed system.

- How architecture of a system can be evaluated.

5.1 Role of Software Architecture

What is architecture? Generally speaking, architecture of a system provides a very high level view of the parts of the system and how they are related to form the whole system. That is, architecture partitions the system in logical parts such that each part can be comprehended independently, and then describes the system in terms of these parts and the relationship between these parts.

Any complex system can be partitioned in many different ways, each providing a useful view and each having different types of logical parts. The same holds true for a software system—there is no unique structure of the system that can be described by its architecture; there are many possible structures.

Due to this possibility of having multiple structures, one of the most widely accepted definitions of software architecture is that *the software architecture of a system is the structure or structures of the system, which comprise software elements, the externally visible properties of those elements, and the relationships among them* [6]. This definition implies that for elements in an architecture, we are only interested in those abstractions that specify those properties that other elements can assume to exist and that are needed to specify relationships. Details on how these properties are supported are not needed for architecture. This is an important capability that allows architecture descriptions to represent a complex system in a succinct form that is easily comprehended.

An architecture description of a system will therefore describe the different structures of the system. The next natural question is why should a team building a software system for some customer be interested in creating and documenting the structures of the proposed system. Some of the important uses that software architecture descriptions play are [6, 23, 54]:

1. *Understanding and communication.* An architecture description is primarily to communicate the architecture to its various stakeholders, which include the users who will use the system, the clients who commissioned the system, the builders who will build the system, and, of course, the architects. Through this description the stakeholders gain an understanding of some macro properties of the system and how the system intends to fulfill the functional and quality requirements. As the description provides a common language between stakeholders, it also becomes the vehicle for

negotiation and agreement among the stakeholders, who may have conflict-
ing goals.

2. *Reuse.* The software engineering world has, for a long time, been working
   toward a discipline where software can be assembled from parts that are
   developed by different people and are available for others to use. If one
   wants to build a software product in which existing components may be
   reused, then architecture becomes the key point at which reuse at the highest level is decided. The architecture has to be chosen in a manner such
   that the components which have to be reused can fit properly and together
   with other components that may be developed. Architecture also facilitates reuse among products that are similar and building product families
   such that the common parts of these different but similar products can be
   reused. Architecture helps specify what is fixed and what is variable in these
   different products, and can help minimize the set of variable elements such
   that different products can share software parts to the maximum. Again,
   it is very hard to achieve this type of reuse at a detail level.

3. *Construction and Evolution.* As architecture partitions the system into
   parts, some architecture-provided partitioning can naturally be used for
   constructing the system, which also requires that the system be broken
   into parts such that different teams (or individuals) can separately work on
   different parts. A suitable partitioning in the architecture can provide the
   project with the parts that need to be built to build the system. As, almost
   by definition, the parts specified in an architecture are relatively independent (the dependence between parts coming through their relationship),
   they can be built independently.

4. *Analysis.* It is highly desirable if some important properties about the behavior of the system can be determined before the system is actually built.
   This will allow the designers to consider alternatives and select the one
   that will best suit the needs. Many engineering disciplines use models to
   analyze design of a product for its cost, reliability, performance, etc. Architecture opens such possibilities for software also. It is possible (though the
   methods are not fully developed or standardized yet) to analyze or predict
   the properties of the system being built from its architecture. For example, the reliability or the performance of the system can be analyzed. Such
   an analysis can help determine whether the system will meet the quality
   and performance requirements, and if not, what needs to be done to meet
   the requirements. For example, while building a website for shopping, it is
   possible to analyze the response time or throughput for a proposed architecture, given some assumptions about the request load and hardware. It
   can then be decided whether the performance is satisfactory or not, and if

not, what new capabilities should be added (for example, a different architecture or a faster server for the back end) to improve it to a satisfactory level.

Not all of these uses may be significant in a project and which of these uses is pertinent to a project depends on the nature of the project. In some projects communication may be very important, but a detailed performance analysis may be unnecessary (because the system is too small or is meant for only a few users). In some other systems, performance analysis may be the primary use of architecture.

5.2 Architecture Views

There is a general view emerging that there is no unique architecture of a system. The definition that we have adopted (given above) also expresses this sentiment. Consequently, there is no one architecture drawing of the system. The situation is similar to that of civil construction, a discipline that is the original user of the concept of architecture and from where the concept of software architecture has been borrowed. For a building, if you want to see the floor plan, you are shown one set of drawings. If you are an electrical engineer and want to see how the electricity distribution has been planned, you will be shown another set of drawings. And if you are interested in safety and firefighting, another set of drawings is used. These drawings are not independent of each other—they are all about the same building. However, each drawing provides a different view of the building, a view that focuses on explaining one aspect of the building and tries to a good job at that, while not divulging much about the other aspects. And no one drawing can express all the different aspects—such a drawing will be too complex to be of any use.

Similar is the situation with software architecture. In software, the different drawings are called views. A view represents the system as composed of some types of *elements* and *relationships* between them. Which elements are used by a view, depends on what the view wants to highlight. Different views expose different properties and attributes, thereby allowing the stakeholders and analysts to properly evaluate those attributes for the system. By focusing only on some aspects of the system, a view reduces the complexity that a reader has to deal with at a time, thereby aiding system understanding and analysis.

A view describes a structure of the system. We will use these two concepts—views and structures—interchangeably. We will also use the term *architectural view* to refer to a view. Many types of views have been proposed. Most of the proposed views generally belong to one of these three types [6, 23]:

− Module

− Component and connector

− Allocation

In a module view, the system is viewed as a collection of code units, each implementing some part of the system functionality. That is, the main elements in this view are modules. These views are code-based and do not explicitly represent any runtime structure of the system. Examples of modules are packages, a class, a procedure, a method, a collection of functions, and a collection of classes. The relationships between these modules are also code-based and depend on how code of a module interacts with another module. Examples of relationships in this view are "is a part of" (i.e., module B is a part of module A), "uses or depends on" (a module A uses services of module B to perform its own functions and correctness of module A depends on correctness of module B), and "generalization or specialization" (a module B is a generalization of a module A).

In a component and connector (C&C) view, the system is viewed as a collection of runtime entities called components. That is, a component is a unit which has an identity in the executing system. Objects (not classes), a collection of objects, and a process are examples of components. While executing, components need to interact with others to support the system services. Connectors provide means for this interaction. Examples of connectors are pipes and sockets. Shared data can also act as a connector. If the components use some middleware to communicate and coordinate, then the middleware is a connector. Hence, the primary elements of this view are components and connectors.

An allocation view focuses on how the different software units are allocated to resources like the hardware, file systems, and people. That is, an allocation view specifies the relationship between software elements and elements of the environments in which the software system is executed. They expose structural properties like which processes run on which processor, and how the system files are organized on a file system.

An architecture description consists of views of different types, with each view exposing some structure of the system. Module views show how the software is structured as a set of implementation units, C&C views show how the software is structured as interacting runtime elements, and allocation views show how software relates to nonsoftware structures. These three types of view of the same system form the architecture of the system.

Note that the different views are not unrelated. They all represent the same system. Hence, there are relationships between elements in one view and elements in another view. These relationships may be simple or may be complex.

For example, the relationship between modules and components may be one to one in that one module implements one component. On the other hand, it may be quite complex with a module being used by multiple components, and a component using multiple modules. While creating the different views, the designers have to be aware of this relationship.

The next question is what are the standard views that should be expressed for describing the architecture of a system? To answer this question, the analogy with buildings may again help. If one is building a simple small house, then perhaps there is no need to have a separate view describing the emergency and the fire system. Similarly, if there is no air conditioning in the building, there need not be any view for that. On the other hand, an office building will perhaps require both of these views, in addition to other views describing plumbing, space, wiring, etc.

However, despite the fact that there are multiple drawings showing different views of a building, there is one view that predominates in construction—that of physical structure. This view forms the basis of other views in that other views cannot really be completed unless this view can be done. Other views may or may not be needed for constructing a building, depending on the nature of the project. Hence, in a sense, the view giving the building structure may be considered as the primary view in that it is almost always used, and other views rely on this view substantially. The view also captures perhaps the most important property to be analyzed in the early stages, namely, that of space organization.

The situation with software architecture is also somewhat similar. As we have said, depending on what properties are of interest, different views of the software architecture are needed. However, of these views, the C&C view has become the defacto primary view, one which is almost always prepared when an architecture is designed (some definitions even view architecture only in terms of C&C views). In this chapter, we will focus primarily on the C&C view.

A note about relationship between architecture and design is in order. As partitioning a system into smaller parts and composing the system from these parts is also a goal of design, a natural question is what is the difference between a design and architecture as both aim to achieve similar objectives and seem to fundamentally rely on the divide and conquer rule? First, it should be clear that architecture is a design in that it is in the solution domain and talks about the structure of the proposed system. Furthermore, an architecture view gives a high-level view of the system, relying on abstraction to convey the meaning— something which design also does. So, architecture is design.

We can view architecture as a very high-level design, focusing only on main components, and the architecture activity as the first step in design. What we term as design is really about the modules that will eventually exist as code. That is, they are a more concrete representation of the implementation (though not yet an implementation). Consequently, during design lower-level issues like the data structures, files, and sources of data, have to be addressed, while such issues are not generally significant at the architecture level. We also take the view that design can be considered as providing the module view of the architecture of the system.

The boundaries between architecture and high-level design are not fully clear. The way the field has evolved, we can say that the line between architecture and design is really up to the designer or the architect. At the architecture level, one needs to show only those parts that are needed to perform the desired evaluation. The internal structure of these parts is not important. On the other hand, during design, designing the structure of the parts that can lead to constructing them is one of the key tasks. However, which parts of the structure should be examined and revealed during architecture and which parts during design is a matter of choice. Generally speaking, details that are not needed to perform the types of analysis we wish to do at the architecture time are unnecessary and should be left for design to uncover.

5.3 Component and Connector View

The C&C architecture view of a system has two main elements—components and connectors. Components are usually computational elements or data stores that have some presence during the system execution. Connectors define the means of interaction between these components. A C&C view of the system defines the components, and which component is connected to which and through what connector. A C&C view describes a runtime structure of the system—what components exist when the system is executing and how they interact during the execution. The C&C structure is essentially a graph, with components as nodes and connectors as edges.

The C&C view is perhaps the most common view of architecture and most box-and-line drawings representing architecture attempt to capture this view. Most often when people talk about the architecture, they refer to the C&C view. Most architecture description languages also focus on the C&C view.

5.3.1 Components

Components are generally units of computation or data stores in the system. A component has a name, which is generally chosen to represent the role of the component or the function it performs. The name also provides a unique identity to the component, which is necessary for referencing details about the component in the supporting documents, as a C&C drawing will only show the component names.

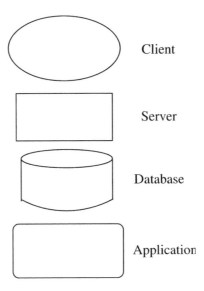

Figure 5.1: Component examples.

A component is of a component type, where the type represents a generic component, defining the general computation and the interfaces a component of that type must have. Note that though a component has a type, in the C&C architecture view, we have components (i.e., actual instances) and not types. Examples of these types are clients, servers, filters, etc. Different domains may have other generic types like controllers, actuators, and sensors (for a control system domain).

In a diagram representing a C&C architecture view of a system, it is highly desirable to have a different representation for different component types, so the different types can be identified visually. In a box-and-line diagram, often all components are represented as rectangular boxes. Such an approach will require that types of the components are described separately and the reader has to read the description to figure out the types of the components. It is much better to use a different symbol/notation for each different component type. Some of the common symbols used for representing commonly found component types are shown in Figure 5.1.

To make sure that the meanings of the different symbols are clear to the reader, it is desirable to have a key of the different symbols to describe what

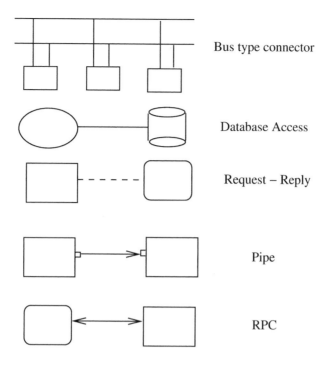

Figure 5.2: Connector examples.

type of component a symbol represents.

5.3.2 Connectors

The different components of a system are likely to interact while the system is in operation to provide the services expected of the system. After all, components exist to provide parts of the services and features of the system, and these must be combined to deliver the overall system functionality. For composing a system from its components, information about the interaction between components is necessary.

Interaction between components may be through a simple means supported by the underlying process execution infrastructure of the operating system. For example, a component may interact with another using the procedure call mechanism (a connector), which is provided by the runtime environment for the programming language. However, the interaction may involve more complex mechanisms as well. Examples of such mechanisms are remote procedure call, TCP/IP ports, and a protocol like HTTP. These mechanisms require a fair amount of underlying runtime infrastructure, as well as special programming within the components to use the infrastructure. Consequently, it is extremely important to identify and explicitly represent these connectors. Specification of connectors will help identify the suitable infrastructure needed to implement an architecture, as well as clarify the programming needs for components using them.

Note that connectors need not be binary and a connector may provide an n-way communication between multiple components. For example, a broadcast bus may be used as a connector, which allows a component to broadcast its message to all the other components. Some of the common symbols used for representing commonly found connector types are shown in Figure 5.2.

A connector also has a name that should describe the nature of interaction the connector supports. A connector also has a type, which is a generic description of the interaction, specifying properties like whether it is a binary or n-way, types of interfaces it supports, etc. If a protocol is used by a connector type, it should be explicitly stated.

It is worth pointing out that the implementation of a connector may be quite complex. If the connector is provided by the underlying system, then the components just have to ensure that they use the connectors as per their specifications. If, however, the underlying system does not provide a connector used in an architecture, then as mentioned above, the connector will have to be implemented as part of the project to build the system. That is, during the development, not only will the components need to be developed, but resources will have to be assigned to also develop the connector. (This situation might arise for a specialized system that requires connectors that are specific to the problem domain.) Generally, while creating an architecture, it is wise for the architect to use the connectors which are available on the systems on which the software will be deployed.

5.3.3 An Example

Suppose we have to design and build a simple system for taking an on-line survey of students on a campus. There is a set of multiple-choice questions, and the proposed system will provide the survey form to the student, who can fill and submit it on-line. We also want that when the user submits the form, he/she is also shown the current result of the survey, that is, what percentage of students so far have filled which options for the different questions.

The system is best built using the Web; this is the likely choice of any developer. For this simple system, a traditional 3-tier architecture is proposed. It consists of a client which will display the form that the student can complete and submit, and will also display the results. The second component is the server, which processes the data submitted by the student, and saves it on the database, which is the third component. The server also queries the database to get the outcome of the survey and sends the results in proper format (HTML) back to the client, which then displays the result. The C&C view is shown in Figure 5.3.

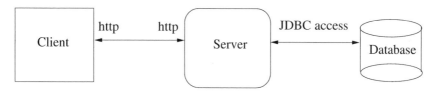

Figure 5.3: Architecture of the survey system.

Note that the client, server, and database are all different types of components, and hence are shown using different symbols. Note also that the connectors between the components are also of different types. The diagram makes the different types clear, making the diagram stand alone and easy to comprehend.

Note that at the architecture level, a host of details are not discussed. How is the URL of the survey set? What are the modules that go into building these components and what language are they written in? Questions like these are not the issues at this level.

Note also that the connector between the client and the server explicitly says that http is to be used. And the diagram also says that it is a Web client. This implies that it is assumed that there will be a Web browser running on the machines from which the student will take the survey. Having the http as the connector also implies that there is a proper http server running, and that the server of this system will be suitably attached to it to allow access by clients. In other words, the entire infrastructure of browser and the http server, for the purposes of this application, mainly provides the connector between the client and the server (and a virtual machine to run the client of the application).

There are some implications of choice of this connector on the components. The client will have to be written in a manner that it can send the request using http (this will imply using some type of scripting language or HTML forms). Similarly, it also implies that the server has to take its request from the http server in the format specified by the http protocol. Furthermore, the server has to send its results back to the client in the HTML format. These are all constraints on implementing this architecture. Hence, when discussing it and finally accepting it, the implications for the infrastructure as well as the implementation should be fully understood and actions should be taken to make sure that these assumptions are valid.

The above architecture has no security and a student can take the survey as many times as he wishes. Furthermore, even a nonstudent can take the survey. Now suppose the Dean of Students wants that this system be open only to registered students, and that each student is allowed to take the survey at most once. To identify the students, it was explained that each student has an account, and their account information is available from the main proxy server of the institute.

Now the architecture will have to be quite different. The proposed architecture now has a separate login form for the user, and a separate server component which does the validation. For validation, it goes to the proxy for checking if the login and password provided are valid. If so, the server returns a cookie to the client (which stores it as per the cookie protocol). When the student completes the survey form, the cookie information validates the user, and the server checks if this student has already completed the survey. The architecture for this system is shown in Figure 5.4.

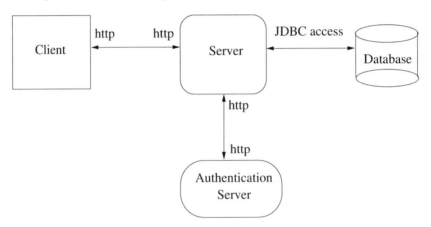

Figure 5.4: Architecture for the survey system with authentication.

Note that even though we are saying that the connection between the client and the server is that of http, it is somewhat different from the connection in the earlier architecture. In the first architecture, plain http is sufficient. In this one, as cookies are also needed, the connector is really http + cookies. So, if the user disables cookies, the required connector is not available and this architecture will not work.

Now suppose we want the system to be extended in a different way. It was found that the database server is somewhat unreliable, and is frequently down. It was also felt that when the student is given the result of the survey when he submits the form, a somewhat outdated result is acceptable, as the results are really statistical data and a little inaccuracy will not matter. We assume that the survey result can be outdated by about 5 data points (even if it does not

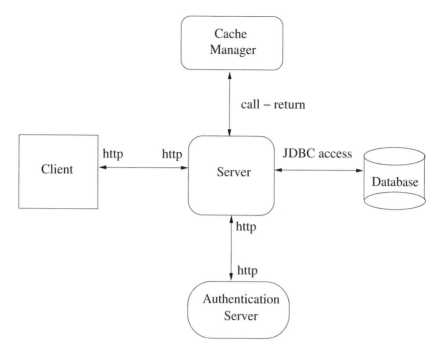

Figure 5.5: Architecture for the survey system with cache.

include data of 5 surveys, it is OK). What the Dean wanted was to make the
system more reliable, and provide some facility for completing the survey even
when the database is down.

To make the system more reliable, the following strategy was proposed.
When the student submits the survey, the server interacts with the database as
before. The results of the survey, however, are also stored in the cache by the
server. If the database is down or unavailable, the survey data is stored locally
in a cache component, and the result saved in the cache component is used to
provide the result to the student. (This can be done for up to 5 requests, after
which the survey cannot be completed.) So, now we have another component
in the server called the cache manager. And there is a connection between the
server and this new component of the call/return type. This architecture is
shown in Figure 5.5.

It should be clear that by using the cache, the availability of the system is
improved. The cache will also have an impact on performance. These exten-
sions show how architecture affects both availability and performance, and how
properly selecting or tuning the architecture can help meet the quality goals (or
just improve the quality of the system). (Of course, detail-level decisions like
how a particular module is implemented also have implications on performance,

but they are quite distinct and orthogonal to the architecture-level decisions.) We will later do a formal evaluation of these different architectures to see the impact of architectural decisions on some quality attributes.

5.4 Architecture Styles for C&C View

It should be clear that different systems will have different architecture. There are some general architectures that have been observed in many systems and that seem to represent general structures that are useful for architecture of a class of problems. These are called *architectural styles*. A style defines a family of architectures that satisfy the constraints of that style [6, 23, 76]. In this section we discuss some common styles for the C&C view which can be useful for a large set of problems [23, 76]. These styles can provide ideas for creating an architecture view for the problem at hand. Styles can also be combined to form richer views.

5.4.1 Pipe and Filter

Pipe-and-filter style of architecture is well suited for systems that primarily do data transformation whereby some input data is received and the goal of the system is to produce some output data by suitably transforming the input data. A system using pipe-and-filter architecture achieves the desired transformation by applying a network of smaller transformations and composing them in a manner such that together the overall desired transformation is achieved.

The pipe-and-filter style has only one component type called the filter. It also has only one connector type, called the pipe. A filter performs a data transformation, and sends the transformed data to other filters for further processing using the pipe connector. In other words, a filter receives the data it needs from some defined input pipes, performs the data transformation, and then sends the output data to other filters on the defined output pipes. A filter may have more than one input and more than one output. Filters can be independent and asynchronous entities, and as they are concerned only with the data arriving on the pipe, a filter need not know the identity of the filter that sent the input data or the identity of the filter that will consume the data they produce.

The pipe connector is a unidirectional channel which conveys streams of data received on one end to the other end. A pipe does not change the data in any manner but merely transports it to the filter on the receiver end in the order in which the data elements are received. As filters can be asynchronous and should work without the knowledge of the identity of the producer or the consumer, buffering and synchronization needs to ensure smooth functioning of the producer-consumer relationship embodied in connecting two filters by a pipe is ensured by the pipe. The filters merely consume and produce data.

There are some constraints that this style imposes. First, as mentioned above, the filters should work without knowing the identity of the consumer or the producer; they should only require the data elements they need. Second, a pipe, which is a two-way connector, must connect an output port of a filter to an input port of another filter.

A pure pipe-and-filter structure will also generally have a constraint that a filter has independent thread of control which processes the data as it comes. Implementing this will require suitable underlying infrastructure to support a pipe mechanism which buffers the data and does the synchronization needed (for example, blocking the producer when the buffer is full and blocking the consumer filter when the buffer is empty). For using this pipe, the filter builder must be fully aware of the properties of the pipe, particularly with regard to buffering and synchronization, input and output mechanisms, and the symbols for end of data.

However, there could be situations in which the constraint that a filter process the data as it comes may not be required. Without this constraint, pipe-and-filter style view may have filters that produce the data completely before passing it on, or which start their processing only after complete input is available. In such a system the filters cannot operate concurrently, and the system is like a batch-processing system. However, it can considerably simplify the pipes and easier mechanisms can be used for supporting them.

Let's consider an example of a system needed to count the frequency of different words in a file. An architecture using the pipes-and-filter style for a system to achieve this is given in Figure 5.6.

Figure 5.6: Pipe-and-filter example.

This architecture proposes that the input data be first split into a sequence of words by a component Sequencer. This sequence of words is then sorted by the component Sorting, which passes the output of sorted words to another filter (Counting) that counts the number of occurrences of the different words.

This structure of sorting the words first has been chosen as it will make the task of determining the frequency more efficient, even though it involves a sort operation. It should be clear that this proposed architecture can implement the desired functionality. Later in the chapter we will further discuss some implementation issues related to this architecture.

As can be seen from this example, pipe-and-filter architectural style is well suited for data processing and transformation. Consequently, it is useful in text processing applications. Signal processing applications also find it useful as such applications typically perform encoding, error correction, and other transformations on the data.

The pipe-and-filter style, due to the constraints, allows a system's overall transformation to be composed of smaller transformations. Or viewing it in another manner, it allows a desired transformation to be factored into smaller transformations, and then filters built for the smaller transformations. That is, it allows the techniques of functional composition and decomposition to be utilized, something that is mathematically appealing.

5.4.2 Shared-Data Style

In this style, there are two types of components—data repositories and data accessors. Components of data repository type are where the system stores shared data—these could be file systems or databases. These components provide a reliable and permanent storage, take care of any synchronization needs for concurrent access, and provide data access support. Components of data accessors type access data from the repositories, perform computation on the data obtained, and if they want to share the results with other components, put the results back in the depository. In other words, the accessors are computational elements that receive their data from the repository and save their data in the repository as well. These components do not directly communicate with each other—the data repository components are the means of communication and data transfer between them.

There are two variations of this style possible. In the blackboard style, if some data is posted on the data repository, all the accessor components that need to know about it are informed. In other words, the shared data source is an active agent as well which either informs the components about the arrival of interesting data, or starts the execution of the components that need to act upon this new data. In databases, this form of style is often supported through triggers. The other is the repository style, in which the data repository is just a passive repository which provides permanent storage and related controls for data accessing. The components access the repository as and when they want.

As can be imagined, many database applications use this architectural style. Databases, though originally more like repositories, now act both as repositories as well as blackboards as they provide triggers and can act as efficient data storage as well. Many Web systems frequently follow this style at the back end—in response to user requests, different scripts (data accessors) access and update some shared data. Many programming environments are also organized this way: the common representation of the program artifacts is stored in the repository and the different tools access it to perform the desired translations or to obtain the desired information. (Some years back there was a standard defined for the common repository to facilitate integration of tools.)

As an example of a system using this style of architecture, let us consider a student registration system in a university. The system clearly has a central repository which contains information about courses, students, prerequisites, etc. It has an Administrator component that sets up the repository, rights to different people, etc. The Registration component allows students to register and update the information for students and courses. The Approvals component is for granting approvals for those courses that require instructor's consent. The Reports component produces the report regarding the students registered in different courses at the end of the registration. The component Course Feedback is used for taking feedback from students at the end of the course. This architecture is shown in Figure 5.7.

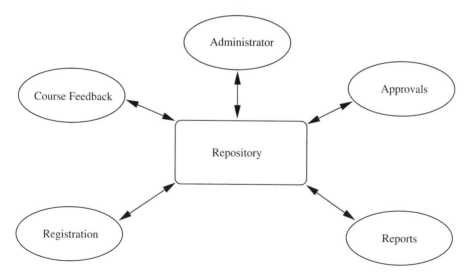

Figure 5.7: Shared data example.

Note that the different computation components do not need to communicate with each other and do not even need to know about each other's presence.

For example, if later it is decided that the scheduling of courses can be auto-mated based on data on registration (and other information about classrooms etc.), then another component called Scheduling can be simply added. No ex-isting computation component needs to change or be informed about the new component being added. (This example is based on a system that is actually used in the author's university.)

There is really only one connector type in this style—read/write. Note, how-ever, that this general connector style may take more precise form in particular architectures. For example, though a database can be viewed as supporting read and updates, for a program interacting with it, the database system may provide transaction services as well. Connectors using this transaction service allow complete transactions (which may involve multiple reads and writes and preserve atomicity) to be performed by an application.

Note also that as in many other cases, the connectors involve a consider-able amount of underlying infrastructure. For example, read and writes to a file system involve a fair amount of file system software involving issues like directories, buffering, locking, and synchronization. Similarly, a considerable amount of software goes into databases to support the type of connections it provides for query, update, and transactions. We will see another use of this style later when we discuss the case studies.

5.4.3 Client-Server Style

Another very common style used to build systems today is the client-server style. Client-server computing is one of the basic paradigms of distributed com-puting and this architecture style is built upon this paradigm.

In this style, there are two component types—clients and servers. A con-straint of this style is that a client can only communicate with the server, and cannot communicate with other clients. The communication between a client component and a server component is initiated by the client when the client sends a request for some service that the server supports. The server receives the request at its defined port, performs the service, and then returns the results of the computation to the client who requested the service.

There is one connector type in this style—the request/reply type. A con-nector connects a client to a server. This type of connector is asymmetric—the client end of the connector can only make requests (and receive the reply), while the server end can only send replies in response to the requests it gets through this connector. The communication is frequently synchronous—the client waits for the server to return the results before proceeding. That is, the client is blocked at the request, until it gets the reply.

A general form of this style is an *n-tier* structure. In this style, a client sends a request to a server, but the server, in order to service the request, sends some request to another server. That is, the server also acts as a client for the next tier. This hierarchy can continue for some levels, providing an n-tier system. A common example of this is the 3-tier architecture. In this style, the clients that make requests and receive the final results reside in the client tier. The middle tier, called the business tier, contains the component that processes the data submitted by the clients and applies the necessary business rules. The third tier is the database tier in which the data resides. The business tier interacts with the database tier for all its data needs.

Most often, in a client-server architecture, the client and the server component reside on different machines. Even if they reside on the same machine, they are designed in a manner such that they can exist on different machines. Hence, the connector between the client and the server is expected to support the request/result type of connection across different machines. Consequently, these connectors are internally quite complex and involve a fair amount of networking to support. Many of the client-server systems today use TCP ports for their connectors. The Web uses the HTTP for supporting this connector.

Note that there is a distinction between a layered architecture and a tiered architecture. The tiered style is a component and connector architecture view in which each tier is a component, and these components communicate with the adjacent ones through a defined protocol. A layered architecture is a module view providing how modules are organized and used. In the layered organization, modules are organized in layers with modules in a layer allowed to invoke services only of the modules in the layer below. Hence, layered and tiered represent two different views. We can have an n-tiered architecture in which some tier(s) have a layered architecture. For example, in a client-server architecture, the server might have a layered architecture, that is, modules that compose the server are organized in the layered style.

5.4.4 Some Other Styles

Publish-Subscribe Style   In this style, there are two types of components. One type of component subscribes to a set of defined events. Other types of components generate or publish events. In response to these events, the components that have published their intent to process the event, are invoked. This type of style is most natural in user interface frameworks, where many events are defined (like mouse click) and components are assigned to these events. When that event occurs, the associated component is executed. As is the case with most connectors, it is the task of the runtime infrastructure to ensure that this type of connector (i.e., publish-subscribe) is supported. This style can be seen as a special case of the blackboard style, except that the repository aspect is not being used.

Peer-to-peer style, or object-oriented style   If we take a client-server style, and generalize each component to be a client as well as a server, then we have this style. In this style, components are peers and any component can request a service from any other component. The object-oriented computation model represents this style well. If we view components as objects, and connectors as method invocations, then we have this style. This model is the one that is primarily supported through middleware connectors like CORBA or .NET.

Communicating processes style   Perhaps the oldest model of distributed computing is that of communicating processes. This style tries to capture this model of computing. The components in this model are processes or threads, which communicate with each other either with message passing or through shared memory. This style is used in some form in many complex systems which use multiple threads or processes.

5.5 Documenting Architecture Design

So far we have focused on representing views through diagrams. While designing, diagrams are indeed a good way to explore options and encourage discussion and brainstorming between the architects. But when the designing is over, the architecture has to be properly communicated to all stakeholders for negotiation and agreement. This requires that architecture be precisely documented with enough information to perform the types of analysis the different stakeholders wish to make to satisfy themselves that their concerns have been adequately addressed. Without a properly documented description of the architecture, it is not possible to have a clear common understanding. Hence, properly documenting an architecture is as important as creating one. In this section, we discuss what an architecture document should contain. Our discussion is based on the recommendations in [6, 23, 54].

Just like different projects require different views, different projects will need different level of detail in their architecture documentation. In general, however, a document describing the architecture should contain the following:

– System and architecture context

– Description of architecture views

– Across views documentation

We know that an architecture for a system is driven by the system objectives and the needs of the stakeholders. Hence, the first aspect that an architecture document should contain is identification of stakeholders and their concerns. This portion should give an overview of the system, the different stakeholders, and the system properties for which the architecture will be evaluated. A context diagram that establishes the scope of the system, its boundaries, the key actors that interact with the system, and sources and sinks of data can also be very useful. A context diagram is frequently represented by showing the system in the center, and showing its connections with people and systems, including sources and sinks of data.

With the context defined, the document can proceed with describing the different structures or views. As stated before, multiple views of different types may be needed, and which views are chosen depends on the needs of the project and its stakeholders. The description of views in the architecture documentation will almost always contain a pictorial representation of the view, which is often the *primary presentation of the view*. As discussed earlier, in any view diagram it is desirable to have different symbols for different element types and provide a key for the different types, such that the type of the different components (represented using the symbols) is clear to a reader. It is, of course, highly desirable to keep the diagram simple and uncluttered. If necessary, to keep the complexity of the view manageable, a hierarchical approach can be followed to make the main view simple (and provide further details as structure of the elements).

However, a pictorial representation is not a complete description of the view. It gives an intuitive idea of the design, but is not sufficient for providing the details. For example, the purpose and functionality of a module or a component is indicated only by its name which is not sufficient. Hence, supporting documentation is needed for the view diagrams. This supporting documentation should have some or all of the following:

– *Element Catalog.* Provides more information about the elements shown in the primary representation. Besides describing the purpose of the element, it should also describe the elements' interfaces (remember that all elements have interfaces through which they interact with other elements). All the different interfaces provided by the elements should be specified. Interfaces should have unique identity, and the specification should give both syntactic and semantic information. Syntactic information is often in terms of signatures, which describe all the data items involved in the interface and their types. Semantic information must describe what the interface does. The description should also clearly state the error conditions that the interface can return.

- *Architecture Rationale.* Though a view specifies the elements and the relationship between them, it does not provide any insight into why the architect chose the particular structure. Architecture rationale gives the reasons for selecting the different elements and composing them in the way it was done. This section may also provide some discussion on the alternatives that were considered and why they were rejected. This discussion, besides explaining the choices, is also useful later when an analyst making a change wonders why the architecture should not be changed in some manner (that might make the change easy).

- *Behavior.* A view gives the structural information. It does not represent the actual behavior or execution. Consequently, in a structure, all possible interactions during an execution are shown. Sometimes, it is necessary to get some idea of the actual behavior of the system in some scenarios. Such a description is useful for arguing about properties like deadlock. Behavior description can be provided to help aid understanding of the system execution. Often diagrams like collaboration diagrams or sequence diagrams (we will discuss these further in Chapter 6 on OO design) are used.

- *Other Information.* This may include a description of all those decisions that have not been taken during architecture creation but have been deliberately left for the future, such as, the choice of a server or protocol. If this is done, then it must be specified as fixing these will have impact on the architecture.

We know that the different views are related. In what we have discussed so far, the views have been described independently. The architecture document, therefore, besides describing the views, should also describe the relationship between the different views. This is the primary purpose of the across view documentation. Essentially, this documentation describes the relationship between elements of the different views (for example, how modules in a module view relate to components in a component view, or how components in a C&C view relate to processes in a process view). This part of the document can also describe the rationale of the overall architecture, why the selected views were chosen, and any other information that cuts across views.

However, often the relationship between the different views is straightforward or very strong. In such situations, the different structures may look very similar and describing the views separately can lead to a repetition. In such situations, for practical reasons, it is better to combine different views into one. Besides eliminating the duplication, this approach can also help clearly show the strong relationship between the two views (and in the process also reduce the across view documentation). Combined views are also useful for some analysis which requires multiple views, for example, performance analysis, which frequently requires both the C&C view as well as the allocation view. So, sometimes, it may be desirable to show some combined views.

Combining of views, however, should be done only if the relationship between the views is strong and straightforward. Otherwise, putting multiple views in one diagram will clutter the view and make it confusing. The objective of reveal multiple views in one is not merely to reduce the number of views, but is to be done primarily to aid understanding and showing the relationships. An example of combining is when there are multiple modules in the module view that form the different layers in the layer view. In such a situation, it is probably more natural to show one view consisting of the layers, and overlaying the module structure on the layers, that is, showing the module structure within the layers. Many layered systems' architectures actually use this approach. In such a situation, it is best to show them together, creating a hybrid style in which both a module view and a C&C view are captured. Overall, if the mapping can be shown easily and in a simple manner, then different views should be combined for the sake of simplicity and compactness. If, however, the relationship between the different views is complex (for example, a many-to-many relationship between elements of the different views), then it is best to keep them separate and specify the relationship separately.

The general structure discussed here can provide a guide for organizing the architecture document. However, the main purpose of the document is to clearly communicate the architecture to the stakeholders such that the desired analysis can be done. And if some of these sections are redundant for that purpose, they may not be included. Similarly, if more information needs to be provided, then it should be done.

Finally, a word on the language chosen for describing different parts of the architecture. Here the choice varies from the formal architecture description languages (ADLs) to informal notation. Many people now use UML to represent the architecture, which allows various possibilities to show the primary description of the view and also allows annotation capability for supporting document. We believe that any method can be used, as long as the objective is met. To allow flexibility, we suggest using a problem-specific notation, but following the guidelines for good view representation, and using a combination of header definitions and text for the supporting documentation.

5.6 Evaluating Architectures

Architecture of a software system impacts some of the key nonfunctional quality attributes like modifiability, performance, reliability, portability, etc. The architecture has a much more significant impact on some of these properties than the design and coding choices. That is, even though choices of algorithms, data structures, etc., are important for many of these attributes, often they have less of an impact than the architectural choices. Clearly then, evaluating a proposed architecture for these properties can have a beneficial impact on the project—any architectural changes that are required to meet the desired goals for these attributes can be done during the architecture design itself.

There are many nonfunctional quality attributes. Not all of them are affected by architecture significantly. Some of the attributes on which architecture has a significant impact are performance, reliability and availability, security (some aspects of it), modifiability, reusability, and portability. Attributes like usability are only mildly affected by architecture.

How should a proposed architecture be evaluated for these attributes? For some attributes like performance and reliability, it is possible to build formal models using techniques like queuing networks and use them for assessing the value of the attribute. However, these models require information beyond the architecture description, generally in forms of execution times, and reliability of each component.

Another approach is procedural—a sequence of steps is followed to subjectively evaluate the impact of the architecture on some of the attributes. One such informal analysis approach that is often used is as follows. First identify the attributes of interest for which an architecture should be evaluated. These attributes are usually determined from stakeholders' interests—the attributes the different stakeholders are most interested in. These attributes are then listed in a table. Then for each attribute, an experience-based, subjective (or quantitative) analysis is done, to assess the level supported by the architecture. The analysis might mention the level for each attribute (e.g., good, average, poor), or might simply mention whether it is satisfactory or not. Based on the outcome of this analysis, the architecture is either accepted or rejected. If rejected, it may be enhanced to improve the performance for the attribute for which the proposed architecture was unsatisfactory. Many techniques have been proposed for evaluation, and a survey of them is given in [29].

5.7 Summary

— Architecture of a software system provides a very high-level view of the
  system in terms of parts of the system and how they are related to form the
  whole system.

— Depending on how the system is partitioned, we get a different architectural
  view of the system. Consequently, the architecture of a software system is
  defined as the structures of the system which comprise software elements,
  their externally visible properties, and relationships among them.

— Architecture facilitates development of a high-quality system. It also allows
  analysis of many of the system properties like performance that depend
  mostly on architecture to be done early in the software life cycle.

— There are three main architectural views of a system—module, component
  and connector, and allocation. In a module view, the system is viewed as
  a structure of programming modules like packages, classes, functions, etc.
  In a component and connector (C&C) view, the system is a collection of
  runtime entities called components, which interact with each other through
  the connectors. An allocation view describes how the different software units
  are allocated to hardware resources in the system.

— C&C view is most common, and is often the centerpiece of the architecture
  description. This view is often described by block diagrams specifying the
  different components and the different connectors between the components.

— There are some common styles for a C&C view which have been found useful
  for creating this architecture view for a system. These include pipe and filter,
  shared data, client-server, publish-subscribe, peer to peer, and communicating processes styles. Each of these styles describes the types of components
  and connectors that exist and the constraints on how they are used.

  — The pipe and filter has one type of component (filter) and one type of
    connector (pipe) and components can be connected through the pipe.

  — The client-server style has two types of components (client and server)
    and there is one connector (request/reply). A client can only communicate
    with the server, and an interaction is initiated by a client.

  — In shared data style the two component types are repository and data
    accessors. Data accessors read/write the repository and share information
    among themselves through the repository.

— The architecture forms the foundation for the system and rest of the design
  and development activities, and needs to be properly documented. A proper

architecture document should describe the context in which the architecture was designed, the different architectural views that were created, and how the different views relate to each other. The architecture description should specify the different types of elements and their external behavior, and the architecture rationale.

— Architecture should be evaluated to see that it satisfies the requirements. A common approach is to do a subjective evaluation with respect to the desired properties.

Self-Assessment Exercises

1. Why is architecture not just one structure consisting of different parts and their relationship?
2. What are the different architectural styles for the component and connector structure of a system?
3. Consider an interactive website which provides many different features to perform various tasks. Show that the architecture for this can be represented as a shared-data style as well as client-server style. Which one will you prefer and why?
4. What should an architecture document for a system contain.
5. Suggest how you will evaluate a proposed architecture from a modifiability perspective.

6
Design

The design activity begins when the requirements document for the software to be developed is available and the architecture has been designed. During design we further refine the architecture. Generally, design focuses on what we have called the *module view* in Chapter 5. That is, during design we determine what modules the system should have and which have to be developed. Often, the module view may effectively be a module structure of each component in the architecture. In that case, the design exercise determines the module structure of the components. However, this simple mapping of components and modules may not always hold. In that case we have to ensure that the module view created in design is consistent with the architecture.

The design of a system is essentially a blueprint or a plan for a solution for the system. Here we consider a system to be a set of modules with clearly defined behavior which interact with each other in a defined manner to produce some behavior or services for its environment.

The design process for software systems often has two levels. At the first level the focus is on deciding which modules are needed for the system, the specifications of these modules, and how the modules should be interconnected. This is what may be called the module design or the high-level design. In the second level, the internal design of the modules, or how the specifications of the module can be satisfied, is decided. This design level is often called detailed design or logic design. Detailed design essentially expands the system design to contain a more detailed description of the processing logic and data structures so that the design is sufficiently complete for coding.

A *design methodology* is a systematic approach to creating a design by

P. Jalote, *A Concise Introduction to Software Engineering*,
DOI: 10.1007/978-1-84800-302-6_6, © Springer-Verlag London Limited 2008

applying of a set of techniques and guidelines. Most design methodologies focus on the module design, but do not reduce the design activity to a sequence of steps that can be blindly followed by the designer.

In this chapter, we will discuss:

– The key design concepts of modularity, cohesion, coupling, and open-closed principle.

– The structure chart notation for expressing the structure of a function-oriented system.

– The structured design methodology for designing the structure chart of the system being developed.

– Some key concepts related to object-orientation, and the unified modeling language (UML) that can be used to express an object-oriented design.

– A methodology of creating the object-oriented design for a system utilizing UML.

– Some guidelines for making a detailed design.

– How a design is verified.

– Some metrics for quantifying the complexity of a design.

6.1 Design Concepts

The design of a system is *correct* if a system built precisely according to the design satisfies the requirements of that system. Clearly, the goal during the design phase is to produce correct designs. However, correctness is not the sole criterion during the design phase, as there can be many correct designs. The goal of the design process is not simply to produce *a* design for the system. Instead, the goal is to find the *best* possible design within the limitations imposed by the requirements and the physical and social environment in which the system will operate.

To evaluate a design, we have to specify some evaluation criteria. We will focus on modularity of a system, which is decided mostly by design, as the main criterion for evaluation.

A system is considered *modular* if it consists of discrete modules so that each module can be implemented separately, and a change to one module has minimal impact on other modules.

Modularity is clearly a desirable property. Modularity helps in system debugging—isolating the system problem to a module is easier if the system is modular; in system repair—changing a part of the system is easy as it affects few other parts; and in system building—a modular system can be easily built by "putting its modules together."

A software system cannot be made modular by simply chopping it into a set of modules. For modularity, each module needs to support a well-defined abstraction and have a clear interface through which it can interact with other modules. To produce modular designs, some criteria must be used to select modules so that the modules support well-defined abstractions and are solvable and modifiable separately. Coupling and cohesion are two modularization criteria, which are often used together. We also discuss the open-closed principle, which is another criterion for modularity.

6.1.1 Coupling

Two modules are considered independent if one can function completely without the presence of the other. Obviously, if two modules are independent, they are solvable and modifiable separately. However, all the modules in a system cannot be independent of each other, as they must interact so that together they produce the desired external behavior of the system. The more connections between modules, the more dependent they are in the sense that more knowledge about one module is required to understand or solve the other module. Hence, the fewer and simpler the connections between modules, the easier it is to understand one without understanding the other. The notion of coupling [79, 88] attempts to capture this concept of "how strongly" different modules are interconnected.

Coupling between modules is the strength of interconnections between modules or a measure of interdependence among modules. In general, the more we must know about module A in order to understand module B, the more closely connected A is to B. "Highly coupled" modules are joined by strong interconnections, while "loosely coupled" modules have weak interconnections. Independent modules have no interconnections. To solve and modify a module separately, we would like the module to be loosely coupled with other modules. The choice of modules decides the coupling between modules. Because the modules of the software system are created during system design, the coupling between modules is largely decided during system design and cannot be reduced during implementation.

Coupling increases with the complexity and obscurity of the interface between modules. To keep coupling low we would like to minimize the number of interfaces per module and the complexity of each interface. An interface of a module is used to pass information to and from other modules. Coupling is reduced if only the defined entry interface of a module is used by other modules, for example, passing information to and from a module exclusively through parameters. Coupling would increase if a module is used by other modules via an indirect and obscure interface, like directly using the internals of a module or using shared variables.

Complexity of the interface is another factor affecting coupling. The more complex each interface is, the higher will be the degree of coupling. For example, complexity of the entry interface of a procedure depends on the number of items being passed as parameters and on the complexity of the items. Some level of complexity of interfaces is required to support the communication needed between modules. However, often more than this minimum is used. For example, if a field of a record is needed by a procedure, often the entire record is passed, rather than just passing that field of the record. By passing the record we are increasing the coupling unnecessarily. Essentially, we should keep the interface of a module as simple and small as possible.

The type of information flow along the interfaces is the third major factor affecting coupling. There are two kinds of information that can flow along an interface: data or control. Passing or receiving control information means that the action of the module will depend on this control information, which makes it more difficult to understand the module and provide its abstraction. Transfer of data information means that a module passes as input some data to another module and gets in return some data as output. This allows a module to be treated as a simple input-output function that performs some transformation on the input data to produce the output data. In general, interfaces with only data communication result in the lowest degree of coupling, followed by interfaces that only transfer control data. Coupling is considered highest if the data is hybrid, that is, some data items and some control items are passed between modules. The effect of these three factors on coupling is summarized in Table 6.1 [79].

Table 6.1: Factors affecting coupling.

	Interface Complexity	Type of Connection	Type of Communication
Low	Simple obvious	To module by name	Data
			Control
High	Complicated obscure	To internal elements	Hybrid

The manifestation of coupling in OO systems is somewhat different as objects are semantically richer than functions. In OO systems, three different types of coupling exist between modules [30]:

- Interaction coupling

- Component coupling

- Inheritance coupling

Interaction coupling occurs due to methods of a class invoking methods of other classes. In many ways, this situation is similar to a function calling another function and hence this coupling is similar to coupling between functional modules discussed above. Like with functions, the worst form of coupling here is if methods directly access internal parts of other methods. Coupling is lowest if methods communicate directly through parameters. Within this category, as discussed above, coupling is lower if only data is passed, but is higher if control information is passed since the invoked method impacts the execution sequence in the calling method. Also, coupling is higher if the amount of data being passed is increased. So, if whole data structures are passed when only some parts are needed, coupling is being unnecessarily increased. Similarly, if an object is passed to a method when only some of its component objects are used within the method, coupling increases unnecessarily. The least coupling situation therefore is when communication is with parameters only, with only necessary variables being passed, and these parameters only pass data.

Component coupling refers to the interaction between two classes where a class has variables of the other class. Three clear situations exist as to how this can happen. A class C can be component coupled with another class C1, if C has an instance variable of type C1, or C has a method whose parameter is of type C1, or if C has a method which has a local variable of type C1. Note that when C is component coupled with C1, it has the potential of being component coupled with all subclasses of C1 as at runtime an object of any subclass may actually be used. It should be clear that whenever there is component coupling, there is likely to be interaction coupling. Component coupling is considered to be weakest (i.e. most desired) if in a class C, the variables of class C1 are either in the signatures of the methods of C, or are some attributes of C. If interaction is through local variables, then this interaction is not visible from outside, and therefore increases coupling.

Inheritance coupling is due to the inheritance relationship between classes. Two classes are considered inheritance coupled if one class is a direct or indirect subclass of the other. If inheritance adds coupling, one can ask the question why not do away with inheritance altogether. The reason is that inheritance may reduce the overall coupling in the system. Let us consider two situations. If a class A is coupled with another class B, and if B is a hierarchy with B1 and

B2 as two subclasses, then if a method m() is factored out of B1 and B2 and put in the superclass B, the coupling drops as A is now only coupled with B, whereas earlier it was coupled with both B1 and B2. Similarly, if B is a class hierarchy which supports specialization-generalization relationship, then if new subclasses are added to B, no changes need to be made to a class A which calls methods in B. That is, for changing B's hierarchy, A need not be disturbed. Without this hierarchy, changes in B would most likely result in changes in A.

Within inheritance coupling there are some situations that are worse than others. The worst form is when a subclass B1 modifies the signature of a method in B (or deletes the method). This situation can easily lead to a runtime error, besides violating the true spirit of the is-a relationship. If the signature is preserved but the implementation of a method is changed, that also violates the is-a relationship, though may not lead to a runtime error, and should be avoided. The least coupling scenario is when a subclass only adds instance variables and methods but does not modify any inherited ones.

6.1.2 Cohesion

We have seen that coupling is reduced when the relationships among elements in different modules are minimized. That is, coupling is reduced when elements in different modules have little or no bonds between them. Another way of achieving this effect is to strengthen the bond between elements of the same module by maximizing the relationship between elements of the same module. Cohesion is the concept that tries to capture this intramodule [79, 88]. With cohesion, we are interested in determining how closely the elements of a module are related to each other.

Cohesion of a module represents how tightly bound the internal elements of the module are to one another. Cohesion of a module gives the designer an idea about whether the different elements of a module belong together in the same module. Cohesion and coupling are clearly related. Usually, the greater the cohesion of each module in the system, the lower the coupling between modules is. This correlation is not perfect, but it has been observed in practice. There are several levels of cohesion:

- Coincidental

- Logical

- Temporal

- Procedural

- Communicational

– Sequential

– Functional

Coincidental is the lowest level, and functional is the highest. Coincidental cohesion occurs when there is no meaningful relationship among the elements of a module. Coincidental cohesion can occur if an existing program is "modularized" by chopping it into pieces and making different pieces modules. If a module is created to save duplicate code by combining some part of code that occurs at many different places, that module is likely to have coincidental cohesion.

A module has logical cohesion if there is some logical relationship between the elements of a module, and the elements perform functions that fall in the same logical class. A typical example of this kind of cohesion is a module that performs all the inputs or all the outputs. In such a situation, if we want to input or output a particular record, we have to somehow convey this to the module. Often, this will be done by passing some kind of special status flag, which will be used to determine what statements to execute in the module. Besides resulting in hybrid information flow between modules, which is generally the worst form of coupling between modules, such a module will usually have tricky and clumsy code. In general, logically cohesive modules should be avoided, if possible.

Temporal cohesion is the same as logical cohesion, except that the elements are also related in time and are executed together. Modules that perform activities like "initialization," "cleanup," and "termination" are usually temporally bound. Even though the elements in a temporally bound module are logically related, temporal cohesion is higher than logical cohesion, because the elements are all executed together. This avoids the problem of passing the flag, and the code is usually simpler.

A procedurally cohesive module contains elements that belong to a common procedural unit. For example, a loop or a sequence of decision statements in a module may be combined to form a separate module. Procedurally cohesive modules often occur when modular structure is determined from some form of flowchart. Procedural cohesion often cuts across functional lines. A module with only procedural cohesion may contain only part of a complete function or parts of several functions.

A module with communicational cohesion has elements that are related by a reference to the same input or output data. That is, in a communicationally bound module, the elements are together because they operate on the same input or output data. An example of this could be a module to "print and punch record." Communicationally cohesive modules may perform more than one function. However, communicational cohesion is sufficiently high as to be generally acceptable if alternative structures with higher cohesion cannot be easily identified.

When the elements are together in a module because the output of one forms the input to another, we get sequential cohesion. If we have a sequence of elements in which the output of one forms the input to another, sequential cohesion does not provide any guidelines on how to combine them into modules.

Functional cohesion is the strongest cohesion. In a functionally bound module, all the elements of the module are related to performing a single function. By function, we do not mean simply mathematical functions; modules accomplishing a single goal are also included. Functions like "compute square root" and "sort the array" are clear examples of functionally cohesive modules.

How does one determine the cohesion level of a module? There is no mathematical formula that can be used. We have to use our judgment for this. A useful technique for determining if a module has functional cohesion is to write a sentence that describes, fully and accurately, the function or purpose of the module. Modules with functional cohesion can always be described by a simple sentence. If we cannot describe it using a simple sentence, the module is not likely to have functional cohesion.

Cohesion in object-oriented systems has three aspects [30]:

— Method cohesion

— Class cohesion

— Inheritance cohesion

Method cohesion is the same as cohesion in functional modules. It focuses on why the different code elements of a method are together within the method. The highest form of cohesion is if each method implements a clearly defined function, and all statements in the method contribute to implementing this function.

Class cohesion focuses on why different attributes and methods are together in this class. The goal is to have a class that implements a single concept or abstraction with all elements contributing toward supporting this concept. In general, whenever there are multiple concepts encapsulated within a class, the cohesion of the class is not as high as it could be, and a designer should try to change the design to have each class encapsulate a single concept.

One symptom of the situation where a class has multiple abstractions is that the set of methods can be partitioned into two (or more) groups, each accessing a distinct subset of the attributes. That is, the set of methods and attributes can be partitioned into separate groups, each encapsulating a different concept. Clearly, in such a situation, by having separate classes encapsulating separate concepts, we can have modules with improved cohesion.

In many situations, even though two (or more) concepts may be encapsulated within a class, there are some methods that access attributes of both the encapsulated concepts. This happens when the class represents different entities which have a relationship between them. For cohesion, it is best to represent them as two separate classes with relationship among them. That is, we should have multiple classes, with some methods in these classes accessing objects of the other class. In a way, this improvement in cohesion results in an increased coupling. However, for modifiability and understandability, it is better if each class encapsulates a single concept.

Inheritance cohesion focuses on the reason why classes are together in a hierarchy. The two main reasons for inheritance are to model generalization-specialization relationship, and for code reuse. Cohesion is considered high if the hierarchy supports generalization-specialization of some concept (which is likely to naturally lead to reuse of some code). It is considered lower if the hierarchy is primarily for sharing code with weak conceptual relationship between superclass and subclasses. In other words, it is desired that in an OO system the class hierarchies should be such that they support clearly identified generalization-specialization relationship.

6.1.3 The Open-Closed Principle

This is a design concept which came into existence more in the OO context. Like with cohesion and coupling, the basic goal here is again to promote building of systems that are easily modifiable, as modification and change happen frequently and a design that cannot easily accommodate change will result in systems that will die fast and will not be able to easily adapt to the changing world.

The basic principle, as stated by Bertrand Meyer, is "Software entities should be open for extension, but closed for modification"[66]. A module being "open for extension" means that its behavior can be extended to accommodate new demands placed on this module due to changes in requirements and system functionality. The module being "closed for modification" means that the existing source code of the module is not changed when making enhancements.

Then how does one make enhancements to a module without changing the existing source code? This principle restricts the changes to modules to extension only, i.e. it allows addition of code, but disallows changing of existing code. If this can be done, clearly, the value is tremendous. Code changes involve heavy risk and to ensure that a change has not "broken" things that were working often requires a lot of regression testing. This risk can be minimized if no changes are made to existing code. But if changes are not made, how will enhancements be made? This principle says that enhancements should be made by adding new code, rather than altering old code.

There is another side benefit of this. Programmers typically prefer writing new code rather than modifying old code. But the reality is that systems that are being built today are being built on top of existing software. If this principle is satisfied, then we can expand existing systems by mostly adding new code to old systems, and minimizing the need for changing code.

This principle can be satisfied in OO designs by properly using inheritance and polymorphism. Inheritance allows creating new classes that will extend the behavior of existing classes without changing the original class. And it is this property that can be used to support this principle. As an example, consider an application in which a client object (of type Client) interacts with a printer object (of class Printer1) and invokes the necessary methods for completing its printing needs. The class diagram for this will be as shown in Figure 6.1.

Figure 6.1: Example without using subtyping.

In this design, the client directly calls the methods on the printer object for printing something. Now suppose the system has to be enhanced to allow another printer to be used by the client. Under this design, to implement this change, a new class Printer2 will have to be created and the code of the client class will have to be changed to allow using object of Printer2 type as well. This design does not support the open-closed principle as the Client class is not closed against change.

The design for this system, however, can be done in another manner that supports the open-closed principle. In this design, instead of directly implementing the Printer1 class, we create an abstract class Printer that defines the interface of a printer and specifies all the methods a printer object should support. Printer1 is implemented as a specialization of this class. In this design, when Printer2 is to be added, it is added as another subclass of type Printer. The client does not need to be aware of this subtype as it interacts with objects of type Printer. That is, the client only deals with a generic Printer, and its interaction is the same whether the object is actually of type Printer1 or Printer2. The class diagram for this is shown in Figure 6.2.

It is this inheritance property of OO that is leveraged to support the open-closed principle. The basic idea is to have a class encapsulate the abstraction

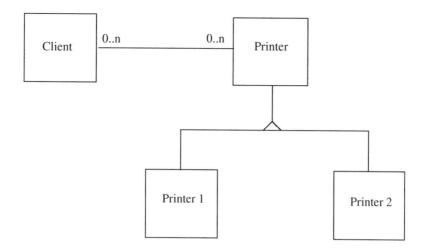

Figure 6.2: Example using subtyping.

of some concept. If this abstraction is to be extended, the extension is done by creating new subclasses of the abstraction, thereby keeping all the existing code unchanged.

If inheritance hierarchies are built in this manner, they are said to satisfy the Liskov Substitution Principle [65]. According to this principle, if a program is using object o1 of a (base) class C, that program should remain unchanged if o1 is replaced by an object o2 of a class C1, where C1 is a subclass of C. If this principle is satisfied for class hierarchies, and hierarchies are used properly, then the open-closed principle can be supported. It should also be noted that recommendations for both inheritance coupling and inheritance cohesion support that this principle be followed in class hierarchies.

6.2 Function-Oriented Design

Creating the software system design is the major concern of the design phase. Many design techniques have been proposed over the years to provide some discipline in handling the complexity of designing large systems. The aim of design methodologies is not to reduce the process of design to a sequence of mechanical steps but to provide guidelines to aid the designer during the design process. We discuss the structured design methodology [79, 88] for developing function-oriented system designs. The methodology employs the structure chart notation for creating the design. So before we discuss the methodology, we describe this notation.

6.2.1 Structure Charts

Graphical design notations are frequently used during the design process to represent design or design decisions, so the design can be communicated to stakeholders in a succinct manner and evaluated. For a function-oriented design, the design can be represented graphically by structure charts.

The structure of a program is made up of the modules of that program together with the interconnections between modules. Every computer program has a structure, and given a program its structure can be determined. The structure chart of a program is a graphic representation of its structure. In a structure chart a module is represented by a box with the module name written in the box. An arrow from module A to module B represents that module A invokes module B. B is called the *subordinate* of A, and A is called the *superordinate* of B. The arrow is labeled by the parameters received by B as input and the parameters returned by B as output, with the direction of flow of the input and output parameters represented by small arrows. The parameters can be shown to be data (unfilled circle at the tail of the label) or control (filled circle at the tail). As an example, consider the structure of the following program, whose structure is shown in Figure 6.3.

```
main()
{
    int sum, n, N, a[MAX];
    readnums(a, &N); sort(a, N); scanf(&n);
    sum = add_n(a, n); printf(sum);
}

readnums(a, N)
int a[], *N;
{
    :
}

sort(a, N)
int a[], N;
{
    :
    if (a[i] > a[t]) switch(a[i], a[t]);
    :
}

/* Add the first n numbers of a */
add_n(a, n)
int a[], n;
{
    :
```

}

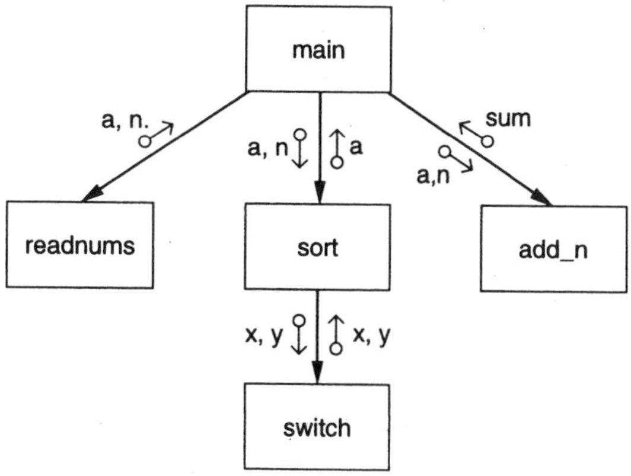

Figure 6.3: The structure chart of the sort program.

In general, procedural information is not represented in a structure chart, and the focus is on representing the hierarchy of modules. However, there are situations where the designer may wish to communicate certain procedural information explicitly, like major loops and decisions. Such information can also be represented in a structure chart. For example, let us consider a situation where module A has subordinates B, C, and D, and A repeatedly calls the modules C and D. This can be represented by a looping arrow around the arrows joining the subordinates C and D to A, as shown in Figure 6.4. All the subordinate modules activated within a common loop are enclosed in the same looping arrow.

Major decisions can be represented similarly. For example, if the invocation of modules C and D in module A depends on the outcome of some decision, that is represented by a small diamond in the box for A, with the arrows joining C and D coming out of this diamond, as shown in Figure 6.4.

Modules in a system can be categorized into few classes. There are some modules that obtain information from their subordinates and then pass it to their superordinate. This kind of module is an *input module*. Similarly, there are *output modules*, which take information from their superordinate and pass it on to its subordinates. As the names suggest, the input and output modules are typically used for input and output of data from and to the environment. The input modules get the data from the sources and get it ready to be

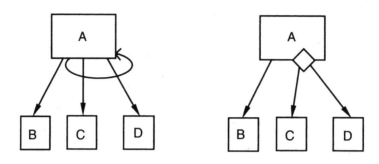

Figure 6.4: Iteration and decision representation.

processed, and the output modules take the output produced and prepare it for proper presentation to the environment. Then there are modules that exist solely for the sake of transforming data into some other form. Such a module is called a *transform module*. Most of the computational modules typically fall in this category. Finally, there are modules whose primary concern is managing the flow of data to and from different subordinates. Such modules are called *coordinate modules*. A module can perform functions of more than one type of module.

A structure chart is a nice representation for a design that uses functional abstraction. It shows the modules and their call hierarchy, the interfaces between the modules, and what information passes between modules. So, for a software system, once its structure is decided, the modules and their interfaces and dependencies get fixed. The objective of the structured design methodology is to control the eventual structure of the system by fixing the structure during design. The aim is to design a system so that programs implementing the design would have a hierarchical structure, with functionally cohesive modules and as few interconnections between modules as possible.

6.2.2 Structured Design Methodology

No design methodology reduces design to a series of steps that can be mechanically executed. All design methodologies are, at best, a set of guidelines that, if applied, will most likely produce a design that is modular and simple.

The basic principle behind the structured design methodology, as with most other methodologies, is problem partitioning. Structured design methodology partitions the system at the very top level into various subsystems, one for managing each major input, one for managing each major output, and one for each major transformation. The modules performing the transformation deal with data at an abstract level, and hence can focus on the conceptual problem of how to perform the transformation without bothering with how to obtain clean inputs or how to present the output.

The rationale behind this partitioning is that in many systems, particularly data processing systems, a good part of the system code deals with managing the inputs and outputs. The modules dealing with inputs have to deal with issues of screens, reading data, formats, errors, exceptions, completeness of information, structure of the information, etc. Similarly, the modules dealing with output have to prepare the output in presentation formats, make charts, produce reports, etc. Hence, for many systems, it is indeed the case that a good part of the software has to deal with inputs and outputs. The actual transformation in the system is frequently not very complex—it is dealing with data and getting it in proper form for performing the transformation or producing the output in the desired form that requires considerable processing.

This partitioning is at the heart of the structured design methodology. There are four major steps in the methodology:

1. Restate the problem as a data flow diagram

2. Identify the input and output data elements

3. First-level factoring

4. Factoring of input, output, and transform branches

We will now discuss each of these steps in more detail.

Restate the Problem as a Data Flow Diagram To use this methodology, the first step is to construct the data flow diagram for the problem. We studied data flow diagrams in Chapter 3. However, there is a fundamental difference between the DFDs drawn during requirements analysis and those drawn during structured design. In the requirements analysis, a DFD is drawn to model the problem domain. The analyst has little control over the problem, and hence his task is to extract from the problem all the information and then represent it as a DFD.

During design activity, we are no longer modeling the problem domain, but are dealing with the solution domain and developing a model for the eventual system. That is, the DFD during design represents how the data will flow in the system when it is built. In this modeling, the major transforms or functions in the software are decided, and the DFD shows the major transforms that the software will have and how the data will flow through different transforms. A DFD of an ATM is shown in Figure 6.5.

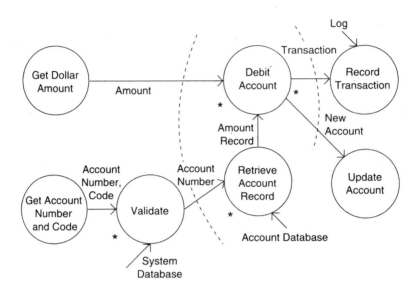

Figure 6.5: Data flow diagram of an ATM.

There are two major streams of input data in this diagram. The first is the account number and the code, and the second is the amount to be debited. Notice the use of * at different places in the DFD. For example, the transform "validate," which verifies if the account number and code are valid, needs not only the account number and code, but also information from the system database to do the validation. And the transform debit account has two outputs, one used for recording the transaction and the other to update the account.

Identify the Most Abstract Input and Output Data Elements Most systems have some basic transformations that perform the required operations. However, in most cases the transformation cannot be easily applied to the actual physical input and produce the desired physical output. Instead, the input is first converted into a form on which the transformation can be applied with ease. Similarly, the main transformation modules often produce outputs that have to be converted into the desired physical output. The goal of this second step is to separate the transforms in the data flow diagram that convert the input or output to the desired format from the ones that perform the actual transformations.

For this separation, once the data flow diagram is ready, the next step is to identify the highest abstract level of input and output. *The most abstract input data elements* are those data elements in the data flow diagram that are farthest removed from the physical inputs but can still be considered inputs to the system. The most abstract input data elements often have little resemblance to the actual physical data. These are often the data elements obtained after operations like error checking, data validation, proper formatting, and conversion are complete.

Most abstract input data elements are recognized by starting from the physical inputs and traveling toward the outputs in the data flow diagram, until the data elements are reached that can no longer be considered incoming. The aim is to go as far as possible from the physical inputs, without losing the incoming nature of the data element. This process is performed for each input stream. Identifying the most abstract data items represents a value judgment on the part of the designer, but often the choice is obvious.

Similarly, we identify the *most abstract output data elements* by starting from the outputs in the data flow diagram and traveling toward the inputs. These are the data elements that are most removed from the actual outputs but can still be considered outgoing. These data elements may also be considered the logical output data items, and the transforms in the data flow diagram after these data items are basically to convert the logical output into a form in which the system is required to produce the output.

There will usually be some transforms left between the most abstract input and output data items. These *central transforms* perform the basic transformation for the system, taking the most abstract input and transforming it into the most abstract output. The purpose of having central transforms deal with the most abstract data items is that the modules implementing these transforms can concentrate on performing the transformation without being concerned with converting the data into proper format, validating the data, and so forth.

Consider now the data flow diagram of the automated teller shown in Figure 6.5. The two most abstract inputs are the dollar amount and the validated account number. The validated account number is the most abstract input, rather than the account number read in, as it is still the input—but with a guarantee that the account number is valid. The two abstract outputs are obvious. The abstract inputs and outputs are marked in the data flow diagram.

First-Level Factoring   Having identified the central transforms and the most abstract input and output data items, we are ready to identify some modules for the system. We first specify a main module, whose purpose is to invoke the subordinates. The main module is therefore a coordinate module. For each of the most abstract input data items, an immediate subordinate module to the main module is specified. Each of these modules is an input module, whose purpose is to deliver to the main module the most abstract data item for which it is created.

Similarly, for each most abstract output data item, a subordinate module that is an output module that accepts data from the main module is specified. Each of the arrows connecting these input and output subordinate modules is labeled with the respective abstract data item flowing in the proper direction.

Finally, for each central transform, a module subordinate to the main one is specified. These modules will be transform modules, whose purpose is to accept data from the main module, and then return the appropriate data back to the main module. The data items coming to a transform module from the main module are on the incoming arcs of the corresponding transform in the data flow diagram. The data items returned are on the outgoing arcs of that transform. Note that here a module is created for a transform, while input/output modules are created for data items.

Let us examine the data flow diagram of the ATM. We have already seen that this has two most abstract inputs, two most abstract outputs, and two central transforms. Drawing a module for each of these, we get the structure chart shown in Figure 6.6.

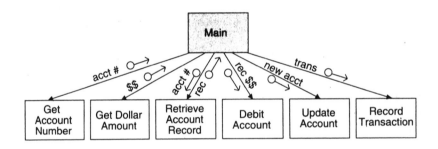

Figure 6.6: First-level factoring for ATM.

As we can see, the first-level factoring is straightforward, after the most abstract input and output data items are identified in the data flow diagram. The main module is the overall control module, which will form the main program or procedure in the implementation of the design. It is a coordinate module that invokes the input modules to get the most abstract data items, passes these to the appropriate transform modules, and delivers the results of the transform modules to other transform modules until the most abstract data items are obtained. These are then passed to the output modules.

Factoring the Input, Output, and Transform Branches   The first-level factoring results in a very high level structure, where each subordinate module has a lot of processing to do. To simplify these modules, they must be factored into subordinate modules that will distribute the work of a module. Each of the input, output, and transformation modules must be considered for factoring. Let us start with the input modules.

The purpose of an input module, as viewed by the main program, is to produce some data. To factor an input module, the transform in the data flow diagram that produced the data item is now treated as a central transform. The process performed for the first-level factoring is repeated here with this new central transform, with the input module being considered the main module. A subordinate input module is created for each input data stream coming into this new central transform, and a subordinate transform module is created for the new central transform. The new input modules now created can then be factored again, until the physical inputs are reached. Factoring of input modules will usually not yield any output subordinate modules.

The factoring of the output modules is symmetrical to the factoring of the input modules. For an output module we look at the next transform to be applied to the output to bring it closer to the ultimate desired output. This now becomes the central transform, and an output module is created for each data stream going out of this transform. During the factoring of output modules, there will usually be no input modules.

If the data flow diagram of the problem is sufficiently detailed, factoring of the input and output modules is straightforward. However, there are no such rules for factoring the central transforms. The goal is to determine subtransforms that will together compose the overall transform and then repeat the process for the newly found transforms, until we reach the atomic modules. Factoring the central transform is essentially an exercise in functional decomposition and will depend on the designers' experience and judgment.

One way to factor a transform module is to treat it as a problem in its own right and start with a data flow diagram for it. The inputs to the data flow diagram are the data coming into the module and the outputs are the data being returned by the module. Each transform in this data flow diagram represents a subtransform of this transform. The central transform can be factored by creating a subordinate transform module for each of the transforms in this data flow diagram. This process can be repeated for the new transform modules that are created, until we reach atomic modules.

6.2.3 An Example

As an example, consider the problem of determining the number of different words in an input file. The data flow diagram for this problem is shown in Figure 6.7.

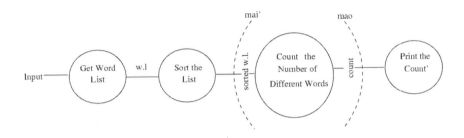

Figure 6.7: DFD for the word-counting problem.

This problem has only one input data stream, the input file, while the desired output is the count of different words in the file. To transform the input to the desired output, the first thing we do is form a list of all the words in the file. It is best to then sort the list, as this will make identifying different words easier. This sorted list is then used to count the number of different words, and the output of this transform is the desired count, which is then printed. This sequence of data transformation is what we have in the data flow diagram.

The arcs in the data flow diagram are the most abstract input and most abstract output. The choice of the most abstract input is obvious. We start following the input. First, the input file is converted into a word list, which is essentially the input in a different form. The sorted word list is still basically the input, as it is still the same list, in a different order. This appears to be the most abstract input because the next data (i.e., count) is not just another form of the input data. The choice of the most abstract output is even more obvious; count is the natural choice (a data that is a form of input will not usually be a candidate for the most abstract output). Thus, we have one central transform, count-number-of-different-words, which has one input and one output data item.

The structure chart after the first-level factoring of the word counting problem is shown in Figure 6.8.

In this structure, there is one input module, which returns the sorted word list to the main module. The output module takes from the main module the value of the count. There is only one central transform in this example, and a

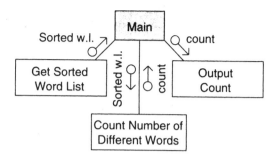

Figure 6.8: First-level factoring.

module is drawn for that. Note that the data items traveling to and from this transformation module are the same as the data items going in and out of the central transform.

The factoring of the input module get-sorted-list in the first-level structure is shown in Figure 6.9. The transform producing the input returned by this module (i.e., the sort transform) is treated as a central transform. Its input is the word list. Thus, in the first factoring we have an input module to get the list and a transform module to sort the list. The input module can be factored further, as the module needs to perform two functions, getting a word and then adding it to the list. Note that the looping arrow is used to show the iteration.

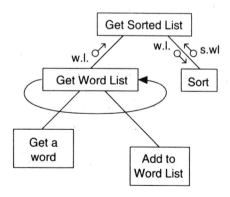

Figure 6.9: Factoring the input module.

In this example, there is only one transform after the most abstract output, so factoring for output need not be done.

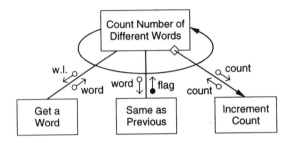

Figure 6.10: Factoring the central transform.

The factoring of the central transform count-the-number-of-different-words is shown in Figure 6.10. This was a relatively simple transform, and we did not need to draw the data flow diagram. To determine the number of words, we have to get a word repeatedly, determine if it is the same as the previous word (for a sorted list, this checking is sufficient to determine if the word is different from other words), and then count the word if it is different. For each of the three different functions, we have a subordinate module, and we get the structure shown in Figure 6.10.

6.3 Object-Oriented Design

Object-oriented (OO) approaches for software development have become extremely popular in recent years. Much of the new development is now being done using OO techniques and languages. There are many advantages that OO systems offer. An OO model closely represents the problem domain, which makes it easier to produce and understand designs. As requirements change, the objects in a system are less immune to these changes, thereby permitting changes more easily. Inheritance and close association of objects in design to problem domain entities encourage more re-use, i.e., new applications can use existing modules more effectively, thereby reducing development cost and cycle time. Object-oriented approaches are believed to be more natural and provide richer structures for thinking and abstraction. Common design patterns have also been uncovered that allow reusability at a higher level. (Design patterns is an advanced topic which we will not discuss further; interested readers are referred to [38].)

The object-oriented design approach is fundamentally different from the function-oriented design approaches primarily due to the different abstraction that is used. It requires a different way of thinking and partitioning. It can be said that thinking in object-oriented terms is most important for producing truly object-oriented designs.

In this section, we will first discuss some important concepts that form the basis of object-orientation. We will then describe the UML notation that can be used while doing an object-oriented design, followed by an OO design methodology.

6.3.1 OO Concepts

Here we very briefly discuss the main concepts behind object-orientation. Readers familiar with an OO language will be familiar with these concepts.

Classes and Objects   Classes and objects are the basic building blocks of an OO design, just like functions (and procedures) are for a function-oriented design. Objects are entities that encapsulate some state and provide services to be used by a client, which could be another object, program, or a user. The basic property of an object is *encapsulation*: it encapsulates the data and information it contains and supports a well-defined abstraction. The set of services that can be requested from outside the object forms the *interface* of the object. An object may have operations defined only for internal use that cannot be used from outside. Such operations do not form part of the interface.

A major advantage of encapsulation is that access to the encapsulated data is limited to the operations defined on the data. Hence, it becomes much easier to ensure that the integrity of data is preserved, something very hard to do if any program from outside can directly manipulate the data structures of an object. Encapsulation and separation of the interface and its implementation, also allows the implementation to be changed without affecting the clients as long as the interface is preserved.

The encapsulated data for an object defines the *state* of the object. An important property of objects is that this state *persists*, in contrast to the data defined in a function or procedure, which is generally lost once the function stops being active (finishes its current execution). In an object, the state is preserved and it persists through the life of the object, i.e., unless the object is actively destroyed.

The state and services of an object together define its *behavior*. We can say that the behavior of an object is how an object reacts in terms of state changes when it is acted on, and how it acts on other objects by requesting services and operations. Generally, for an object, the defined operations together specify the behavior of the object.

Objects represent the basic runtime entities in an OO system; they occupy space in memory that keeps its state and is operated on by the defined operations on the object. A *class*, on the other hand, defines a possible set of objects. We have seen that objects have some attributes, whose values constitute much of the state of an object. What attributes an object has are defined by the class of the object. Similarly, the operations allowed on an object or the services it provides, are defined by the class of the object. But a class is merely a definition that does not create any objects and cannot hold any values.

Each object, when it is created, gets a private copy of the instance variables, and when an operation defined on the class is performed on the object, it is performed on the state of the particular object.

The relationship between a class and objects of that class is similar to the relationship between a type and elements of that type. A class represents a set of objects that share a common structure and a common behavior, whereas an object is an instance of a class.

Relationships among Objects An object, as a stand-alone entity, has very limited capabilities—it can only provide the services defined on it. Any complex system will be composed of many objects of different classes, and these objects will interact with each other so that the overall system objectives are met. In object-oriented systems, an object interacts with another by sending a *message* to the object to perform some service it provides. On receiving the request message, the object invokes the requested service or the method and sends the result, if needed. This form of client-server interaction is a direct fall out of encapsulation and abstraction supported by objects.

If an object invokes some services in other objects, we can say that the two objects are *related* in some way to each other. If an object uses some services of another object, there is an *association* between the two objects. This association is also called a *link*—a link exists from one object to another if the object uses some services of the other object. Links frequently show up as pointers when programming. A link captures the fact that a message is flowing from one object to another. However, when a link exists, though the message flows in the direction of the link, information can flow in both directions (e.g., the server may return some results).

With associations comes the issue of visibility, that is, which object is visible to whom. The basic issue here is that if there is a link from object A to object B, for A (client object) to be able to send a message to B (supplier object), B must be visible to A in the final program. There are different ways to provide this visibility. Some of the important possibilities are [15]:

– The supplier object is global to the client.

– The supplier object is a parameter to some operation of the client that sends the message.

– The supplier object is a part of the client object.

– The supplier object is locally declared in some operation.

Links between objects capture the client/server type of relationship. Another type of relationship between objects is *aggregation*, which reflects the whole/part-of relationship. Though not necessary, aggregation generally implies containment. That is, if an object A is an aggregation of objects B and C, then objects B and C will generally be within object A (though there are situations where the conceptual relationship of aggregation may not get reflected as actual containment of objects). The main implication of this is that a contained object cannot survive without its containing object. With links, that is not the case.

Inheritance and Polymorphism   Inheritance is a relation between classes that allows for definition and implementation of one class based on the definition of existing classes [62]. When a class B inherits from another class A, B is referred to as the *subclass* or the *derived class* and A is referred to as the *superclass* or the *base class*.   In general, a subclass B will have two parts: a derived part and an incremental part [62]. The derived part is the part inherited from A and the incremental part is the new code and definitions that have been specifically added for B. This is shown in Figure 6.11 [62]. Objects of type B have the derived part as well as the incremental part. Hence, by defining only the incremental part and inheriting the derived part from an existing class, we can define objects that contain both.

Inheritance is often called an "is a" relation, implying that an object of type B is also an instance of type A. That is, an instance of a subclass, though more than an instance of the superclass, is also an instance of the superclass.

The inheritance relation between classes forms a hierarchy. As discussed earlier, it is important that the hierarchy represent a structure present in the application domain and is not created simply to reuse some parts of an existing class. And the hierarchy should be such that an object of a class is also an object of all its superclasses in the problem domain.

The power of inheritance lies in the fact that all common features of the subclasses can be accumulated in the superclass. In other words, a feature is

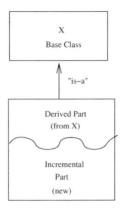

Figure 6.11: Inheritance.

placed in the higher level of abstractions. Once this is done, such features can be inherited from the parent class and used in the subclass directly. This implies that if there are many abstract class definitions available, when a new class is needed, it is possible that the new class is a specialization of one or more of the existing classes. In that case, the existing class can be tailored through inheritance to define the new class.

Inheritance can be broadly classified as being of two types: strict inheritance and nonstrict inheritance [77]. In *strict inheritance* a subclass takes all the features from the parent class and adds additional features to specialize it. That is, all data members and operations available in the base class are also available in the derived class. This form supports the "is-a" relation and is the easiest form of inheritance. *Nonstrict inheritance* occurs when the subclass does not have all the features of the parent class or some features have been redefined. These forms do not satisfy Liskov's substitution principle.

A class hierarchy need not be a simple tree structure. It may be a graph, which implies that a class may inherit from multiple classes. This type of inheritance, when a subclass inherits from many superclasses, is called *multiple inheritance*. Multiple inheritance complicates matters and its use is generally discouraged. We will assume that multiple inheritance is not to be used.

Inheritance brings in *polymorphism*, a general concept widely used in type theory, that deals with the ability of an object to be of different types. In OO programming, polymorphism comes in the form that a reference can refer to objects of different types at different times. In object-oriented systems, with inheritance, polymorphism cannot be avoided—it must be supported. The reason is the "is a" relation supported by inheritance—an object x declared to be of class B is also an object of any class A that is the superclass of B. Hence, anywhere an instance of A is expected, x can be used.

With polymorphism, an entity has a static type and a dynamic type [62]. The static type of an object is the type of which the object is declared in the program text, and it remains unchanged. The dynamic type of an entity, on the other hand, can change from time to time and is known only at reference time. Once an entity is declared, at compile time the set of types that this entity belongs to can be determined from the inheritance hierarchy that has been defined. The dynamic type of the object will be one of this set, but the actual dynamic type will be defined at the time of reference of the object.

This type of polymorphism requires *dynamic binding* of operations. Dynamic binding means that the code associated with a given procedure call is not known until the moment of the call [62]. Let us illustrate with an example. Suppose x is a polymorphic reference whose static type is B but whose dynamic type could be either A or B. Suppose that an operation $O()$ is defined in the class A, which is redefined in the class B. Now when the operation $O()$ is invoked on x, it is not known statically what code will be executed. That is, the code to be executed for the statement $x.O()$ is decided at runtime, depending on the dynamic type of x—if the dynamic type is A, the code for the operation $O()$ in class A will be executed; if the dynamic type is B, the code for operation $O()$ in class B will be executed. This dynamic binding can be used quite effectively during application development to reduce the size of the code.

This feature polymorphism, which is essentially overloading of the feature (i.e., a feature can mean different things in different contexts and its exact meaning is determined only at runtime) causes no problem in strict inheritance because all features of a superclass are available in the subclasses. But in nonstrict inheritance, it can cause problems, because a child may lose a feature. Because the binding of the feature is determined at runtime, this can cause a runtime error as a situation may arise where the object is bound to the superclass in which the feature is not present.

6.3.2 Unified Modeling Language (UML)

UML is a graphical notation for expressing object-oriented designs [35]. It is called a modeling language and not a design notation as it allows representing various aspects of the system, not just the design that has to be implemented. For an OO design, a specification of the classes that exist in the system might suffice. However, while modeling, during the design process, the designer also tries to understand how the different classes are related and how they interact to provide the desired functionality. This aspect of modeling helps build designs that are more likely to satisfy the requirements of the system. Due to the ability of UML to create different models, it has become an aid for understanding the system, designing the system, as well as a notation for representing design.

Though UML has now evolved into a fairly comprehensive and large modeling notation, we will focus on a few central concepts and notations relating to classes and their relationships and interactions. For a more detailed discussion on UML, the reader is referred to [35].

Class Diagram   The class diagram of UML is the central piece in a design or model. As the name suggests, these diagrams describe the classes that are there in the design. As the final code of an OO implementation is mostly classes, these diagrams have a very close relationship with the final code. There are many tools that translate the class diagrams to code skeletons, thereby avoiding errors that might get introduced if the class diagrams are manually translated to class definitions by programmers. A class diagram defines

1. *Classes that exist in the system*—besides the class name, the diagrams are capable of describing the key fields as well as the important methods of the classes.

2. *Associations between classes*—what types of associations exist between different classes.

3. *Subtype, supertype relationship*—classes may also form subtypes giving type hierarchies using polymorphism. The class diagrams can represent these hierarchies also.

A class itself is represented as a rectangular box which is divided into three areas. The top part gives the class name. By convention the class name is a word with the first letter in uppercase. (In general, if the class name is a combination of many words, then the first letter of each word is in uppercase.) The middle part lists the key attributes or fields of the class. These attributes are the state holders for the objects of the class. By convention, the name of the attributes starts in lowercase, and if multiple words are joined, then each new word starts in uppercase. The bottom part lists the methods or operations of the class. These represent the behavior that the class can provide. Naming convention is same as for attributes but to show that it is a function, the names end with "( )". (The parameters of the methods can also be specified, if desired.)

If a class is an interface (having specifications but no body,) this can be specified by marking the class with the stereotype "$<< interface >>$", which is generally written above the class name. Similarly, if a class/method/attribute has some properties that we want to specify, it can be done by tagging the entity by specifying the property next to the entity name within "{" and "}" or by using some special symbol. Examples of a class with some tagged values, and an interface, are shown in Figure 6.12.

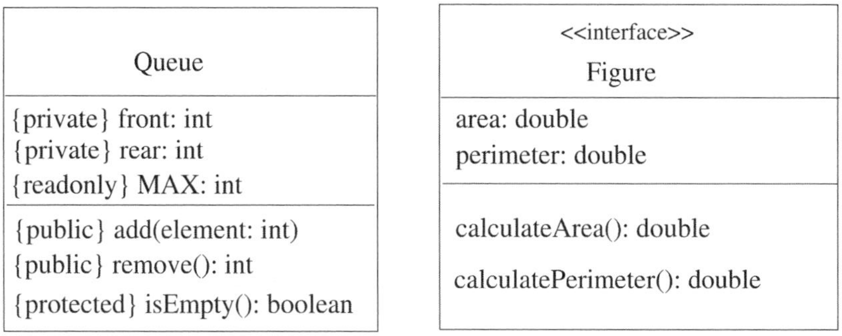

Queue
{private} front: int {private} rear: int {readonly} MAX: int
{public} add(element: int) {public} remove(): int {protected} isEmpty(): boolean

<<interface>> Figure
area: double perimeter: double
calculateArea(): double calculatePerimeter(): double

Figure 6.12: Class, stereotypes, and tagged values.

The divided-box notation is to describe the key features of a class as a stand-alone entity. However, classes have relationships between them, and objects of different classes interact. Therefore, to model a system or an application, we must represent relationship between classes. One common relationship is the generalization-specialization relationship between classes, which finally gets reflected as the inheritance hierarchy. In this hierarchy, properties of general significance are assigned to a more general class—the superclass—while properties which can specialize an object further are put in the subclass. All properties of the superclass are inherited by the subclass, so a subclass contains its own properties as well as those of the superclass.

The generalization-specialization relationship is specified by having arrows coming from the subclass to the superclass, with the empty triangle-shaped arrowhead touching the superclass. Often, when there are multiple subclasses of a class, this may be specified by having one arrowhead on the superclass, and then drawing lines from this to the different subclasses. In this hierarchy, often specialization is done on the basis of some *discriminator*—a distinguishing property that is used to specialize superclass into different subclasses. In other words, by using the discriminator, objects of the superclass type are partitioned into sets of objects of different subclass types. The discriminator used for the generalization-specialization relationship can be specified by labeling the arrow. An example of how this relationship is modeled in UML is shown in Figure 6.13.

In this example, the `IITKPerson` class represents all people belonging to the IITK. These are broadly divided into two subclasses—**Student** and **Employee**, as both these types have many different properties (some common ones also) and different behavior. Similarly, students have two different

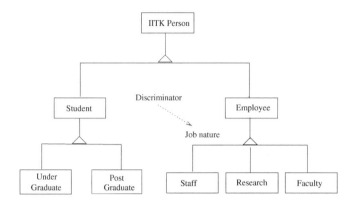

Figure 6.13: A class hierarchy.

subclasses, `UnderGraduate` and `PostGraduate`, both requiring some different attributes and having different constraints. The `Employee` class has subtypes representing the faculty, staff, and research staff. (This hierarchy is from an actual working system developed for the Institute.)

Besides the generalization-specialization relationship, another common relationship is association, which allows objects to communicate with each other. An association between two classes means that an object of one class needs some services from objects of the other class to perform its own service. The relationship is that of peers in that objects of both the classes can use services of the other. The association is shown by a line between the two classes. An association may have a name which can be specified by labeling the association line. (The association can also be assigned some attributes of its own.) And if the roles of the two ends of the association need to be named, that can also be done. In an association, an end may also have multiplicity allowing relationships like 1 to 1, 1 to many, etc., to be modeled. Where there is a fixed multiplicity, it is represented by putting a number at that end; a zero or many multiplicity is represented by a "*".

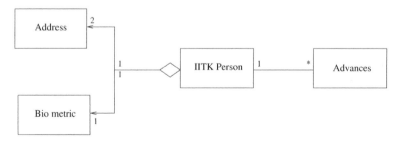

Figure 6.14: Aggregation and association among classes.

Another type of relationship is the part-whole relationship which represents the situation when an object is composed of many parts, each part itself being an object. This situation represents containment or aggregation, i.e., object of a class is contained inside the object of another class. (Containment and aggregation can be treated separately and shown differently, but we will consider them as the same.) For representing this aggregation relationship, the class which represents the "whole" is shown at the top and a line emanating from a little diamond connecting it to classes which represent the parts. Often in an implementation this relationship is implemented in the same manner as an association, hence, this relationship is also sometimes modeled as an association.

The association and aggregation are shown in Figure 6.14, expanding the example given above. An object of IITKPerson type contains two objects of type Address, representing the permanent address and the current address. It also contains an object of type BiometricInfo, which keeps information like the person's picture and signature. As these objects are common to all people, they belong in the parent class rather than a subclass. An IITKPerson is allowed to take some advances from the Institute to meet expenses for travel, medical, etc. Hence, Advances is a different class (which, incidently, has a hierarchy of its own) to which IITKPerson class has a 1-to-m association. (These relations are also from the system.)

Class diagrams focus on classes, and should not be confused with *object diagram*. Objects are specific instances of classes. Sometimes, it is desirable to model specific objects and the relationship between them, and for that object diagrams are used. An object is represented like a class, except that its name also specifies the name of the class to which it belongs. Generally, the object name starts in lowercase, and the class name is specified after a colon. To further clarify, the entire name is underlined. An example is myList: List. The attributes of an object may have specific values. These values can be specified by giving them along with the attribute name (e.g., name = "John").

Sequence and Collaboration Diagrams   Class diagrams represent the static structure of the system. That is, they capture the structure of the code that may implement it, and how the different classes in the code are related. Class diagrams, however, do not represent the dynamic behavior of the system. That is, how the system behaves when it performs some of its functions cannot be represented by class diagrams. This is done through *sequence diagrams* or *collaboration diagrams*, together called *interaction diagrams*. An interaction diagram typically captures the behavior of a use case and models how the different objects in the system collaborate to implement the use case. Let us first discuss sequence diagrams, which is perhaps more common of the two interaction diagrams.

A sequence diagram shows the series of messages exchanged between some objects, and their temporal ordering, when objects collaborate to provide some desired system functionality (or implement a use case). The sequence diagram is generally drawn to model the interaction between objects for a particular use case. Note that in a sequence diagram (and also in collaboration diagrams), it is objects that participate and not classes. When capturing dynamic behavior, the role of classes are limited as during execution it is objects that exist.

In a sequence diagram, all the objects that participate in the interaction are shown at the top as boxes with object names. For each object, a vertical bar representing its lifeline is drawn downwards. A message from one object to another is represented as an arrow from the lifeline of one to the lifeline of the other. Each message is labeled with the message name, which typically should be the name of a method in the class of the target object. An object can also make a self call, which is shown as a message starting and ending in the same object's lifeline. To clarify the sequence of messages and relative timing of each, time is represented as increasing as one moves farther away downwards from the object name in the object life. That is, time is represented by the y-axis, increasing downwards.

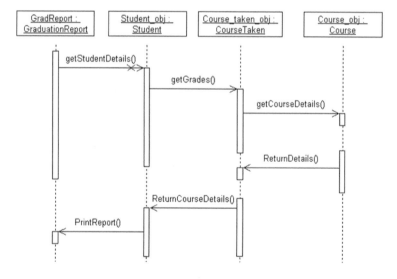

Figure 6.15: Sequence diagram for printing a graduation report.

Using the lifeline of objects and arrows, one can model objects' lives and how messages flow from one object to another. However, frequently a message is sent from one object to another only under some condition. This condition can be represented in the sequence diagram by specifying it within brackets

before the message name. If a message is sent to multiple receiver objects, then
this multiplicity is shown by having a "*" before the message name.

Each message has a return, which is when the operation finishes and returns
the value (if any) to the invoking object. Though often this message can be
implied, sometimes it may be desirable to show the return message explicitly.
This is done by using a dashed arrow. An example sequence diagram is shown in
Figure 6.15. This example concerns printing the graduation report for students.
The object for `GradReport` (which has the responsibility for printing the report)
sends a message to the `Student` objects for the relevant information, which
request the `CourseTaken` objects for the courses the student has taken. These
objects get information about the courses from the `Course` objects.

A collaboration diagram also shows how objects communicate. Instead of
using a timeline-based representation that is used by sequence diagrams, a collaboration diagram looks more like a state diagram. Each object is represented
in the diagram, and the messages sent from one object to another are shown
as *numbered* arrows from one object to the other. In other words, the chrono-
logical ordering of messages is captured by message numbering, in contrast to
a sequence diagram where ordering of messages is shown pictorially. As should
be clear, the two types of interaction diagrams are semantically equivalent and
have the same representation power. The collaboration diagram for the above
example is shown in Figure 6.16. Over the years, however, sequence diagrams
have become more popular, as people find the visual representation of sequenc-
ing quicker to grasp.

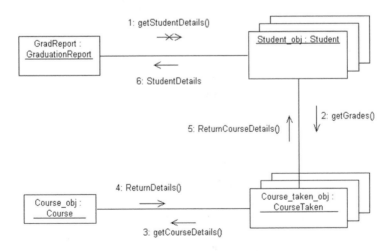

Figure 6.16: Collaboration diagram for printing a graduation report.

As we can see, an interaction diagram models the internal dynamic behavior of the system, when the system performs some function. The internal dynamics of the system is represented in terms of how the objects interact with each other. Through an interaction diagram, one can clearly see how a system internally implements an operation, and what messages are sent between different objects. If a convincing interaction diagram cannot be constructed for a system operation with the classes that have been identified in the class diagram, then it is safe to say that the system structure is not capable of supporting this operation and that it must be enhanced. So, it can be used to validate if the system structure being designed through class diagrams is capable of providing the desired services.

As a system has many functions, each involving different objects in different ways, there will be a dynamic model for each of these functions or use cases. In other words, whereas one class diagram can capture the structure of the system's code, for the dynamic behavior many diagrams are needed. However, it may not be feasible or practical to draw the interaction diagram for each use case scenario. Typically, during design, an interaction diagram of some key use cases or functions will be drawn to make sure that the classes that exist can indeed support the desired use cases, and to understand their dynamics.

Other Diagrams and Capabilities   UML is an extensible and quite elaborate modeling notation. Above we have discussed notation related to two of the most common models developed while modeling a system—class diagrams and interaction diagrams. These two together help model the static structure of the system as well as the dynamic behavior. There are, however, many other aspects that might need to be modeled for which extra notation is required. UML provides notation for many different types of models.

In modeling and building systems, as we have seen, components may also be used. Components encapsulate "larger" elements, and are semantically simpler than classes. Components often encapsulate subsystems and provide clearly defined interfaces through which these components can be used by other components in the system. While designing an architecture, as we have seen, components are very useful. UML provides a notation for specifying a component, and a separate notation for specifying a subsystem. In a large system, many classes may be combined together to form packages, where a package is a collection of many elements, possibly of different types. UML also provides a notation to specify packages. These are shown in Figure 6.17.

As discussed in Chapter 5, the deployment view of the system is distinct from the component or module view. In a deployment view, the focus is on what software element uses which hardware, that is, how the system is deployed. UML has notation for representing a deployment view. The main element is a

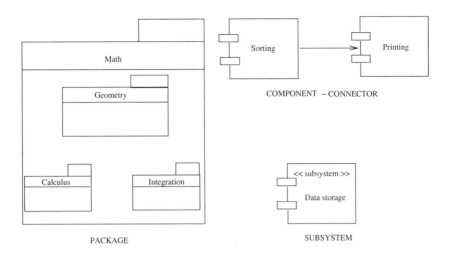

Figure 6.17: Subsystems, Components, and packages

node, represented as a named cube, which represents a computing resource like the CPU which physically exists. The name of the cube identifies the resource as well as its type. Within the cube for the node the software elements it deploys (which can be components, packages, classes, etc.) are shown using their respective notation. If different nodes communicate with each other, this is shown by connecting the nodes with lines.

The notation for packages, deployment view, etc., provides structural views of the system from different perspectives. UML also provides notation to express different types of behavior. A *state diagram* is a model in which the entity being modeled is viewed as a set of states, with transitions between the states taking place when some event occurs. A state is represented as a rectangle with rounded edges or as ellipses or circles; transitions are represented by arrows connecting two states. Details can also be attached to transitions. State diagrams are often used to model the behavior of objects of a class—the state represents the different states of the object and transition captures the performing of the different operations on that object. So, whereas interaction diagrams capture how objects collaborate, a state diagram models how an object itself evolves as operations are performed on it. This can help clearly understand and specify the behavior of a class.

Activity Diagram. This is another diagram for modeling dynamic behavior. It aims to model a system by modeling the activities that take place in it when the system executes for performing some function. Each activity is represented as an oval, with the name of the activity within it. From the activity, the system proceeds to other activities. Often, which activity to perform next depends on some decision. This decision is shown as a diamond leading to multiple activities (which are the options for this decision). Repeated execution of some activities can also be shown. These diagrams are like flow-charts, but also have notation to specify parallel execution of activities in a system by specifying an activity splitting into multiple activities or many activities joining (synchronizing) after their completion.

UML is an extensible notation allowing a modeler the flexibility to represent newer concepts as well. There are many situations in which a modeler needs some notation which is similar to an existing one but is not exactly the same. For example, in some cases, one may want to specify if a class is an abstract class or an interface. Instead of having special notation for these concepts, UML has the concept of a stereotype, through which existing notation can be used to model different concepts. An existing notation, for example of a class, can be used to represent some other similar concept by specifying it as a stereotype by giving the name of the new concept within $<<$ and $>>$. We have already seen an example earlier. A metaclass can be specified in a similar manner; and so can a utility class (one which has some utility functions which are directly used and whose objects are not created).

Tagged values can be used to specify additional properties of the elements to which they are attached. They can be attached to any name, and are specified within "{ }". Though tagged values can be anything a modeler wants, it is best to limit its use to a few clearly defined (and pre-agreed) properties like *private, abstract, query, readonly*, etc. Notes can also be attached to the different elements in a model. We have earlier seen the use of some tagged values in Figure 6.12.

Use case diagrams are also a part of the UML. We discussed use cases in an earlier chapter. In a use case diagram, each use case is shown as a node, and the relationship between actors and use cases is shown by arcs. They are mostly used to provide a high-level summary of use cases.

6.3.3 A Design Methodology

Many design and analysis methodologies have been proposed. As we stated earlier, a methodology basically uses the concepts (of OO in this case) to provide guidelines for the design activity. Though methodologies are useful, they do not reduce the activity of design to a sequence of steps that can be followed mechanically. We briefly discuss one methodology here. Even though it is one of the earlier methodologies, its basic concepts are still applicable [15].

We assume that during architecture design the system has been divided into high-level subsystems or components. The problem we address is how to produce an object-oriented design for a subsystem.

As we discussed earlier, the OO design consists of specification of all the classes and objects that will exist in the system implementation. A complete OO design should be such that in the implementation phase, only further details about methods or attributes need to be added. A few low-level objects may be added later, but most of the classes and objects and their relationships are identified during design. An approach for creating an OO design consists of the following sequence of steps:

- Identify classes and relationships between them.

- Develop the dynamic model and use it to define operations on classes.

- Develop the functional model and use it to define operations on classes.

- Identify internal classes and operations.

- Optimize and package.

Identifying Classes and Relationships Identifying the classes and their relationships requires identification of object types in the problem domain, the structures between classes (both inheritance and aggregation), attributes of the different classes, associations between the different classes, and the services each class needs to provide to support the system. Basically, in this step we are trying to define the initial class diagram of the design.

To identify analysis objects, start by looking at the problem and its description. In the descriptions consider the phrases that represent entities. Include an entity as an object if the system needs to remember something about it, the system needs some services from it to perform its own services, or it has multiple attributes. If the system does not need to keep information about some real-world entity or does not need any services from the entity, it need not be considered as an object for design. Carefully consider objects that have only one attribute; such objects can frequently be included as attributes in other objects. Though in the analysis we focus on identifying objects, in modeling, classes for these objects are represented.

Classes have attributes. Attributes add detail about the class and are the repositories of data for an object. For example, for an object of class Person, the attributes could be the name, sex, and address. The data stored in forms of values of attributes are hidden from outside the objects and are accessed and manipulated only by the service functions for that object. Which attributes should be used to define the class of an object depends on the problem and what needs to be done. For example, while modeling a hospital system, for the class Person attributes of height, weight, and date of birth may be needed, although these may not be needed for a database for a county that keeps track of populations in various neighborhoods.

To identify attributes, consider each class and see which attributes are needed by the problem domain. This is frequently a simple task. Then position each attribute properly using the structures; if the attribute is a common attribute, it should be placed in the superclass, while if it is specific to a specialized object, it should be placed with the subclass. While identifying attributes, new classes may also get defined or old classes may disappear (e.g., if you find that a class really is an attribute of another).

For a class diagram, we also need to identify the structures and associations between classes. To identify the classification structure, consider the classes that have been identified as a generalization and see if there are other classes that can be considered as specializations of this. The specializations should be meaningful for the problem domain. For example, if the problem domain does not care about the material used to make some objects, there is no point in specializing the classes based on the material they are made of. Similarly, consider classes as specializations and see if there are other classes that have similar attributes. If so, see if a generalized class can be identified of which these are specializations. Once again, the structure obtained must naturally reflect the hierarchy in the problem domain; it should not be "extracted" simply because some classes have some attributes with the same names.

To identify assembly structure, a similar approach is taken. Consider each object of a class as an assembly and identify its parts. See if the system needs to keep track of the parts. If it does, then the parts must be reflected as objects; if not, then the parts should not be modeled as separate objects. Then, consider an object of a class as a part and see to which class's object it can be considered as belonging. Once again, this separation is maintained only if the system needs it. As before, the structures identified should naturally reflect the hierarchy in the problem domain and should not be "forced."

For associations we need to identify the relationship between instances of various classes. For example, an instance of the class Company may be related to an instance of the class Person by an "employs" relationship. This is similar to what is done in ER modeling. And like in ER modeling, an instance connection may be of 1:1 type representing that one instance of this type is related to exactly one instance of another class. Or it could be 1:M, indicating that one instance of this class may be related to many instances of the other class. There are M:M connections, and there are sometimes multiway connections, but these are not very common. The associations between objects are derived from the problem domain directly once the objects have been identified. An association may have attributes of its own; these are typically attributes that do not naturally belong to either object. Although in many situations they can be "forced" to belong to one of the two objects without losing any information, it should not be done unless the attribute naturally belongs to the object.

Dynamic Modeling   The class diagram obtained gives the initial module-level design. This design will be further shaped by the events in the system, as the design has to ensure that the expected behavior for the events can be supported. Modeling the dynamic behavior of the system will help in further refining the design.

The dynamic model of a system aims to specify how the state of various objects changes when events occur. An event is something that happens at some time instance. For an object, an event is essentially a request for an operation. An event typically is an occurrence of something and has no time duration associated with it. Each event has an initiator and a responder. Events can be internal to the system, in which case the event initiator and the event responder are both within the system. An event can be an external event, in which case the event initiator is outside the system (e.g., the user or a sensor).

A scenario is a sequence of events that occur in a particular execution of the system, as we have seen while discussing use cases in Chapter 3. From the scenarios, the different events being performed on different objects can be identified, which are then used to identify services on objects. The different scenarios together can completely characterize the behavior of the system. If the design is such that it can support all the scenarios, we can be sure that the desired dynamic behavior of the system can be supported by the design. This is the basic reason for performing dynamic modeling. With use cases, dynamic modeling involves preparing interaction diagrams for the important scenarios.

It is best to start by modeling scenarios being triggered by external events. The scenarios should not necessarily cover all possibilities, but the major ones should be considered. First the main success scenarios should be modeled, then scenarios for "exceptional" cases should be modeled. For example, in a restaurant, the main success scenario for placing an order could be the following sequence of actions: customer reads the menu; customer places the order; order is sent to the kitchen for preparation; ordered items are served; customer requests a bill for the order; bill is prepared for this order; customer is given the bill; customer pays the bill. An "exception" scenario could be if the ordered item was not available or if the customer cancels his order.

From each scenario, events have to be identified. Events are interactions with the outside world and object-to-object interactions. All the events that have the same effect on the flow of control in the system are grouped as a single event type. Each event type is then allocated to the object classes that initiate it and that service the event. With this done, a scenario can be represented as a sequence (or collaboration) diagram showing the events that will take place on the different objects in the execution corresponding to the scenario. A possible sequence diagram of the main success scenario of the restaurant is given in Figure 6.18.

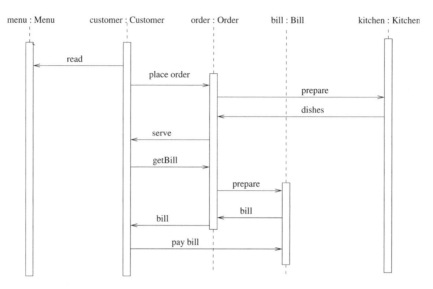

Figure 6.18: A sequence diagram for the restaurant.

Once the main scenarios are modeled, various events on objects that are needed to support executions corresponding to the various scenarios are known. This information is then used to expand our view of the classes in the design. Generally speaking, for each event in the sequence diagrams, there will be an operation on the object on which the event is invoked. So, by using the scenarios and sequence diagrams we can further refine our view of the objects and add operations that are needed to support some scenarios but may not have been identified during initial modeling. For example, from the event trace diagram in Figure 6.18, we can see that "place order" and "getBill" will be two operations required on the object of type `Order` if this interaction is to be supported.

The effect of these different events on a class itself can be modeled using the state diagrams. We believe that the state transition diagram is of limited use during system design but may be more useful during detailed design. Hence, we will discuss state modeling of classes later.

Functional Modeling   A functional model of a system specifies how the output values are computed in the system from the input values, without considering the control aspects of the computation. This represents the functional view of the system—the mapping from inputs to outputs and the various steps involved in the mapping. Generally, when the transformation from the inputs to outputs is complex, consisting of many steps, the functional modeling is likely to be useful. In systems where the transformation of inputs to outputs is not complex, functional model is likely to be straightforward.

As we have seen, the functional model of a system can be represented by a data flow diagram (DFD). We have used DFDs in problem modeling, and the structured design methodology, discussed earlier. Just as with dynamic modeling, the basic purpose of doing functional modeling is to use the model to make sure that the object model can perform the transformations required from the system. As processes represent operations and in an object-oriented system, most of the processing is done by operations on classes, all processes should show up as operations on classes. Some operations might appear as single operations on an object; others might appear as multiple operations on different classes, depending on the level of abstraction of the DFD. If the DFD is sufficiently detailed, most processes will occur as operations on classes. The DFD also specifies the abstract signature of the operations by identifying the inputs and outputs.

Defining Internal Classes and Operations   The classes identified so far are the ones that come from the problem domain. The methods identified on the objects are the ones needed to satisfy all the interactions with the environment and the user and to support the desired functionality. However, the final design is a blueprint for implementation. Hence, implementation issues have to be considered. While considering implementation issues, algorithm and optimization issues arise. These issues are handled in this step.

First, each class is critically evaluated to see if it is needed in its present form in the final implementation. Some of the classes might be discarded if the designer feels they are not needed during implementation.

Then the implementation of operations on the classes is considered. For this, rough algorithms for implementation might be considered. While doing this, a complex operation may get defined in terms of lower-level operations on simpler classes. In other words, effective implementation of operations may require heavy interaction with some data structures and the data structure to be considered an object in its own right. These classes that are identified while considering implementation concerns are largely support classes that may be needed to store intermediate results or to model some aspects of the object whose operation is to be implemented.

Once the implementation of each class and each operation on the class has been considered and it has been satisfied that they can be implemented, the system design is complete. The detailed design might also uncover some very low-level objects, but most such objects should be identified during system design.

Optimize and Package   During design, some inefficiencies may have crept in. In this final step, the issue of efficiency is considered, keeping in mind that the final structures should not deviate too much from the logical structure produced. Various optimizations are possible and a designer can exercise his judgment keeping in mind the modularity aspects also.

6.3.4 Examples

Before we apply the methodology on some examples, it should be remembered again that no design methodology reduces the activity of producing a design to a series of steps that can be mechanically executed; each step requires some amount of engineering judgment. Methodologies are essentially guidelines to help the designer in the design activity; they are not hard-and-fast rules. The examples we present here are relatively small, and all aspects of the methodology do not get reflected in them.

The Word Counting Problem   Let us first consider the word counting problem discussed earlier as an example for Structured Design methodology. The initial analysis clearly shows that there is a `File` object, which is an aggregation of many `Word` objects. Further, one can consider that there is a `Counter` object, which keeps track of the number of different words. It is a matter of preference and opinion whether `Counter` should be an object, or counting should be implemented as an operation. If counting is treated as an operation, the question will be to which object it belongs. As it does not belong "naturally" to either the class `Word` or the class `File`, it will have to be "forced" into one of the classes. For this reason, we have kept `Counter` as a separate object. The basic problem statement finds only these three objects. However, further analysis for services reveals that some history mechanism is needed to check if the word is unique. The class diagram obtained after doing the initial modeling is shown in Figure 6.19.

Now let us consider the dynamic modeling for this problem. This is essentially a batch processing problem, where a file is given as input and some output is given by the system. Hence, the use case and scenario for this problem are straightforward. For example, the scenario for the "normal" case can be:

- System prompts for the file name; user enters the file name.

- System checks for existence of the file.

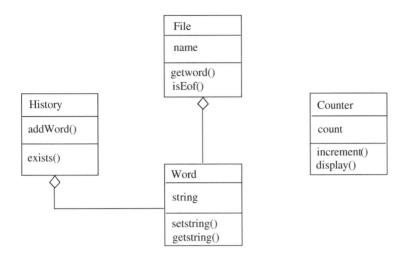

Figure 6.19: Class diagram for the word counting problem.

– System reads the words from the file.

– System prints the count.

From this simple scenario, no new operations are uncovered, and our class diagram stays unchanged. Now we consider the functional model. One possible functional model is shown in Figure 6.20. The model reinforces the need for some object where the history of what words have been seen is recorded. This object is used to check the uniqueness of the words. It also shows that various operations like increment(), isunique(), and addToHistory() are needed. These operations should appear as operations in classes or should be supported by a combination of operations. In this example, most of these processes are reflected as operations on classes and are already incorporated in the design.

Now we are at the last two steps of design methodology, where implementation and optimization concerns are used to enhance the object model. First decision we take is that the history mechanism will be implemented by a binary search tree. Hence, instead of the class History, we have a different class Btree. Then, for the class Word, various operations are needed to compare different words. Operations are also needed to set the string value for a word and retrieve it. The final class diagram is similar in structure to the one shown in Figure 6.19, except for these changes.

The final step of the design activity is to specify this design. This is not a part of the design methodology, but it is an essential step, as the design specification is what forms the major part of the design document. The design specification, as mentioned earlier, should specify all the classes that are in the design, all methods of the classes along with their interfaces. We use C++ class

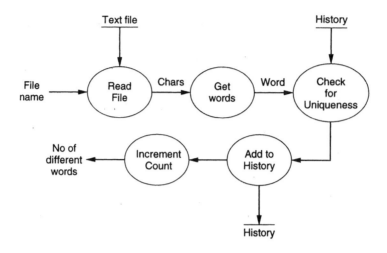

Figure 6.20: Functional model for the word counting problem.

structures for our specification. The final specification of this design is given below. This specification can be used as a basis of implementing the design.

```
class Word  {
    private :
        char *string; // string representing the word
    public:
        bool operator == ( Word ); // Checks for equality
        bool operator < ( Word );
        bool operator > ( Word );
        Word operator = ( Word ); // The assignment operator
        void setWord ( char * ); // Sets the string for the word
        char *getWord ( ); // gets the string for the word
};

class File {
    private:
        FILE inFile;
        char *fileName;
    public:
        Word getWord ( ); // get a word; Invokes operations of Word
        bool isEof ( ); // Checks for end of file
        void fileOpen ( char * );
};
```

```
class Counter {
    private:
        int counter;
    public:
        void increment ( );
        void display ( );
};

class Btree: GENERIC in <ELEMENT_TYPE>  {
    private:
        ELEMENT_TYPE element;
        Btree < ELEMENT_TYPE > *left;
        Btree < ELEMENT_TYPE > *right;
    public:
        void insert( ELEMENT_TYPE ); // to insert an element
        bool lookup( ELEMENT_TYPE ); // to check if an element exists
};
```

As we can see, all the class definitions complete with data members and operations and all the major declarations are given in the design specification. Only the implementation of the methods is not provided. This design was later implemented in C++. The conversion to code required only minor additions and modifications to the design. The final code was about 240 lines of C++ code (counting noncomment and nonblank lines only).

Rate of Returns Problem   Let us consider a slightly larger problem: of determining the rate of returns on investments. An investor has made investments in some companies. For each investment, in a file, the name of the company, all the money he has invested (in the initial purchase as well as in subsequent purchases), and all the money he has withdrawn (through sale of shares or dividends) are given, along with the dates of each transaction. The current value of the investment is given at the end, along with the date. The goal is to find the rate of return the investor is getting for each investment, as well as the rate of return for the entire portfolio. In addition, the amounts he has invested initially, amounts he has invested subsequently, amounts he has withdrawn, and the current value of the portfolio also is to be output.

This is a practical problem that is frequently needed by investors, and a rate of returns calculator can easily form an important component of a larger financial management system. The computation of rate of return is not straightforward and cannot be easily done through spreadsheets. Hence, such a software can be of practical use.

Initial problem analysis easily throws up a few object classes of interest— Portfolio, Investment, and Transaction. A portfolio consists of many investments, and an investment consists of many transactions. Hence, the class

Portfolio is an aggregation of many Investments, and an Investment is an aggregation of many Transactions. A transaction can be of Withdrawal type or Deposit type, resulting in a class hierarchy, with Investment being the superclass and Withdrawal and Deposit subclasses.

For an object of class Investment, the major operation we need to perform is to find the rate of return. For the class Portfolio we need to have operations to compute rate of return, total initial investment, total withdrawal, and total current value of the portfolio. Hence, we need operations for these. The class diagram obtained from analysis of the problem is shown in Figure 6.21.

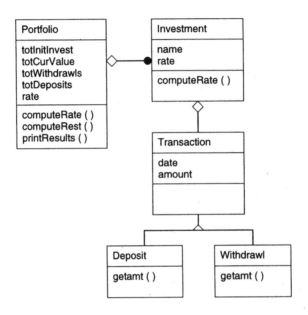

Figure 6.21: Class diagram for rate of return problem.

In this problem, as the interaction with the environment is not much, the dynamic model is not significant. Hence, we omit the dynamic modeling for this problem. A possible functional model is given in Figure 6.22. The classes are then enhanced to make sure that each of the processes of the functional model is reflected as operations on various objects. As we can see, most of the processes already exist as operations.

Now we have to perform the last two steps of the design methodology, where implementation and optimization concerns are used to enhance the classes. While considering the implementation of computation of total initial investment, computation of overall return rate, overall withdrawals, and so on, we notice that for all of these, appropriate data from each investment is needed.

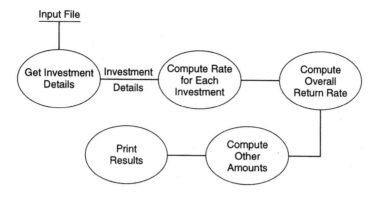

Figure 6.22: Functional model for the rate of return problem.

Hence, to the class `Investments`, appropriate operations need to be added. Further, we note that all the computations for total initial investment, total current value, and so on are all done together, and each of these is essentially adding values from various investments. Hence, we combine them in a single operation in `Portfolio` and a corresponding single operation in `Investment`. Studying the class hierarchy, we observe that the only difference in the two sub-classes `Withdrawal` and `Deposit` is that in one case the amount is subtracted and in the other it is added. In such a situation, the two types can be easily considered a single type by keeping the amount as negative for a withdrawal and positive for a deposit. So we remove the subclasses, thereby simplifying the design and implementation. Instead of giving the class diagram for the final design, we provide the specification of the classes:

```
class Transaction {
    private:
        int amount; // money amount for the transaction
        int month; // month of the transaction
        int year; // year of the transaction
    public:
        getAmount();
        getMonth();
        getYear();
        Transaction(amount, month, year); // sets values
};


class Investment {
```

```
    private:
        char *investmentName; // Name of the company
        Transaction *transactArray; // List of transactions
        int noOfTransacts; // Total number of transactions
        float rateOfReturn; // rate of return
    public:
        getTransactDetails();  // Set details of transactions
        computeRate();
        float getRate(); // Return the rate of the returns
        compute(initVal, totWithdrawls, totCurVal, totDeposits);
                // Returns these values for this investment
};

class Portfolio {
    private:
        Investment *investArray; // List of investments
        int noOfInvestments; // Total number of investments
        int totalInitInvest;
        int totalDeposits;
        int totalCurVal;
        int totalWithdrawl;
        float RateOfReturns; // Overall rate of returns
    public:
        getInvestDetails( char * fname ); // Parse the input file
        computeRate(); // Compute rates of return
        compute(); // Compute other totals
        printResults(); // Print return rates, total values, etc.
};
```

The design is self-explanatory. This design was later implemented in C++ code, and we found that only minor implementation details got added during the implementation, showing the correctness and completeness of the design. The final size of the program was about 470 lines of C++ code (counting noncomment and nonblank lines only).

6.4 Detailed Design

In the previous two sections we discussed two different approaches for system design—one based on functional abstraction and one based on objects. In system design we concentrate on the modules in a system and how they interact with each other. Once the modules are identified and specified during the high-level design, the internal logic that will implement the given specifications can be designed, and is the focus of this section.

The detailed design activity is often not performed formally and archived as it is almost impossible to keep the detailed design document consistent with the code. Due to this, developing the detailed design is useful for the more complex and important modules, and is often done informally by the programmer as part of the personal process of developing code.

6.4.1 Logic/Algorithm Design

The basic goal in detailed design is to specify the logic for the different modules that have been specified during system design. Specifying the logic will require developing an algorithm that will implement the given specifications. Here we consider some principles for designing algorithms or logic that will implement the given specifications.

The term *algorithm* is quite general and is applicable to a wide variety of areas. For software we can consider an algorithm to be an unambiguous procedure for solving a problem [42]. A *procedure* is a finite sequence of well-defined steps or operations, each of which requires a finite amount of memory and time to complete. In this definition we assume that termination is an essential property of procedures. From now on we will use procedures, algorithms, and logic interchangeably.

There are a number of steps that one has to perform while developing an algorithm [42]. The starting step in the design of algorithms is *statement of the problem*. The problem for which an algorithm is being devised has to be precisely and clearly stated and properly understood by the person responsible for designing the algorithm. For detailed design, the problem statement comes from the system design. That is, the problem statement is already available when the detailed design of a module commences. The next step is development of a mathematical *model* for the problem. In modeling, one has to select the mathematical structures that are best suited for the problem. It can help to look at other similar problems that have been solved. In most cases, models are constructed by taking models of similar problems and modifying the model to suit the current problem. The next step is the *design of the algorithm*. During this step the data structure and program structure are decided. Once the algorithm is designed, its correctness should be verified.

No clear procedure can be given for designing algorithms. Having such a procedure amounts to automating the problem of algorithm development, which is not possible with the current methods. However, some heuristics or methods can be provided to help the designer design algorithms for modules. The most common method for designing algorithms or the logic for a module is to use the *stepwise refinement technique* [84].

The stepwise refinement technique breaks the logic design problem into a series of steps, so that the development can be done gradually. The process starts by converting the specifications of the module into an abstract description of an algorithm containing a few abstract statements. In each step, one or several statements in the algorithm developed so far are decomposed into more detailed instructions. The successive refinement terminates when all instructions are sufficiently precise that they can easily be converted into programming language statements. During refinement, both data and instructions have to be refined. A guideline for refinement is that in each step the amount of decomposition should be such that it can be easily handled and that represents one or two design decisions. Generally, detailed design is not specified using formal programming languages, but using languages that have formal programming language like outer structures (like loops, conditionals, etc.), but a freer format for internal description. This allows the designer to focus on the logic and not its representation in the programming language.

6.4.2 State Modeling of Classes

For object-oriented design, the approach just discussed for obtaining the detailed design can be used for designing the logic of methods. But a class is not a functional abstraction and cannot be viewed as merely a collection of functions (methods).

The technique for getting a more detailed understanding of the class as a whole, without talking about the logic of different methods, has to be different from the refinement-based approach. An object of a class has some state and many operations on it. To better understand a class, the relationship between the state and various operations and the effect of interaction of various operations have to be understood. This can be viewed as one of the objectives of the detailed design activity for object-oriented development. Once the overall class is better understood, the algorithms for its various methods can be developed.

A method to understand the behavior of a class is to view it as a finite state automaton, which consists of states and transitions between states. When modeling an object, the state is the value of its attributes, and an event is the performing of an operation on the object. A *state diagram* relates events and states by showing how the state changes when an event is performed. A state diagram for an object will generally have an initial state, from which all states are reachable (i.e., there is a path from the initial state to all other states).

A state diagram for an object does not represent all the actual states of the object, as there are many possible states. A state diagram attempts to represent only the logical states of the object. A *logical state* of an object is a combination of all those states from which the behavior of the object is similar

for all possible events. Two logical states will have different behavior for at
least one event. For example, for an object that represents a stack, all states
that represent a stack of size more than 0 and less than some defined maximum
are similar as the behavior of all operations defined on the stack will be similar
in all such states (e.g., push will add an element, pop will remove one, etc.).
However, the state representing an empty stack is different as the behavior of
top and pop operations are different now (an error message may be returned).
Similarly, the state representing a full stack is different. The state model for
this bounded size stack is shown in Figure 6.23.

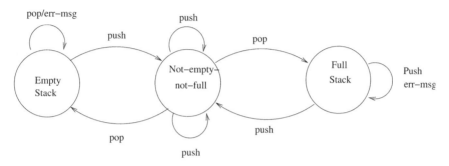

Figure 6.23: FSA model of a stack.

The finite state modeling of objects is an aid to understand the effect of
various operations defined on the class on the state of the object. A good understanding of this can aid in developing the logic for each of the operations. To
develop the logic of operations, regular approaches for algorithm development
can be used. The model can also be used to validate if the logic for an operation
is correct. As we will see later, a state model can be used for generating test
cases for validation.

6.5 Verification

The output of the design activity should be verified before proceeding with the
activities of the next phase. If the design is expressed in some formal notation
for which analysis tools are available, then through tools it can be checked
for internal consistency (e.g., those modules used by another are defined, the
interface of a module is consistent with the way others use it, data usage is
consistent with declaration, etc.) If the design is not specified in a formal,
executable language, it cannot be processed through tools, and other means
for verification have to be used. The most common approach for verification is

design review. We discuss this approach here.

The purpose of design reviews is to ensure that the design satisfies the requirements and is of good quality. If errors are made during the design process, they will ultimately reflect themselves in the code and the final system. As the cost of removing faults caused by errors that occur during design increases with the delay in detecting the errors, it is best if design errors are detected early, before they manifest themselves in the system. Detecting errors in design is the purpose of design reviews.

The system design review process is similar to the inspection process, in that a group of people get together to discuss the design with the aim of revealing design errors or undesirable properties. The review group must include a member of both the system design team and the detailed design team, the author of the requirements document, the author responsible for maintaining the design document, and an independent software quality engineer. As with any review, it should be kept in mind that the aim of the meeting is to uncover design errors, not to try to fix them; fixing is done later.

The number of ways in which errors can enter a design is limited only by the creativity of the designer. The most important design error, however, is that the design does not fully support some requirements. For example, some exception case scenario cannot be handled, or some design constraint has not been satisfied. For design quality, modularity is the main criterion. However, since there is a need to validate whether performance requirements can be met by a design, efficiency is another key property for which a design is evaluated.

6.6 Metrics

Here we discuss some of the metrics that can be extracted from a design and that could be useful for evaluating the design. We do not discuss the standard metrics of effort or defect that are collected (as per the project plan) for project monitoring.

Size is always a product metric of interest. For size of a design, the *total number of modules* is a commonly used metric. (By using an average size of a module, from this metric the final size in LOC can be estimated and compared with project estimates.)

Another metric of interest is complexity. A possible use of complexity metrics at design time is to improve the design by reducing the complexity of the modules that have been found to be most complex. This will directly improve the testability and maintainability. We describe some of the metrics that have been proposed to quantify the complexity of design. We first discuss metrics for function-oriented design and then for OO design.

6.6.1 Complexity Metrics for Function-Oriented Design

Network Metrics   Network metrics is a complexity metric that tries to capture how "good" the structure chart is. As coupling of a module increases if it is called by more modules, a good structure is considered one that has exactly one caller. That is, the call graph structure is simplest if it is a pure tree. The more the structure chart deviates from a tree, the more complex the system. Deviation of the tree is then defined as the *graph impurity* of the design [87]. Graph impurity can be defined as

$$Graph\ impurity = n - e - 1$$

where n is the number of nodes in the structure chart and e is the number of edges. As in a pure tree the total number of nodes is one more than the number of edges, the graph impurity for a tree is 0. Each time a module has a fan-in of more than one, the graph impurity increases. The major drawback of this approach is that it ignores the common use of some routines like library or support routines. An approach to handle this is not to consider the lowest-level nodes for graph impurity because most often the lowest-level modules are the ones that are used by many different modules, particularly if the structure chart was factored. Library routines are also at the lowest level of the structure chart (even if they have a structure of their own, it does not show in the structure chart of the application using the routine).

Other network metrics have also been defined. For most of these metrics, significant correlations with properties of interest have not been established. Hence, their use is limited to getting some idea about the structure of the design.

Information Flow Metrics   The network metrics of graph impurity had the basis that as the graph impurity increases, the coupling increases. However, it is not a very good approximation for coupling, as coupling of a module increases with the complexity of the interface and the total number of modules a module is coupled with, whether it is the caller or the callee. So, if we want a metric that is better at quantifying coupling between modules, it should handle these. The information flow metrics attempt to define the complexity in terms of the total information flowing through a module.

In one of the earliest works on information flow metrics [48, 49], the complexity of a module is considered as depending on the intramodule complexity and the intermodule complexity. The intramodule complexity is approximated by the size of the module in lines of code. The intermodule complexity of a module depends on the total information flowing in the module (*inflow*) and the total information flowing out of the module (*outflow*). The inflow of a module is the total number of abstract data elements flowing in the module (i.e., whose values are used by the module), and the outflow is the total number of abstract data elements that are flowing out of the module (i.e., whose values are defined by this module and used by other modules). The module design complexity, D_c, is defined as

$$D_c = size * (inflow * outflow)^2.$$

The term ($inflow*outflow$) refers to the total number of combinations of input source and output destination. This term is squared, as the interconnection between the modules is considered a more important factor (compared to the internal complexity) determining the complexity of a module. This is based on the common experience that the modules with more interconnections are harder to test or modify compared to other similar-size modules with fewer interconnections.

The metric defined earlier defines the complexity of a module purely in terms of the total amount of data flowing in and out of the module and the module size. A variant of this was proposed based on the hypothesis that the module complexity depends not only on the information flowing in and out, but also on the number of modules to or from which it is flowing. The module size is considered an insignificant factor, and complexity D_c for a module is defined as [89]

$$D_c = fan\_in * fan\_out + inflow * outflow$$

where fan_in represents the number of modules that call this module and fan_out is the number of modules this module calls.

How can this metric be used in design? One method for highlighting the modules was suggested in [89]. Let *avg_complexity* be the average complexity of the modules in the design being evaluated, and let *std_deviation* be the standard deviation in the design complexity of the modules of the system. The proposed method classifies the modules in three categories: error-prone, complex, and normal. If D_c is the complexity of a module, it can be classified as follows:

Error-prone	If $D_c > avg\_complexity + std\_deviation$
Complex	If $avg\_complexity < D_c < avg\_complexity$
	$\qquad\qquad + std\_deviation$
Normal	Otherwise

Note that this definition of error-prone and complex is independent of the metric definition used to compute the complexity of modules. With this approach, a design can be evaluated by itself, not for overall design quality, but to draw attention to the error-prone and complex modules. This information can then be used to redesign the system to reduce the complexity of these modules (which also results in overall complexity reduction). This approach has been found to be very effective in identifying error-prone modules [89].

6.6.2 Complexity Metrics for OO Design

A few attempts have been made to propose metrics for object-oriented software [1, 21, 64]. Here we present some metrics that have been proposed for evaluating the complexity of an OOD. As design of classes is the central issue in OOD and the major output of any OOD methodology is the class definition, these metrics focus on evaluating classes. The metrics discussed here were proposed in [21]. We discuss some of these metrics that were experimentally found to be most useful in predicting fault-proneness [3].

Weighted Methods per Class (WMC)   The effort in developing a class will in some sense will be determined by the number of methods the class has and the complexity of the methods. Hence, a complexity metric that combines the number of methods and the complexity of methods can be useful in estimating the overall complexity of the class. The weighted methods per class (WMC) metric does precisely this.

Suppose a class C has methods $M_1, M_2, ..., M_n$ defined on it. Let the complexity of the method M_i be c_i. As a method is like a regular function or procedure, any complexity metric that is applicable for functions can be used to define c_i (e.g., estimated size, interface complexity, and data flow complexity). The WMC is defined as

$$WMC = \sum_{i=1}^{i=n} c_i.$$

If the complexity of each method is considered to be 1, WMC gives the total number of methods in the class.

Depth of Inheritance Tree (DIT)   Inheritance is, as we have mentioned, one of the unique features of the object-oriented paradigm. As we have said before, inheritance is one of the main mechanisms for reuse in OOD—the deeper a particular class is in a class hierarchy, the more methods it has available for reuse, thereby providing a larger reuse potential. At the same time, as we have mentioned, inheritance increases coupling, which makes changing a class harder. In other words, a class deep in the hierarchy has a lot of methods it can inherit, which makes it difficult to predict its behavior. For both these reasons, it is useful to have some metric to quantify inheritance. The depth of inheritance tree (DIT) is one such metric. The DIT of a class C in an inheritance hierarchy is the depth from the root class in the inheritance tree. In other words, it is the length of the shortest path from the root of the tree to the node representing C or the number of ancestors C has. In case of multiple inheritance, the DIT metric is the maximum length from a root to C.

Coupling between Classes (CBC)   Coupling between classes (CBC) is a metric that tries to quantify coupling that exists between classes. The CBC value for a class C is the total number of other classes to which the class is coupled. Two classes are considered coupled if methods of one class use methods or instance variables defined in the other class. In general, whether two classes are coupled can easily be determined by looking at the code and the definitions of all the methods of the two classes. However, note that there are indirect forms of coupling (through pointers, etc.) that are hard to identify by evaluating the code.

Response for a Class (RFC)   Although the CBC for a class captures the number of other classes to which this class is coupled, it does not quantify the "strength" of interconnection. In other words, it does not explain the degree of connection of methods of a class with other classes. Response for a class (RFC) tries to quantify this by capturing the total number of methods that can be invoked from an object of this class.

The RFC value for a class C is the cardinality of the response set for a class. The response set of a class C is the set of all methods that can be invoked if a message is sent to an object of this class. This includes all the methods of C and of other classes to which any method of C sends a message. It is clear that even if the CBC value of a class is 1 (that is, it is coupled with only one class), the RFC value may be quite high, indicating that the "volume" of interaction between the two classes is very high. It should be clear that it is likely to be harder to test classes that have higher RFC values.

6.7 Summary

– The design of a system is a plan for a solution such that if the plan is implemented, the implemented system will satisfy the requirements of the system and will preserve its architecture. The module-level design specifies the modules that should be there in the system to implement the architecture, and the *detailed design* the processing logic of modules.

– A system is considered modular if each module has a well-defined abstraction and if change in one module has minimal impact on other modules. Two criteria used for evaluating the modularity of a design are *coupling* and *cohesion*. Coupling reflects how interdependent are modules on each other, while cohesion is a measure of the strength with which the different elements of a module are related. In general, in a design coupling should be minimized and cohesion maximized. A design should also support the open-closed principle, that is, the modules are such that they are open for extension but closed for modification.

– A structure chart for a procedural system represents the modules in the system and the call relationship between them.

– The structured design methodology gives guidelines on how to create a design (represented as a structure chart) such that the modules have minimum dependence on each other (low coupling) and a high level of cohesion. For this, the methodology partitions the system at the very top level into various subsystems, one for managing each major input, one for managing each major output, and one for each major transformation. This cleanly partitions the system into parts each independently dealing with different concerns.

– The Universal Modeling Language (UML) has various types of diagrams to model different properties, which allow both static structure as well as dynamic behavior to be modeled. For representing the static structure, the main diagram is the class diagram, which represents the classes in the system and relationships between the classes. For modeling the dynamic behavior, sequence or collaboration diagrams may be used to show how a scenario is implemented by involving different objects.

– Using the UML notation, OO designs of a system can be created. The OO design methodology focuses on identifying classes and relationships between them, and validating the class definitions using dynamic and functional modeling.

– In detailed design of procedures, the logic for implementing the procedure is specified in a semiformal notation. For classes, state diagrams can be used to model the relationships between methods.

− The most common method for verifying a design is design reviews, in which a team of people reviews the design for the purpose of finding defects.

− There are a number of metrics that can be used to evaluate the complexity of a design. Network metrics evaluate the structure chart and consider deviation from the tree as the metric signifying the quality of design. The information flow complexity metrics define design complexity based on the internal complexity of the module and the number of connections between modules. These can be used to identify error-prone modules, and improve the design by reducing their complexity. For the complexity of an object-oriented design, metrics like weighted methods per class, the depth of inheritance tree of a class, and maximum depth in the class hierarchy of this class can be used.

Self-Assessment Exercises

1. What is the relationship between an architecture and module-level design?
2. Given a design that implements the SRS, what criteria will you use to evaluate the quality of this design?
3. Consider a program containing many modules. If a global variable x must be used to share data between two modules A and B, how would you design the interfaces of these modules to minimize coupling?
4. What is the cohesion of the following module? How would you change the module to increase cohesion?

> procedure file (file_ptr, file_name, op_name);
> begin
>   case op_name of
>   "open": perform activities for opening the file.
>   "close": perform activities for opening the file.
>   "print": print the file
>   end case
> end

5. Draw the structure chart for the following program:

```
main();
{    int x, y;
     x = 0; y = 0;
     a(); b(); }
a()
{    x = x+y; y = y+5; }
b()
{    x = x+5; y = y+x; a(); }
```

How would you modify this program to improve the modularity?

6. List some practices that you will follow while developing a software system using an object-oriented approach to increase cohesion and reduce coupling.

7. Finally in an object-oriented implementation, mostly classes are coded. Then during design, what is the role of dynamic modeling using UML?

8. How will you measure the information flow complexity of a full design specified as a structure chart?

9. Describe two metrics for quantifying complexity of an object-oriented design. How will you use one of them to identify highly-complex or error-prone modules?

7

Coding and Unit Testing

The goal of the coding or programming activity is to implement the design in the best possible manner. The coding activity affects both testing and maintenance profoundly. As we saw earlier, the time spent in coding is a small percentage of the total software cost, while testing and maintenance consume the major portion. Thus, it should be clear that the goal during coding should not be just to reduce the implementation cost, but help reduce the cost of later phases. During coding, it should be kept in mind that the programs should not be constructed so that they are easy to write, but in a manner that they are easy to read and understand. A program is read a lot more often and by a lot more people during the later phases.

Having readability and understandability as a clear objective of the coding activity can itself help in achieving it. A famous experiment by Weinberg showed that if programmers are specified a clear objective for the program, they usually satisfy it [82]. In the experiment, five different teams were given the same problem for which they had to develop programs. However, each of the teams was specified a different objective, which it had to satisfy. The different objectives given were: minimize the effort required to complete the program, minimize the number of statements, minimize the memory required, maximize the program clarity, and maximize the output clarity. It was found that in most cases each team did the best for the objective that was specified to it. The rank of the different teams for the different objectives is shown in Table 7.1.

The experiment clearly shows that if objectives are clear, programmers tend to achieve that objective. Hence, if readability is an objective of the coding activity, then it is likely that programmers will develop easily understandable

P. Jalote, *A Concise Introduction to Software Engineering*,
DOI: 10.1007/978-1-84800-302-6_7, © Springer-Verlag London Limited 2008

Table 7.1: The Weinberg experiment.

	Resulting Rank (1 = Best)				
	O1	O2	O3	O4	O5
Minimize effort to complete (O1)	1	4	4	5	3
Minimize number of statements (O2)	2–3	1	2	3	5
Minimize memory required (O3)	5	2	1	4	4
Maximize program clarity (O4)	4	3	3	2	2
Maximize output clarity (O5)	2–3	5	5	1	1

programs. It also shows that if the focus is on minimizing coding effort, program clarity takes a big hit. For our purposes, ease of understanding and modification are the basic goals of the programming activity.

In this chapter we will discuss:

— Some principles like structured programming, information hiding, use of coding standards, which can help develop more readable programs.

— Some programmer-level processes like incremental development and test-driven development, for efficiently developing high-quality code.

— How to manage evolving code by using proper source code control and refactoring.

— How to unit test modules using unit testing frameworks.

— A structured code inspection process that can be used effectively to improve the quality of the code.

7.1 Programming Principles and Guidelines

The main task before a programmer is to write readable code with few bugs in it. An additional goal is to write code quickly. Writing solid code is a skill that can only be acquired by practice. However, based on experience, some general rules and guidelines can be given for the programmer. Good programming (producing correct and simple programs) is a practice independent of the target programming language, although well-structured programming languages make the programmer's job simpler. In this section, we will discuss some concepts and practices that can help a programmer write higher-quality code that is also easier to understand.

7.1.1 Structured Programming

As stated earlier the basic objective of the coding activity is to produce programs that are easy to understand. It has been argued by many that structured programming practice helps develop programs that are easier to understand. The structured programming movement started in the 1970s, and much has been said and written about it. Now the concept pervades so much that it is generally accepted—even implied—that programming should be structured. Though a lot of emphasis has been placed on structured programming, the concept and motivation behind structured programming are often not well understood. Structured programming is often regarded as "goto-less" programming. Although extensive use of gotos is certainly not desirable, structured programs *can* be written with the use of gotos. Here we provide a brief discussion on what structured programming is.

A program has a static structure as well as a dynamic structure. The static structure is the structure of the text of the program, which is just a linear organization of statements of the program. The dynamic structure of the program is the sequence of statements executed during the execution of the program. In other words, both the static structure and the dynamic behavior are sequences of statements; while the sequence representing the static structure of a program is fixed, the sequence of statements it executes can change from execution to execution.

It will clearly be easier to understand the dynamic behavior if the structure in the dynamic behavior resembles the static structure. The closer the correspondence between execution and text structure, the easier the program is to understand, and the more different the structure during execution, the harder it will be to argue about the behavior from the program text. The goal of structured programming is to ensure that the static structure and the dynamic structures are the same. That is, the objective of structured programming is to write programs so that the sequence of statements executed during the execution of a program is the same as the sequence of statements in the text of that program. As the statements in a program text are linearly organized, the objective of structured programming becomes developing programs whose control flow during execution is linearized and follows the linear organization of the program text.

The real motivation for structured programming, however, was formal verification of programs. To show that a program is correct, we need to show that when the program executes, its behavior is what is expected. For specifying the behavior, we need to specify the conditions the output of the program should satisfy. As a program will usually not operate on an arbitrary set of input data and may produce valid results only for some range of inputs, we generally need to also state the input conditions in which the program is to be invoked and for which the program is expected to produce valid results. The assertion about the expected final state of a program is called the *post-condition* of that program, and the assertion about the input condition is called the *pre-condition* of the program. Often, in program verification, determining the pre-condition for which the post-condition will be satisfied is the goal of proof.

Using Hoare's notation [50], for verifying a program, the basic assertion about a program segment is of the form

$$P\{S\}Q.$$

The interpretation of this is that if assertion P is true before executing S, then assertion Q will be true after executing S, if the execution of S terminates. Assertion P is the pre-condition of the program and Q is the post-condition. These assertions are about the values taken by the variables in the program before and after its execution. The assertions generally do not specify a particular value for the variables, but they specify the general properties of the values and the relationships among them.

For verification of larger programs, we would like to make assertions about the program from assertions about its components or statements. If the program is a sequence of statements, then determining the semantics of a composite program becomes easier. If a statement S is composed of two statements S1 and S2, which are to be executed in sequence, then from the semantics of S1 and S2, we can easily determine the semantics of S (this rule is called *rule of composition* in [50]) as follows:

$$\frac{P1\{ S1\}Q1, Q1 \Rightarrow P2, P2\{S2\}R2}{P1\{S1; S2\}R2}$$

The explanation of this notation is that if what is stated in the numerator can be proved, the denominator can be inferred. Using this rule, if we have proved P1{S1}Q1 and P2{S2}R2, then to determine the semantics of S1;S2, all we need to show is that $Q1 \Rightarrow P2$, and then we can claim that if before execution the pre-condition P1 holds, then after execution of S1;S2 the post-condition Q2 will hold. In other words, to prove P{S1;S2}R, once we have determined the behaviors of S1 and S2, we just need one additional step. This allows building proofs of larger programs from proofs of its elements. Note that the rule handles a strict sequence of statements only. So, if we want to apply this, we need to construct the program as a sequence of statements. And that is the verification motivation of wanting to linearize the control flow in a program.

Clearly, no meaningful program can be written as a sequence of simple statements without any branching or repetition (which also involves branching). So, how is the objective of linearizing the control flow to be achieved? By making use of structured constructs. In structured programming, a statement is not a simple assignment statement, it is a structured statement. The key property of a structured statement is that it has a *single-entry* and a *single-exit*. That is, during execution, the execution of the (structured) statement starts from one defined point and the execution terminates at one defined point. With single-entry and single-exit statements, we can view a program as a sequence of (structured) statements. And if all statements are structured statements, then during execution, the sequence of execution of these statements will be the same as the sequence in the program text. Hence, by using single-entry and single-exit statements, the correspondence between the static and dynamic structures can be obtained. The most commonly used single-entry and single-exit statements are

> *Selection:* if B then S1 else S2
> if B then S1
> *Iteration:* While B do S
> repeat S until B
> *Sequencing:* S1; S2; S3;...

It can be shown that these three basic constructs are sufficient to program any conceivable algorithm. Modern languages have other such constructs that help linearize the control flow of a program, which, generally speaking, makes it easier to understand a program. Hence, programs should be written so that, as far as possible, single-entry, single-exit control constructs are used. The basic goal, as we have tried to emphasize, is to make the logic of the program simple to understand. No hard-and-fast rule can be formulated that will be applicable under all circumstances. Structured programming practice forms a good basis and guideline for writing programs clearly.

A final note about the structured constructs. Any piece of code with a single-entry and single-exit cannot be considered a structured construct. If that is the case, one could always define appropriate units in any program to make it appear as a sequence of these units (in the worst case, the whole program could be defined to be a unit). The basic objective of using structured constructs is to linearize the control flow so that the execution behavior is easier to understand and argue about. In linearized control flow, if we understand the behavior of each of the basic constructs properly, the behavior of the program can be considered a composition of the behaviors of the different statements. For this approach to work, it is implied that we can clearly understand and specify the behavior of each construct. This requires that we be able to succinctly capture or describe the behavior of each construct. Unless we can do this, it will not be possible to compose them. Clearly, for an arbitrary structure, we cannot do this merely because it has a single-entry and single-exit. It is from this viewpoint that the structures mentioned earlier are chosen as structured statements. There are well-defined rules that specify how these statements behave during execution, which allows us to argue about larger programs.

Overall, it can be said that structured programming leads to programs that are easier to understand than unstructured programs, and that such programs are easier to formally prove. However, it should be kept in mind that structured programming is not an end in itself. Our basic objective is that the program be easy to understand. And structured programming is a safe approach for achieving this objective. Still, there are some common programming practices that are now well understood that make use of unstructured constructs (e.g., break statement, continue statement). Although efforts should be made to avoid using statements that effectively violate the single-entry single-exit property, if the use of such statements is the simplest way to organize the program, then from the point of view of readability, the constructs should be used. The main point is that any unstructured construct should be used only if the structured alternative is harder to understand. This view can be taken only because we are focusing on readability. If the objective was formal verifiability, structured programming will probably be necessary.

7.1.2 Information Hiding

A software solution to a problem always contains data structures that are meant to represent information in the problem domain. That is, when software is developed to solve a problem, the software uses some data structures to capture the information in the problem domain.

In general, only certain operations are performed on some information. That is, a piece of information in the problem domain is used only in a limited number of ways in the problem domain. For example, a ledger in an accountant's office has some very defined uses: debit, credit, check the current balance, etc. An operation where all debits are multiplied together and then divided by the sum of all credits is typically not performed. So, any information in the problem domain typically has a small number of defined operations performed on it.

When the information is represented as data structures, the same principle should be applied, and only some defined operations should be performed on the data structures. This, essentially, is the principle of information hiding. The information captured in the data structures should be hidden from the rest of the system, and only the access functions on the data structures that represent the operations performed on the information should be visible. In other words, when the information is captured in data structures and then on the data structures that represent some information, for each operation on the information an access function should be provided. And as the rest of the system in the problem domain only performs these defined operations on the information, the rest of the modules in the software should only use these access functions to access and manipulate the data structures.

Information hiding can reduce the coupling between modules and make the system more maintainable. Information hiding is also an effective tool for managing the complexity of developing software—by using information hiding we have separated the concern of managing the data from the concern of using the data to produce some desired results.

Many of the older languages, like Pascal, C, and FORTRAN, do not provide mechanisms to support data abstraction. With such languages, information hiding can be supported only by a disciplined use of the language. That is, the access restrictions will have to be imposed by the programmers; the language does not provide them. Most modern OO languages provide linguistic mechanisms to implement information hiding.

7.1.3 Some Programming Practices

The concepts discussed above can help in writing simple and clear code with few bugs. There are many programming practices that can also help toward that objective. We discuss here a few rules that have been found to make code easier to read as well as avoid some of the errors.

Control Constructs: As discussed earlier, it is desirable that as much as possible single-entry, single-exit constructs be used. It is also desirable to use a few standard control constructs rather than using a wide variety of constructs, just because they are available in the language.

Gotos: Gotos should be used sparingly and in a disciplined manner. Only when the alternative to using gotos is more complex should the gotos be used. In any case, alternatives must be thought of before finally using a goto. If a goto must be used, forward transfers (or a jump to a later statement) is more acceptable than a backward jump.

Information Hiding: As discussed earlier, information hiding should be supported where possible. Only the access functions for the data structures should be made visible while hiding the data structure behind these functions.

User-Defined Types: Modern languages allow users to define types like the enumerated type. When such facilities are available, they should be exploited where applicable. For example, when working with dates, a type can be defined for the day of the week. Using such a type makes the program much clearer than defining codes for each day and then working with codes.

Nesting: If nesting of if-then-else constructs becomes too deep, then the logic become harder to understand. In case of deeply nested if-then-elses, it is often difficult to determine the if statement to which a particular else clause is associated. Where possible, deep nesting should be avoided, even if it means a little inefficiency. For example, consider the following construct of nested if-then-elses:

```
if C1 then S1
    else if C2 then S2
        else if C3 then S3
            else if C4 then S4;
```

If the different conditions are disjoint (as they often are), this structure can be converted into the following structure:

```
if C1 then S1;
if C2 then S2;
if C3 then S3;
if C4 then S4;
```

This sequence of statements will produce the same result as the earlier sequence (if the conditions are disjoint), but it is much easier to understand. The price is a little inefficiency.

Module Size: We discussed this issue during system design. A programmer should carefully examine any function with too many statements (say more than 100). Large modules often will not be functionally cohesive. There can be no hard-and-fast rule about module sizes; the guiding principle should be cohesion and coupling.

Module Interface: A module with a complex interface should be carefully examined. As a rule of thumb, any module whose interface has more than five parameters should be carefully examined and broken into multiple modules with a simpler interface if possible.

Side Effects: When a module is invoked, it sometimes has side effects of modifying the program state beyond the modification of parameters listed in the module interface definition, for example, modifying global variables. Such side effects should be avoided where possible, and if a module has side effects, they should be properly documented.

Robustness: A program is robust if it does something planned even for exceptional conditions. A program might encounter exceptional conditions in such forms as incorrect input, the incorrect value of some variable, and overflow. If such situations do arise, the program should not just "crash" or "core dump"; it should produce some meaningful message and exit gracefully.

Switch Case with Default: If there is no default case in a "switch" statement, the behavior can be unpredictable if that case arises at some point of time which was not predictable at development stage. Such a practice can result in a bug like NULL dereference, memory leak, as well as other types of serious bugs. It is a good practice to always include a default case.

```
switch (i){
  case 0 : {s=malloc(size)
  }
  s[0] = y; /* NULL dereference if default occurs*/
```

Empty Catch Block: An exception is caught, but if there is no action, it may represent a scenario where some of the operations to be done are not performed. Whenever exceptions are caught, it is a good practice to take some default action, even if it is just printing an error message.

```
try {
  FileInputStream fis = new
  FileInputStream("InputFile");
}
catch (IOException ioe) { }
  // not a good practice
```

Empty if, while Statement: A condition is checked but nothing is done based on the check. This often occurs due to some mistake and should be caught. Other similar errors include empty finally, try, synchronized, empty static method, etc. Such useless checks should be avoided.

```
if (x == 0) {}  /* nothing is done after checking x */
else {
  :
}
```

Read Return to Be Checked: Often the return value from reads is not checked, assuming that the read returns the desired values. Sometimes the result from a read can be different from what is expected, and this can cause failures later. There may be some cases where neglecting this condition may result in some serious error. For example, if read from scanf() is more than expected, then it may cause a buffer overflow. Hence, the value of read should be checked before accessing the data read. (This is the reason why most languages provide a return value for the read operation.)

Return from Finally Block: One should not return from finally block, as it can create false beliefs. For example, consider the code

```
public String foo() {
  try {
      throw new Exception( "An Exception" );
  }
  catch (Exception e) {
      throw e;
  }
  finally {
      return "Some value";
      }
  }
```

In this example, a value is returned both in exception and nonexception scenarios. Hence, at the caller site, the user will not be able to distinguish between
the two. Another interesting case arises when we have a return from try block.
In this case, if there is a return in finally also, then the value from finally is
returned instead of the value from try.

Correlated Parameters: Often there is an implicit correlation between
the parameters. For example, in the code segment given below, "length" represents the size of BUFFER. If the correlation does not hold, we can run into
a serious problem like buffer overflow (illustrated in the code fragment below).
Hence, it is a good practice to validate this correlation rather than assuming
that it holds. In general, it is desirable to do some counter checks on implicit
assumptions about parameters.

```
void (char *src, int length, char destn[]) {
  strcpy (destn, src); /* Can cause buffer overflow
                         if length > MAX_SIZE */
}
```

Trusted Data Sources: Counter checks should be made before accessing
the input data, particularly if the input data is being provided by the user or
is being obtained over the network. For example, while doing the string copy
operation, we should check that the source string is null terminated, or that its
size is as we expect. Similar is the case with some network data which may be
sniffed and prone to some modifications or corruptions. To avoid problems due
to these changes, we should put some checks, like parity checks, hashes, etc.,
to ensure the validity of the incoming data.

Give Importance to Exceptions: Most programmers tend to give less
attention to the possible exceptional cases and tend to work with the main flow
of events, control, and data. Though the main work is done in the main path,
it is the exceptional paths that often cause software systems to fail. To make
a software system more reliable, a programmer should consider all possibilities
and write suitable exception handlers to prevent failures or loss when such

situations occur.

7.1.4 Coding Standards

Programmers spend far more time reading code than writing code. Over the life of the code, the author spends a considerable time reading it during debugging and enhancement. People other than the author also spend considerable effort in reading code because the code is often maintained by someone other than the author. In short, it is of prime importance to write code in a manner that is easy to read and understand. Coding standards provide rules and guidelines for some aspects of programming in order to make code easier to read. Most organizations who develop software regularly develop their own standards.

In general, coding standards provide guidelines for programmers regarding naming, file organization, statements and declarations, and layout and comments. To give an idea of coding standards (often called conventions or style guidelines), we discuss some guidelines for Java, based on publicly available standards (from www.geosoft.no or java.sun.com/docs).

Naming Conventions   Some of the standard naming conventions that are followed often are:

- Package names should be in lowercase (e.g., mypackage, edu.iitk.maths).

- Type names should be nouns and should start with uppercase (e.g., Day, DateOfBirth, EventHandler).

- Variable names should be nouns starting with lowercase (e.g., name, amount).

- Constant names should be all uppercase (e.g., PI, MAX_ITERATIONS).

- Method names should be verbs starting with lowercase (e.g., getValue()).

- Private class variables should have the _ suffix (e.g., "private int value_"). (Some standards will require this to be a prefix.)

- Variables with a large scope should have long names; variables with a small scope can have short names; loop iterators should be named i, j, k, etc.

- The prefix *is* should be used for Boolean variables and methods to avoid confusion (e.g., isStatus should be used instead of status); negative boolean variable names (e.g., isNotCorrect) should be avoided.

- The term *compute* can be used for methods where something is being computed; the term *find* can be used where something is being looked up (e.g., computeMean(), findMin()).

- Exception classes should be suffixed with *Exception* (e.g., OutOfBoundException).

Files   There are conventions on how files should be named, and what files should contain, such that a reader can get some idea about what the file contains. Some examples of these conventions are:

- Java source files should have the extension .java—this is enforced by most compilers and tools.

- Each file should contain one outer class and the class name should be the same as the file name.

- Line length should be limited to less than 80 columns and special characters should be avoided. If the line is longer, it should be continued and the continuation should be made very clear.

Statements   These guidelines are for the declaration and executable statements in the source code. Some examples are given below. Note, however, that not everyone will agree on these. That is why organizations generally develop their own guidelines that can be followed without restricting the flexibility of programmers for the type of work the organization does.

- Variables should be initialized where declared, and they should be declared in the smallest possible scope.

- Declare related variables together in a common statement. Unrelated variables should not be declared in the same statement.

- Class variables should never be declared public.

- Use only loop control statements in a for loop.

- Loop variables should be initialized immediately before the loop.

- Avoid the use of *break* and *continue* in a loop.

- Avoid the use of *do ... while* construct.

- Avoid complex conditional expressions—introduce temporary boolean variables instead.

- Avoid executable statements in conditionals.

Commenting and Layout   Comments are textual statements that are meant for the program reader to aid the understanding of code. The purpose of comments is not to explain in English the logic of the program—if the logic is so complex that it requires comments to explain it, it is better to rewrite and simplify the code instead. In general, comments should explain what the code is doing or why the code is there, so that the code can become almost standalone for understanding the system. Comments should generally be provided for blocks of code, and in many cases, only comments for the modules need to be provided.

Providing comments for modules is most useful, as modules form the unit of testing, compiling, verification, and modification. Comments for a module are often called *prologue* for the module, which describes the functionality and the purpose of the module, its public interface and how the module is to be used, parameters of the interface, assumptions it makes about the parameters, and any side effects it has. Other features may also be included. It should be noted that prologues are useful only if they are kept consistent with the logic of the module. If the module is modified, then the prologue should also be modified, if necessary.

Java provides *documentation comments* that are delimited by "/** ... */", and which could be extracted to HTML files. These comments are mostly used as prologues for classes and its methods and fields, and are meant to provide documentation to users of the classes who may not have access to the source code. In addition to prologue for modules, coding standards may specify how and where comments should be located. Some such guidelines are:

- Single line comments for a block of code should be aligned with the code they are meant for.

- There should be comments for all major variables explaining what they represent.

- A block of comments should be preceded by a blank comment line with just "/*" and ended with a line containing just "*/".

- Trailing comments after statements should be short, on the same line, and shifted far enough to separate them from statements.

Layout guidelines focus on how a program should be indented, how it should use blank lines, white spaces, etc., to make it more easily readable. Indentation guidelines are sometimes provided for each type of programming construct. However, most programmers learn these by seeing the code of others and the code fragments in books and documents, and many of these have become fairly standard over the years. We will not discuss them further except to say that a programmer should use some conventions, and use them consistently.

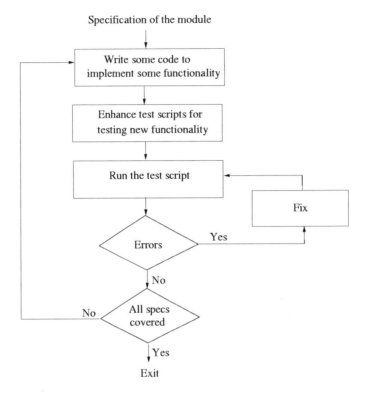

Figure 7.1: An incremental coding process.

7.2 Incrementally Developing Code

The coding activity starts when some form of design has been done and the specifications of the modules to be developed are available. With the design, modules are assigned to developers for coding. When modules are assigned to developers, they use some process for developing the code. Clearly, a wide range of processes are possible for achieving this goal. Here we discuss some effective processes that developers use for incrementally developing code.

7.2.1 An Incremental Coding Process

The process followed by many developers is to write the code for the currently assigned module, and when done, perform unit testing on it and fix the bugs found. Then the code is checked in the project repository to make it available to others in the project. (We will explain the process of checking in later.)

A better process for coding, which is often followed by experienced developers, is to develop the code incrementally. That is, write code for implementing only part of the functionality of the module. This code is compiled and tested with some quick tests to check the code that has been written so far. When the code passes these tests, the developer proceeds to add further functionality to the code, which is then tested again. In other words, the code is developed incrementally, testing it as it is built. This coding process is shown in Figure 7.1.

The basic advantage of developing code incrementally with testing being done after every round of coding is to facilitate debugging—an error found in some testing can be safely attributed to code that was added since the last successful testing. However, for following this process, it is essential that testing be done through test scripts that can be run easily. With these test scripts, testing can be done as frequently as desired, and new test cases can be added easily. These test scripts are also a tremendous aid when code is enhanced in the future—through the test scripts it can be quickly checked that the earlier functionality is still working. These test scripts can also be used with some enhancements for the final unit testing that is often done before checking in the module.

7.2.2 Test-Driven Development

Test-Driven Development (TDD) [8] is a coding process that turns around the common approach to coding. Instead of writing code and then developing test cases to check the code, in TDD it is the other way around—a programmer first writes the test scripts, and then writes the code to pass the tests. The whole process is done incrementally, with tests being written based on the specifications and code being written to pass the tests. The TDD process is shown in Figure 7.2.

This is a relatively new approach, which has been adopted in the extreme programming (XP) methodology [7]. The concept of TDD is, however, general and not tied to any particular methodology.

A few points are worth noting about TDD. First, the approach says that you write just enough code to pass the tests. By following this, the code is always in sync with the tests. This is not always the case with the code-first approach, in which it is all too common to write a long piece of code, but then only write a few tests which cover only some parts of the code. By encouraging that code is written only to pass the tests, the responsibility of ensuring that required functionality is built is shifted to the activity of designing the test cases. That is, it is the task of test cases to check that the code that will be developed has all the functionality needed.

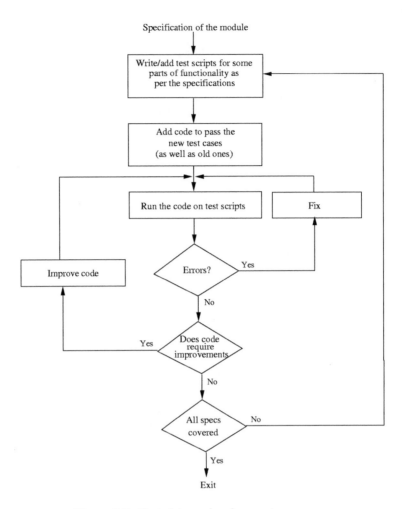

Figure 7.2: Test-driven development process.

This writing of test cases before the code is written makes the development usage-driven. Since test cases have to be written first from the specifications, how the code is to be used gets the attention first. This helps ensure that the interfaces are from the perspective of the user of the code and that key usage scenarios. This can help reduce interface errors.

In TDD, some type of prioritization for code development naturally happens. It is most likely that the first few tests are likely to focus on using the main functionality. Generally, the test cases for lower-priority features or functionality will be developed later. Consequently, code for high-priority features will be developed first and lower-priority items will be developed later. This has the benefit that higher-priority items get done first, but has the drawback that some of the lower-priority features or some special cases for which test cases are not written may not get handled in the code.

As the code is written to satisfy the test cases, the completeness of the code depends on the thoroughness of the test cases. Often it is hard and tedious to write test cases for all the scenarios or special conditions, and it is highly unlikely that a developer will write test cases for all the special cases. In TDD, as the goal is to write enough code to pass the test cases, such special cases may not get handled. Also, as at each step code is being written primarily to pass the tests, it may later be found that earlier algorithms were not well suited. In that case, the code should be improved before new functionality is added, as shown in Figure 7.2.

7.2.3 Pair Programming

Pair programming is also a coding process that has been proposed as a key technique in extreme programming (XP) methodology [7]. In pair programming, code is not written by individual programmers but by a pair of programmers. That is, the coding work is assigned not to an individual but to a pair of individuals. This pair together writes the code.

The process envisaged is that one person will type the program while the other will actively participate and constantly review what is being typed. When errors are noticed, they are pointed out and corrected. When needed, the pair discusses the algorithms, data structures, or strategies to be used in the code to be written. The roles are rotated frequently making both equal partners and having similar roles.

The basic motivation for pair programming is that as code reading and code reviews have been found to be very effective in detecting defects, by having a pair do the programming we have the situation where the code is getting reviewed as it is being typed. That is, instead of writing code and then getting it reviewed by another programmer, we have a programmer who is constantly reviewing the code being written. Like incremental development and testing, we now have incremental reviewing taking place.

Besides ongoing code review, having two programmers apply themselves to the programming task at hand is likely to result in better decisions being taken about the data structures, algorithms, interfaces, logic, etc. Special conditions, which frequently result in errors, are also more likely to be dealt with in a better manner.

The potential drawback of pair programming is that it may result in loss of productivity by assigning two people for a programming task. It is clear that a pair will produce better code as compared to code being developed by a single programmer. The open question is whether this increase in productivity due to improved code quality offsets the loss incurred by putting two people on a task. There are also issues of accountability and code ownership, particularly when the pairs are not fixed and rotate (as has been proposed in XP). Impact of pair programming is an active area of research, particularly for experimental software engineering.

7.3 Managing Evolving Code

During the coding process, the code being written by a programmer (or a pair) evolves—starting from nothing to eventually having a well-tested module. During this process the code undergoes changes. Besides the changes due to the development process, code changes are also needed due to changes in module specifications, which may come about due to requirement changes. In such a dynamic scenario, managing evolving code is a challenge. Here we discuss two aspects of this—how to manage the different versions that get created, and how to maintain code quality under changes.

7.3.1 Source Code Control and Build

In a project many different people develop source code. Each programmer creates different source files, which are eventually combined together to create executables. Programmers keep changing their source files as the code evolves, as we have seen in the processes discussed above, and often make changes in other source files as well. In order to keep control over the sources and their evolution, source code control is almost always used in projects using tools like the CVS on UNIX (www.cvshome.org) or visual source safe (VSS) on Windows (msdn.microsoft.com/vstudio/previous/ssafe). Here we give a brief description of how these tools are used in the coding process. Our discussion is based on CVS.

A modern source code control system contains a repository, which is essentially a controlled directory structure, which keeps the full revision history of all the files produced by the different programmers in the project team. For efficiency, a file history is generally kept as deltas or increments from the base file. This allows any older version of the file to be re-created, thereby giving the flexibility to easily discard a change, should the need arise. The repository is also the "official" source for all the files.

For a project, a repository has to be set up with permissions for different people in the project. The files the repository will contain are also specified—these are the files whose evolution the repository maintains. Programmers use the repository to make their source file changes available, as well as obtain other source files. Some of the types of commands that are generally performed by a programmer are:

Get a local copy. A programmer in a project works on a local copy of the file. Commands are provided to make a local copy from the repository. Making a local copy is generally called a *checkout*. An example command is *cvs checkout < module >*, which copies a set of files that belongs to the *< module >* on the local machine. A user will get the latest copy of the file. However, if a user wants, any older version of a file can be obtained from the repository, as the complete history is maintained. Many users can check out a file.

Make changes to file(s). The changes made to the local file by a programmer remain local until the changes are *committed* back on the repository. By committing (e.g., by *cvs commit < file >*) the changes made to the local file are made to the repository, and are hence available to others. This operation is also referred to as *check in*.

Update a local copy. Changes committed by project members to the repository are not reflected in the local copies that were made before the changes were committed. For getting the changes, the local copies of the files have to be updated (e.g., by *cvs update* command). By an update, all the changes made to the files are reflected in the local copy.

Get reports. Source control tools provide a host of commands to provide different reports on the evolution of the files. These include reports like the difference between the local file and the latest version of the file, all changes made to a file along with the dates and reasons for change (which are typically provided while committing a change).

Note that once the changes are committed, they become available to all members of the team, who are supposed to use the source files from the repository. Hence, it is essential that a programmer commits a source file only when it is in a state that is usable by others. The normal behavior of a project member will be as follows: check out the latest version of the files to be changed; make the planned changes to them; validate that the changes have the desired effect (for which all the files may be copied and the system tried out locally); commit the changes back to the repository.

It should be clear that if two people check out some file and then make changes, there is a possibility of a conflict—different changes are made to the same parts of the file. All tools will detect the conflict when the second person tries to commit the changes, and will inform the user. The user has to manually resolve the conflit, i.e., make the file such that the changes do not conflict with existing changes, and then commit the file. Conflicts are usually rare as they occur only if different changes are made to the same lines in a file.

With a source code control system, a programmer does not need to maintain all the versions—at any time if some changes need to be undone, older versions can be easily recovered. The repositories are always backed up, so they also provide protection against accidental loss. Furthermore, a record of changes is maintained—who made the change and when, why was the change made, what were the actual changes, etc. Most importantly, the repository provides a central place for the latest and authoritative files of the project. This is invaluable for products that have a long life and that evolve over many years.

Besides using the repository for maintaining the different versions, it is also used for constructing the software system from the sources—an activity often called *build*. The build gets the latest version (or the desired version number) of the sources from the repository, and creates the executables from the sources.

Building the final executables from the source files is often done through tools like the Makefile [34], which specify the dependence between files and how the final executables are constructed from the source files. These tools are capable of recognizing that files have changed and will recompile whenever files are changed for creating the executables. With source code control, these tools will generally get the latest copy from the repository, then use it for creating executables.

What we discussed here is one of the simplest approaches to source code control and build. Often, when large systems are being built, more elaborate methods for source code control may be needed.

7.3.2 Refactoring

We have seen that coding often involves making changes to some existing code. Code also changes when requirements change or when new functionality is added. Due to the changes being done to modules, even if we started with a good design, with time we often end up with code whose design is not as good as it could be. And once the design embodied in the code becomes complex, then enhancing the code to accommodate required changes becomes more complex, time consuming, and error prone. In other words, the productivity and quality start decreasing.

Refactoring is the technique to improve existing code and prevent this design decay with time. Refactoring is part of coding in that it is performed during the coding activity, but is not regular coding. Refactoring has been practiced in the past by programmers, but recently it has taken a more concrete shape, and has been proposed as a key step in the XP practice [7]. Refactoring also plays an important role in test-driven development—code improvement step in the TDD process is really doing refactoring. Here we discuss some key concepts and some methods for doing refactoring [36]. More details are available on www.refactoring.com.

Refactoring is defined as a change made to the internal structure of software to make it easier to understand and cheaper to modify without changing its observable behavior [36]. A key point here is that the change is being made to the design embodied in the source code (i.e., the internal structure) exclusively for improvement purposes.

The basic objective of refactoring is to improve the design. However, note that this is not about improving a design during the design stages for creating a design which is to be later implemented (which is the focus of design methodologies), but about improving the design of code that already exists. In other words, refactoring, though done on source code, has the objective of improving the design that the code implements. Therefore, the basic principles of design guide the refactoring process. Consequently, a refactoring generally results in one or more of the following:

1. Reduced coupling

2. Increased cohesion

3. Better adherence to open-closed principle

Refactoring involves changing the code to improve one of the design properties, while keeping the external behavior the same. Refactoring is often triggered by some coding changes that have to be done. If some enhancements are to be made to the existing code, and it is felt that if the code structure was different (better) then the change could have been done easier, that is the time to do refactoring to improve the code structure.

Even though refactoring is triggered by the need to change the software (and its external behavior), it should not be confused or mixed with the changes for enhancements. It is best to keep these two types of changes separate. So, while developing code, if refactoring is needed, the programmer should cease to write new functionality, and first do the refactoring, and then add new code.

The main risk of refactoring is that existing working code may "break" due to the changes being made. This is the main reason why often refactoring is not done. (The other reason is that it may be viewed as an additional and unnecessary cost.) To mitigate this risk, the two golden rules are:

1. Refactor in small steps

2. Have test scripts available to test existing functionality

If a good test suite is available, then whether refactoring preserves existing functionality can be checked easily. Refactoring cannot be done effectively without an automated test suite as without such a suite determining if the external behavior has changed or not will become a costly affair. By doing refactoring in a series of small steps, and testing after each step, mistakes in refactoring can be easily identified and rectified. With this, each refactoring makes only a small change, but a series of refactorings can significantly transform the program structure.

With refactoring, code becomes continuously improving. That is, the design, rather than decaying with time, evolves and improves with time. With refactoring, the quality of the design improves, making it easier to make changes to the code as well as find bugs. The extra cost of refactoring is paid for by the savings achieved later in reduced testing and debugging costs, higher quality, and reduced effort in making changes.

If refactoring is to be practiced, its usage can also ease the design task in the design stages. Often the designers spend considerable effort in trying to make the design as good as possible, try to think of future changes, and try to make the design flexible enough to accommodate all types of future changes they can envisage. This makes the design activity very complex, and often results in complex designs. With refactoring, the designer does not have to be terribly worried about making the best or most flexible design—the goal is to try to come up with a good and simple design. And later if new changes are required that were not thought of before, or if shortcomings are found in the design, the design is changed through refactoring. More often than not, the extra flexibility envisaged and designed is never needed, resulting in a system that is unduly complex.

Note that refactoring is not a technique for bug fixing or for improving code that is in very bad shape. It is done to code that is mostly working—the basic purpose is to make the code live longer by making its structure healthier. It starts with healthy code and instead of letting it become weak, it continues to keep it healthy.

When is refactoring needed? There are some easy-to-spot signs in the code, which are sometimes called "bad smells" [36], that often indicate that some of the desirable design properties may be getting violated or that there is potential of improving the design. In other words, if you "smell" one of these "bad smells," it may be a sign that refactoring is needed. Some of these bad smells from [36] are given here.

1. *Duplicate Code.* This is quite common. One reason for this is that some small functionality is being executed at multiple places (e.g., the age from

date of birth may be computed in each place that needs the date). Another common reason is that when there are multiple subclasses of a class, then each subclass may end up doing a similar thing. Duplicate code means that if this logic or function has to be changed, it will have to be changed in all the places it exists, making changes much harder and costlier.

2. *Long Method.* If a method is large, it often represents the situation where it is trying to do too many things and therefore is not cohesive.

3. *Long Class.* Similarly, a large class may indicate that it is encapsulating multiple concepts, making the class not cohesive.

4. *Long Parameter List.* Complex interfaces are clearly not desirable—they make the code harder to understand. Often, the complexity is not intrinsic but a sign of improper design.

5. *Switch Statements.* In object-oriented programs, if the polymorphism is not being used properly, it is likely to result in a switch statement everywhere the behavior is to be different depending on the property. Presence of similar switch statements in different places is a sign that instead of using class hierarchy, switch statement is being used. Presence of switch statement makes it much harder to extend code—if a new category is to be added, all the switch statements will have to be modified.

6. *Speculative Generality.* Some class hierarchies may exist because the objects in subclasses seem to be different. However, if the behavior of objects of the different subclasses is the same, and there is no immediate reason to think that behaviors might change, then it is a case of unnecessary complexity.

7. *Too Much Communication Between Objects.* If methods in one class are making many calls to methods of another object to find out about its state, this is a sign of strong coupling. It is possible that this may be unnecessary and hence such situations should be examined for refactoring.

8. *Message Chaining.* One method calls another method, which simply passes this call to another object, and so on. This chain potentially results in unnecessary coupling.

These bad smells in general are indicative of a poor design. Clearly there are unlimited possibilities of how code can be refactored to improve its design. There are, however, some "standard" refactorings that can be applied in many of the situations. For a catalog of common refactorings, and steps for performing each of them, the reader is referred to [36].

7.4 Unit Testing

Once a programmer has written the code for a module, it has to be verified before it is used by others. Testing remains the most common method of this verification. At the programmer level the testing done for checking the code the programmer has developed (as compared to checking the entire software system) is called *unit testing.*

Unit testing is like regular testing where programs are executed with some test cases except that the focus is on testing smaller programs or modules which are typically assigned to one programmer (or a pair) for coding. In the programming processes we discussed earlier, the testing was essentially unit testing. A unit may be a function or a small collection of functions for procedural languages, or a class or a small collection of classes for object-oriented languages.

Testing of modules or software systems is a difficult and challenging task. Selection of test cases is a key issue in any form of testing. We will discuss the problem of test case selection in detail in the next chapter when we discuss testing. For now, it suffices that during unit testing the tester, who is generally the programmer, will execute the unit with a variety of test cases and study the actual behavior of the units being tested for these test cases. Based on the behavior, the tester decides whether the unit is working correctly or not. If the behavior is not as expected for some test case, then the programmer finds the defect in the program (an activity called *debugging*), and fixes it. After removing the defect, the programmer will generally execute the test case that caused the unit to fail again to ensure that the fixing has indeed made the unit behave correctly.

An issue with unit testing is that as the unit being tested is not a complete system but just a part, it is not executable by itself. Furthermore, in its execution it may use other modules that have not been developed yet. Due to this, unit testing often requires drivers or stubs to be written. Drivers play the role of the "calling" module and are often responsible for getting the test data, executing the unit with the test data, and then reporting the result. Stubs are essentially "dummy" modules that are used in place of the actual module to facilitate unit testing. So, if a module M uses services from another module N that has not yet been developed, then for unit testing M, some stub for N will have to be written so M can invoke the services in some manner on N so that unit testing can proceed. The need for stubs can be avoided, if coding and testing proceeds in a bottom-up manner—the modules at lower levels are coded and tested first such that when modules at higher levels of hierarchy are tested, the code for lower-level modules is already available.

If incremental coding is practiced, as discussed above, then unit testing needs to be performed every time the programmer adds some code. Clearly, it will be much more efficient if instead of executing the unit and giving the inputs manually, the execution of test cases is automated. Then test cases can be executed easily every time testing needs to be done. Some tools are available to facilitate this. Here we discuss some approaches for unit testing using testing frameworks.

7.4.1 Testing Procedural Units

In the previous chapter we have seen that when using procedural units for modules, a program can be viewed as a structure chart, in which nodes are functions and edges represent a calling relationship. In unit testing, one, or a small collection, of these modules is to be tested with a set of test cases. As the behavior of a module depends on the value of its parameters as well as the overall state of the system of which it is a part (e.g., states of global variables), a test case for a module f() will involve setting both the state of the system on which the behavior of f() depends as well as the value of parameters. The actual values and the state of the system for a test case depend on the purpose for which the tester has designed this test case.

In addition, if a module f() has other modules below it in the structure chart, that is, the module calls other modules, say, g() and h(), then for executing f(), we must have code for g() and h() also available. This is handled in two ways. First is to test in a bottom-up manner, i.e., test the modules at the bottom of the structure chart first, and then move up. In this approach, when testing f(), the tested code for g() and h() will be available and will be used during testing. The other approach is to write *stubs* for g() and h(). Stubs are throwaway code written for the called functions only to facilitate testing of the caller function. Often the stub for a function will just print some statement, if no value is to be returned. If some value is to be returned for the caller to proceed, then often a few values will be hard coded in the stub, and then the caller will ensure that the stub is called with the values for which it has been coded. We will assume that the former approach is being followed, that is, for testing f(), tested code for g() and h() is already available.

Testing of a module f() by a test case will then involve the following steps:

1. Set the system state as needed by this test case.

2. Set value of parameters suitably.

3. Call the procedure f() with the parameters.

4. Compare result of f with expected results.

5. Declare whether the test case has succeeded or failed.

The simplest and commonly used approach for executing this sequence of steps is to write a main() program which executes the first three steps, with the values being given as input by the tester or read from a file or hard coded in the program, and then prints out the important values. The programmer then executes the last two steps, namely, comparing the results with expected and deciding whether the test has succeeded or failed. Due to the need of programmer intervention for evaluating the outputs, and possibly also for giving inputs, this approach is not easy to scale.

Once a test case is designed, this sequence of steps remains fixed and hence is ideal for complete automation. In a testing framework, often a test case will be declared as a function in which this sequence of steps is executed for that test case, including the checking of the outcome and declaring the result—this being done often with the help of assert statements provided by the framework. A test suite is then a collection of these functions, and execution of a test suite means each of the functions is executed. The test suite succeeds if all the test cases succeed. If a test case fails, then the test framework will decide whether to continue executing or stop.

A function for a test case can be easily defined—it will execute the sequence of steps given above. However, executing the module under test with the test cases is not straightforward as a suitable executable will have to be formed which can execute the functions representing the test cases and report the results about success or failure. And one would like to do this without changing the module being tested or the file in which this module is contained. If the source code files remain unchanged during unit testing, then the integration process remains unaffected by unit testing. Otherwise, after unit testing, any changes made to the files will have to be removed. This type of unit testing is facilitated by testing frameworks. For a procedural language like C, some common unit testing frameworks are CuTest, CUnit, Cutest, Check, etc.

With these test frameworks, each test case is defined as a function. The function ends with some assertions (provided by the framework) which test for some conditions to declare whether the test has failed or succeeded. Each function representing a unit test is added to an array or a structure, which is the test suite. Multiple test suites can also be created. Often there is one driver function to which these suites are passed and which then executes all the test cases.

7.4.2 Unit Testing of Classes

In object-oriented programs, the unit to be tested is usually an object of a class. Testing of objects can be defined as the process of exercising the routines provided by an object with the goal of uncovering errors in the implementation of the routines or state of the object or both [78].

To test a class, the programmer needs to create an object of that class, take the object to a particular state, invoke a method on it, and then check whether the state of the object is as expected. This sequence has to be executed many times for a method, and has to be performed for all the methods. All this is facilitated if we use frameworks like the Junit (www.junit.org). Though Junit itself is for Java, similar frameworks have been developed for other languages like C++ and C#. Here we briefly describe how Junit can be used for testing a class and give an example.

For testing of a class CUT (class under test) with Junit, the tester has to create another class which inherits from Junit (e.g., `class CUTtest extends Junit`). The Junit framework has to be imported by this class. This class is the driver for testing CUT. It must have a constructor in which the objects that are needed for the test cases are created; a setUp() method which is typically used for creating any objects and setting up values before executing a test case; a suite(), and a main () that executes the suite() using a TestRunner provided by Junit. Besides these methods, all other methods are actually test cases.

Most of these methods are often named `testxxxx()`. Such a method typically focuses on testing a method under some state (typically the name of the method and/or the state is contained in xxx). This method first sets up the state if not already setup (by setup()), and then executes the method to be tested. To check the results, Junit provides two special methods Assert-True(boolean_expression) and AssertFalse(boolean_expression). By using functions and having a logical expression on the state of the object, the tester can test if the state is correct or not. If all the assertions in all the methods succeed, then Junit declares that the test has passed. If any assert statements fail, Junit declares that testing has failed and specifies the assertion that has failed.

To get an idea of how it works, consider the testing of a class Matrix.java, which provides standard operations on matrices. The main attributes of the class and the main methods are given in Figure 7.3.

For unit testing the Matrix class, clearly we need to test standard operations like creation of a matrix, setting of values, etc. We also need to test whether the operations like add, subtract, multiply, determinant are performing as expected. Each test case we want to execute is programmed by setting the values and then performing the operation. The result of the operation is checked through the assert statements. For example, for testing add(), we create a method testAdd()

```
class Matrix {
    private double [][] matrix;  //Matrix elements
    private int row, col;        //Order of Matrix

    public Matrix(); // Constructor
    public Matrix(int i,int j); // Sets #rows and #cols
    public Matrix(int i,int j,double[][] a); // Sets from 2D array
    public Matrix(Matrix a); //Constructs matrix from another
    public void read(); //read elts from console and set up matrix
    public void setElement(int i,int j,double value); // set elt i,j
    public int noOfRows(); // returns no of rows
    public int noOfCols(); // returns no of cols
    public Matrix add(Matrix a); // adds a to matrix
    public Matrix sub(Matrix a); // subtracts a from matrix
    public Matrix mul(Matrix b); // multiplies b to matrix
    public Matrix transpose(); // transposes the matrix
    public Matrix minor(int a, int b); // returns a x b sub-matrix
    public double determinant(); // determinant of the matrix
    public Matrix inverse() throws Exception; // inverse of the matrix
    public void print(); // prints matrix on console
    public boolean equals(Matrix m); // checks for equality with m
}
```

Figure 7.3: Class Matrix.java.

in which a matrix is added to another. The correct result is stored a priori in another matrix. After addition, it is checked if the result obtained by performing add() is equal to the correct result. The method for this is shown in Figure 7.4. The programmer may want to perform more tests for add(), for which more test methods will be needed. Similarly, methods are written for testing other methods. Some of these tests are also shown in Figure 7.4.

As we can see, Junit encourages automated testing. Not only is the execution of test cases automated, the checking of the results is also automated. This makes running tests fully automatic. By building testing scripts, and continuously updating them as the class evolves, we always have a test script which can be run quickly. So, whenever we make any changes to the code, we can quickly check if the past test cases are running on the click of a button. This becomes almost essential if incremental coding or test-driven development (discussed earlier in the chapter) is to be practiced.

```
import junit.framework.*;
public class MatrixTest extends TestCase {

   Matrix A, B, C, D, E, res;          /* test matrices */

   public MatrixTest(String testcase)
   {
      super(testcase);

      double a[][]=new double[][]{{9,6},{7,5}};
      A = new Matrix(2,2,a);
      double b[][]=new double[][]{{16,21},{3,12}};
      B = new Matrix(2,2,b);
      double d[][]=new double[][]{{2,2,3},{4,8,6},{7,8,9}};
      res=new Matrix();
   }

   public void testAdd()
   {
      double c[][]=new double[][]{{25,27},{10,17}};
      C = new Matrix(2,2,c);
      res=A.add(B);
      assertTrue(res!=null);
      assertTrue(C.equals(res));
   }

   public void testSetGet()
   {
      C=new Matrix(2,2);
      for (int i=0;i<2;i++)
         for (int j=0;j<2;j++)
            C.setElement(i,j,A.getElement(i,j));
      assertTrue(C.equals(A));
   }

   public void testMul()
   {
      double c[][]=new double[][]{{162,261},{127,207}};
      C = new Matrix(2,2,c);
      res=A.mul(B);
      assertTrue(res!=null);
      assertTrue(C.equals(res));
   }
```

Figure 7.4: Testing the Matrix class with Junit.

```
public void testTranspose()
{
   res=A.transpose();
   res=res.transpose();
   assertTrue(res.equals(A));
}

public void testInverseCorrectness()
{
   try{
      res=null;
      res=A.inverse();
      res=res.mul(A);
      double dd[][]=new double[][]{{1,0},{0,1}};
      Matrix DD=new Matrix(2,2,dd);
      assertTrue(res.equals(DD));
   }
   catch (Exception e)
   {assertTrue(false);
   }
}
}
```

Figure 7.4: Testing the Matrix class with Junit (contd.).

7.5 Code Inspection

Code inspection is another technique that is often applied at the unit level. It can be viewed as "static testing" in which defects are detected in the code not by executing the code but through a manual process. Code inspection, unlike testing, is applied almost entirely at the unit level, i.e., only program units are subjected to inspection. Hence, we consider it as another form of unit testing. However, in practice, often both are employed, particularly for critical modules.

It should be pointed out that inspection is a general verification approach that can be applied for detecting defects in any document. However, it was first utilized for detecting defects in the code, and code inspections remain even today an industry best practice which is widely employed. Inspections have been found to help in improving not only quality but also productivity (see reports in [39, 44, 83]). Code inspections were first proposed by Fagan [31, 32]. Now there are books on the topic which describe in great detail how inspections should be conducted [37, 39].

Code inspection is a review of code by a group of peers following a clearly defined process. The basic goal of inspections is to improve the quality of code by finding defects. Some of the key characteristics of inspections are:

- Code inspection is conducted by programmers and for programmers.
- It is a structured process with defined roles for the participants.
- The focus is on identifying defects, not fixing them.
- Inspection data is recorded and used for monitoring the effectiveness of the inspection process.

Inspections are performed by a team of reviewers (or inspectors) including the author, with one of them being the *moderator*. The moderator has the overall responsibility to ensure that the review is done in a proper manner and all steps in the review process are followed. Most methods for inspections are similar with minor variations. Here we discuss the inspection process employed by a commercial organization [58]. The different stages in this process are: planning, self-review, group review meeting, and rework and follow-up. These stages are generally executed in a linear order. We discuss each of these phases now.

7.5.1 Planning

The objective of the planning phase is to prepare for inspection. An inspection team is formed, which should include the programmer whose code is to be reviewed. The team should consist of at least three people, though sometimes four-or-five member teams are also formed. A moderator is appointed.

The author of the code ensures that the code is ready for inspection and that the entry criteria are satisfied. Commonly used entry criteria are that the code compiles correctly and the available static analysis tools have been applied. The moderator checks that the entry criteria are satisfied by the code. A package is prepared that is to be distributed to the inspection team. The package typically consists of code to be inspected, the specifications for which the code was developed, and the checklist that should be used for inspection.

The package for review is given to the reviewers. The moderator may arrange an opening meeting, if needed, in which the author may provide a brief overview of the product and any special areas that need to be looked at carefully.

A checklist that should be used during the inspection may be prepared (or some ready checklist may be used). As the aim of code inspections is to improve quality, in addition to coding defects, there are other quality issues which code inspections usually look for, like efficiency, compliance to coding standards, etc. The type of defects the code inspection should focus on is contained in a checklist that is provided to the inspectors.

7.5.2 Self-Review

In this phase, each reviewer does a *self-review* of the code. During the self-review, a reviewer goes through the entire code and logs all the potential defects he or she finds in the *self-preparation log*. Often the reviewers will mark the defect on the work product itself, and may provide a summary of the self-review in the log. The reviewers also record the time they spent in the self-review. A standard form may be used for the self-preparation log; an example form is shown in Figure 7.5 [58].

Project name and code :			
Work product name and ID:			
Reviewer name:			
Effort spent for preparation (hrs):			
Defect List:			
No. hline	Location	Description	Criticality/Seriousness

Figure 7.5: Self-review log.

Ideally, the self-review should be done in one continuous time span. The recommended time is less than two hours—that is, the work product is small enough that it can be fully examined in less than two hours. This phase of the review process ends when all reviewers have properly performed their self-review and filled the self-review logs.

7.5.3 Group Review Meeting

The basic purpose of the group review meeting is to come up with the final defect list, based on the initial list of defects reported by the reviewers and the new ones found during the discussion in the meeting. The entry criterion for this step is that the moderator is satisfied that all the reviewers are ready for

Project	Xxxxxxxx
Work Product	Class AuctionItem
Size of Product	250 LOC of Java
Review Team	P1, P2, P3
Effort (Person-Hours)	
Preparation	Total 3 person-hrs.
Group Review Meeting	4.5 person-hrs.
Total Effort	**7.5 person-hrs.**
Defects	
Number of Major Defects	3
Number of Minor Defects	8
Total Number of defects	**11**
Review Status	Accepted
Recommendations for next phase	
Comments	Code quality can be improved

Figure 7.6: Summary report of an inspection.

the meeting. The main outputs of this phase are the defect log and the defect summary report.

The moderator first checks to see if all the reviewers are prepared. This is done by a brief examination of the effort and defect data in the self-review logs to confirm that sufficient time and attention has gone into the preparation. When preparation is not adequate, the group review is deferred until all participants are fully prepared.

If everything is ready, the group review meeting is held. The moderator is in charge of the meeting and has to make sure that the meeting stays focused on its basic purpose of defect identification and does not degenerate into a general brainstorming session or personal attacks on the author.

The meeting is conducted as follows. A team member (called the *reader*) goes over the code line by line (or any other convenient small unit), and paraphrases each line to the team. Sometimes no paraphrasing is done and the team just goes over the code line by line. At any line, if any reviewer has any issue from before, or finds any new issue in the meeting while listening to others, the reviewer raises the issue. There could be a discussion on the issue raised. The author accepts the issue as a defect or clarifies why it is not a defect. After discussion an agreement is reached and one member of the review team (called the *scribe*) records the identified defects in the defect log. At the end of the meeting, the scribe reads out the defects recorded in the defect log for a final review by the team members. Note that during the entire process of review, defects are only identified. It is not the purpose of the group to identify solutions—that is done later by the author.

The final defect log is the official record of the defects identified in the inspection and may also be used to track the defects to closure. For analyzing the effectiveness of an inspection, however, only summary-level information is needed, for which a *summary report* is prepared. The summary report describes the code, the total effort spent and its breakup in the different review process activities, total number of defects found for each category, and size. If types of defects were also recorded, then the number of defects in each category can also be recorded in the summary. A partially filled summary report is shown in Figure 7.6 [58].

The summary report is self-explanatory. Total number of minor defects found was 8, and the total number of major defects found was 3. That is, the defect density found is $8/0.250 = 32$ minor defects per KLOC, and $3/0.25 = 12$ major defects per KLOC. From experience, both of these rates are within the range seen in the past; hence it can be assumed that the review was conducted properly. The review team had 3 members, and each had spent about 1.5 hours in individual review and the review meeting lasted 1 hour. This means that the preparation rate was about 180 LOC per hour, and the group review rate was 250 LOC per hour, both of which, from past experience, also seem acceptable.

If the modifications required for fixing the defects and addressing the issues are few, then the group review status is "accepted." If the modifications required are many, a follow-up meeting by the moderator or a re-review might be necessary to verify whether the changes have been incorporated correctly. The moderator recommends what is to be done. In addition, recommendations regarding reviews in the next stages may also be made (e.g., in a detailed-design review it may be recommended code of which modules should undergo inspections).

7.6 Metrics

Traditionally, work on metrics has focused on the final product, namely, the code. In a sense, all metrics for intermediate products of requirements and design are basically used to ensure that the final product has a high quality and the productivity of the project stays high. That is, the basic goal of metrics for intermediate products is to predict or get some idea about the metrics of the final product. For the code, the most commonly used metrics are size and complexity. Here we discuss a few size and complexity measures.

7.6.1 Size Measures

Size of a product is a simple measure, which can be easy to calculate. The main reason for interest in size measures is that size is the major factor that affects the cost of a project. Size in itself is of little use; it is the relationship of size with the cost and quality that makes size an important metric. It is also used to measure productivity during the project (e.g., KLOC per person-month). Final quality delivered by a process is also frequently normalized with respect to size (number of defects per KLOC). For these reasons, size is one of the most important and frequently used metrics.

The most common measure of size is delivered lines of source code, or the number of lines of code (LOC) finally delivered. The trouble with LOC is that the number of lines of code for a project depends heavily on the language used. For example, a program written in assembly language will be large compared to the same program written in a higher-level language, if LOC is used as a size measure. Even for the same language, the size can vary considerably depending on how lines are counted. Despite these deficiencies, LOC remains a handy and reasonable size measure that is used extensively. Currently, perhaps the most widely used counting method for determining the size is to count noncomment, nonblank lines only.

Halstead [46] has proposed metrics for length and volume of a program based on the number of operators and operands. In a program we define the following measurable quantities:

− n_1 is the number of distinct operators

− n_2 is the number of distinct operands

− $f_{1,j}$ is the number of occurrences of the jth most frequent operator

− $f_{2,j}$ is the number of occurrences of the jth most frequent operand

Then the vocabulary n of a program is defined as

$$n = n_1 + n_2.$$

With the measurable parameters listed earlier, two new parameters are defined:

$$N_1 = \sum f_{1,j}, N_2 = \sum f_{2,j}.$$

N_1 is the total occurrences of different operators in the program and N_2 is the total occurrences of different operands. The length of the program is defined as

$$N = N_1 + N_2.$$

From the length and the vocabulary, the volume V of the program is defined as

$$V = N log_2(n).$$

This definition of the volume of a program represents the minimum number of bits necessary to represent the program. $log_2(n)$ is the number of bits needed to represent every element in the program uniquely, and N is the total occurrences of the different elements. Volume is used as a size metric for a program. Experiments have shown that the volume of a program is highly correlated with the size in LOC.

7.6.2 Complexity Metrics

The productivity, if measured only in terms of lines of code per unit time, can vary a lot depending on the complexity of the system to be developed. Clearly, a programmer will produce a lesser amount of code for highly complex system programs, as compared to a simple application program. Similarly, complexity has great impact on the cost of maintaining a program. To quantify complexity beyond the fuzzy notion of the ease with which a program can be constructed or comprehended, some metrics to measure the complexity of a program are needed.

A number of metrics have been proposed for quantifying the complexity of a program [47], and studies have been done to correlate the complexity with maintenance effort. Here we discuss a few of the complexity measures that have been proposed.

Cyclomatic Complexity   Based on the capability of the human mind and the experience of people, it is generally recognized that conditions and control statements add complexity to a program. Given two programs with the same size, the program with the larger number of decision statements is likely to be more complex. The simplest measure of complexity, then, is the number of constructs that represent branches in the control flow of the program, like `if then else`, `while do`, `repeat until`, and `goto` statements.

A more refined measure is the *cyclomatic complexity measure* proposed by McCabe, which is a graph-theoretic–based concept. For a graph G with n nodes, e edges, and p connected components, the cyclomatic number $V(G)$ is defined as

$$V(G) = e - n + p.$$

To use this to define the cyclomatic complexity of a module, the control flow graph G of the module is first drawn. To construct a control flow graph of a program module, break the module into blocks delimited by statements that affect the control flow, like if, while, repeat, and goto. These blocks form the nodes of the graph. If the control from a block i can branch to a block j, then draw an arc from node i to node j in the graph. The control flow of a program can be constructed mechanically. As an example, consider the C-like function for bubble sorting, given next. The control flow graph for this is given in Figure 7.7.

```
0. {
1.      i = 1;
2.      while (i <= n) {
3.              j = i;
4.              while (j <= i) {
5.                      if (A[i] < A[j])
6.                              swap(A[i], A[j]);
7.                      j = j + 1; }
8.      i = i + 1; }
9. }
```

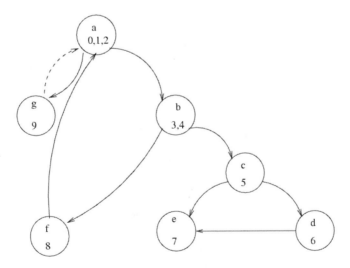

Figure 7.7: Flow graph of the example.

The graph of a module has an entry node and an exit node, corresponding to the first and last blocks of statements (or we can create artificial nodes for simplicity, as in the example). In such graphs there will be a path from the entry node to any node and a path from any node to the exit node (assuming the program has no anomalies like unreachable code). For such a graph, the cyclomatic number can be 0 if the code is a linear sequence of statements without any control statement. If we draw an arc from the exit node to the entry node, the graph will be strongly connected because there is a path between any two nodes. The cyclomatic number of a graph for any program will then be nonzero, and it is desirable to have a nonzero complexity for a simple program without any conditions (after all, there is some complexity in such a program). Hence, for computing the cyclomatic complexity of a program, an arc is added from the exit node to the start node, which makes it a strongly connected graph. For a module, the *cyclomatic complexity* is defined to be the cyclomatic number of such a graph for the module.

As it turns out the cyclomatic complexity of a module (or cyclomatic number of its graph) is equal to the maximum number of linearly independent circuits in the graph. A set of circuits is linearly independent if no circuit is totally contained in another circuit or is a combination of other circuits. So, for calculating the cyclomatic number of a module, we can draw the graph, make it connected by drawing an arc from the exit node to the entry node, and then either count the number of circuits or compute it by counting the number of edges and nodes. In the graph shown in Figure 7.7, the cyclomatic complexity is

$$V(G) = 10 - 7 + 1 = 4.$$

The independent circuits are

> ckt 1: b c e b
> ckt 2: b c d e b
> ckt 3: a b f a
> ckt 4: a g a

It can also be shown that the cyclomatic complexity of a module is the number of decisions in the module plus one, where a decision is effectively any conditional statement in the module [26]. Hence, we can also compute the cyclomatic complexity simply by counting the number of decisions in the module. For this example, as we can see, we get the same cyclomatic complexity for the module if we add 1 to the number of decisions in the module. (The module has three decisions: two in the two `while` statements and one in the `if` statement.)

The cyclomatic number is one quantitative measure of module complexity. It can be extended to compute the complexity of the whole program, though it is more suitable at the module level. McCabe proposed that the cyclomatic complexity of modules should, in general, be kept below 10. The cyclomatic number can also be used as a number of paths that should be tested during testing. Cyclomatic complexity is one of the most widely used complexity measures. Experiments indicate that the cyclomatic complexity is highly correlated to the size of the module in LOC (after all, the more lines of code the greater the number of decisions). It has also been found to be correlated to the number of faults found in modules.

Halstead's Measure   Halstead also proposed a number of other measures based on his software science [46]. Some of these can be considered complexity measures. As given earlier, a number of variables are defined in software science. These are n_1 (number of unique operators), n_2 (number of unique operands), N_1 (total frequency of operators), and N_2 (total frequency of operands). As any program must have at least two operators—one for function call and one for end of statement—the ratio $n_1/2$ can be considered the relative level of difficulty due to the larger number of operators in the program. The ratio N_2/n_2 represents the average number of times an operand is used. In a program in which variables are changed more frequently, this ratio will be larger. As such programs are harder to understand, *ease of reading or writing* is defined as

$$D = \frac{n_1 * N_2}{2 * n_2}.$$

Halstead's complexity measure focused on the internal complexity of a module, as does McCabe's complexity measure. Thus, the complexity of the module's connection with its environment is not given much importance. In Halstead's measure, a module's connection with its environment is reflected in terms of operands and operators. A call to another module is considered an operator, and all the parameters are considered operands of this operator.

Live Variables   In a computer program, a typical assignment statement uses and modifies only a few variables. However, in general the statements have a much larger context. That is, to construct or understand a statement, a programmer must keep track of a number of variables, other than those directly used in the statement. For a statement, such data items are called *live variables*. Intuitively, the more live variables for statements, the harder it will be to understand a program. Hence, the concept of live variables can be used as a metric for program complexity.

First let us define *live variables* more precisely. A variable is considered live from its first to its last reference within a module, including all statements between the first and last statement where the variable is referenced. Using this definition, the set of live variables for each statement can be computed easily by analysis of the module's code. The procedure of determining the live variables can easily be automated.

For a statement, the number of live variables represents the degree of difficulty of the statement. This notion can be extended to the entire module by defining the average number of live variables. The average number of live variables is the sum of the count of live variables (for all executable statements) divided by the number of executable statements. This is a complexity measure for the module.

Live variables are defined from the point of view of data usage. The logic of a module is not explicitly included. The logic is used only to determine the first and last statement of reference for a variable. Hence, this concept of complexity is quite different from cyclomatic complexity, which is based entirely on the logic and considers data as secondary.

Another data usage-oriented concept is *span*, the number of statements between two successive uses of a variable. If a variable is referenced at n different places in a module, then for that variable there are $(n - 1)$ spans. The average span size is the average number of executable statements between two successive references of a variable. A large span implies that the reader of the program has to remember a definition of a variable for a larger period of time (or for more statements). In other words, span can be considered a complexity measure; the larger the span, the more complex the module.

Knot Count   A method for quantifying complexity based on the locations of the control transfers of the program has been proposed in [85]. It was designed largely for FORTRAN programs, where explicit transfer of control is shown by the use of goto statements. A programmer, to understand a given program, typically draws arrows from the point of control transfer to its destination, helping to create a mental picture of the program and the control transfers in it. According to this metric, the more intertwined these arrows become, the more complex the program. This notion is captured in the concept of a "knot."

A *knot* is essentially the intersection of two such control transfer arrows. If each statement in the program is written on a separate line, this notion can be formalized as follows. A jump from line a to line b is represented by the pair (a, b). Two jumps (a, b) and (p, q) give rise to a knot if either min (a, b) < min (p, q) < max (a, b) and max (p, q) > max (a, b); or min (a, b) < max (p, qa) < max (a, b) and min (p, q) < min (a, b).

Problems can arise while determining the knot count of programs using structured constructs. One method is to convert such a program into one that explicitly shows control transfers and then compute the knot count. The basic scheme can be generalized to flow graphs, though with flow graphs only bounds can be obtained.

Topological Complexity   A complexity measure that is sensitive to the nesting of structures has been proposed in [20]. Like cyclomatic complexity, it is based on the flow graph of a module or program. The complexity of a program is considered its maximal intersect number *min*.

To compute the maximal intersect, a flow graph is converted into a strongly connected graph (by drawing an arrow from the terminal node to the initial node). A strongly connected graph divides the graph into a finite number of regions. The number of regions is (edges − nodes + 2). If we draw a line that enters each region exactly once, then the number of times this line intersects the arcs in the graph is the maximal intersect *min*, which is taken to be the complexity of the program.

7.7 Summary

- As reading programs is a much more common activity than writing programs, the goal of the coding activity is to produce programs that are, besides being free of defects, easy to understand and modify.

- Use of structured programming in which the program is a sequence of suitable single-entry single-exit constructs makes programs easy to understand and verify. Other practices like using information hiding, suitable coding standards, and good programming practices also help improve code readability and quality.

- For a developer, it is most effective to develop code incrementally. This can be done by writing code in small increments, and testing and debugging each increment before writing more code. Alternatively, test-driven development may be followed in which test cases are written first and then code is written to pass these test cases. Though coding of a module is generally done by individual programmers, an alternative is pair programming, in which coding is done by a pair of programmers—both together evolving strategies, data structures, algorithms etc.

- Evolving code needs to be properly managed. This can be done through proper source code control tools which allow easy management of the different versions that get created, as well as easy undoing of changes that need to be rolled back.

- As code changes with time, to ensure that the code quality does not continue to degrade due to evolution, refactoring may be done. During refactoring no new functionality is added—only improvement is done so that the design of the code improves by reduction of coupling, increase in cohesion, and better use of hierarchies.

— Unit testing is a very popular and most often used practice by programmers for verifying the code they have written. In unit testing, the programmer tests his/her code in isolation. For procedural languages this is often a small set of procedures or functions, and for object-oriented languages this is generally a class or a small set of classes. Unit testing requires drivers and stubs, and can be facilitated by the use of frameworks which allow automated test script execution. Good frameworks like CUnit and Junit exist for both procedural languages and object-oriented languages.

— A number of metrics exist for quantifying different qualities of code. The most commonly used are size metrics, because they are used to assess the productivity of people and are often used in cost estimation. The most common size measure is lines of code (LOC), which is also used in most cost models. The goal of complexity metrics is to quantify the complexity of software, as complexity is an important factor affecting the productivity of projects and is a factor in cost estimation. A number of different metrics exist, most common being the cyclomatic complexity, which is based on the internal logic of the program and defines complexity as the number of independent cycles in the flow graph of the program.

Self-Assessment Exercises

1. What is structured programming and how does it help improve code readability?

2. How does the use of information hiding and coding standards help improve the readability?

3. Suggest some possibilities on how TDD will function if programming is being done in pairs.

4. Write a class/procedure using TDD (and some testing framework). Have another programmer do the same using the incremental code first approach. Then compare the code for the class/procedure with respect to size of the code, effort required, and the number of test cases used.

5. Consider the code for a class. Describe two situations for this code which will suggest to you that refactoring may be desired. For each of these, suggest the nature of refactoring that you will perform.

6. What is the role of testing frameworks and automated scripts in refactoring?

7. Use your favorite unit testing framework and use it to unit test a procedure/class which requires at least one other procedure/classe.

8. Give a flowchart describing the code inspection process.

9. Write some rules for evaluating the summary report of a code review.

10. Consider the following two algorithms for searching an element E in a sorted array A, which contains n integers. The first procedure implements a simple linear search algorithm. The second performs a binary search. Binary search is generally much more efficient in terms of execution time compared to the linear search.

```
function lin_search (A, E): boolean
var
        i : integer;
        found: boolean;
begin
        found := false;
        i := 1;
        while (not found) and (i ≤ n) do begin
        if (A[i] = E) then found := true;
        i := i + 1;
        end;
        lin_search := found;
end;


function bin_search (A, E): boolean
var
        low, high, mid, i, j : integer;
        found : boolean;
begin
        low := 1;
        high := n;
        found := false;
        while (low ≤ high) and (not found) do begin
                mid := (low + high)/2;
                if E < A[mid] then high := mid - 1
                        else if E > A[mid] then low := mid + 1
                        else found := true;
        end;
        bin_search := found;
end;
```

Determine the cyclomatic complexity and live variable complexity for these two functions. Is the ratio of the two complexity measures similar for the two functions?

11. What is Halstead's size measure for these two modules? Compare this size with the size measured in LOC.

8
Testing

In a software development project, errors can be introduced at any stage during development. Though errors are detected after each phase by techniques like inspections, some errors remain undetected. Ultimately, these remaining errors are reflected in the code. Hence, the final code is likely to have some requirements errors and design errors, in addition to errors introduced during the coding activity. To ensure quality of the final delivered software, these defects will have to be removed.

There are two types of approaches for identifying defects in the software— static and dynamic. In static analysis, the code is not executed but is evaluated through some process or some tools for locating defects. Code inspections, which we discussed in the previous chapter, is one static approach. Another is static analysis of code through the use of tools. In dynamic analysis, code is executed, and the execution is used for determining defects. Testing is the most common dynamic technique that is employed. Indeed, testing is the most commonly used technique for detecting defects, and performs a very critical role for ensuring quality.

During testing, the software under test (SUT) is executed with a finite set of test cases, and the behavior of the system for these test cases is evaluated to determine if the system is performing as expected. The basic purpose of testing is to increase the confidence in the functioning of SUT. And as testing is extremely expensive and can consume unlimited amount of effort, an additional practical goal is to achieve the desired confidence as efficiently as possible. Clearly, the effectiveness and efficiency of testing depends critically on the test cases selected. Much of this chapter therefore is devoted to test case selection.

P. Jalote, *A Concise Introduction to Software Engineering*,
DOI: 10.1007/978-1-84800-302-6_8, © Springer-Verlag London Limited 2008

In this chapter we will discuss:

— Basic concepts and definitions relating to testing, like error, fault, failure, test case, test suite, test harness, etc.

— The testing process—how testing is planned and how testing of a unit is done.

— Test case selection using black-box testing approaches.

— Test case selection using white-box approaches.

— Some metrics like coverage and reliability that can be employed during testing.

8.1 Testing Concepts

In this section we will first define some of the terms that are commonly used when discussing testing. Then we will discuss some basic issues relating to how testing is performed, and the importance of psychology of the tester.

8.1.1 Error, Fault, and Failure

While discussing testing we commonly use terms like *error, fault, failure* etc. Let us start by defining these concepts clearly [52].

The term *error* is used in two different ways. It refers to the discrepancy between a computed, observed, or measured value and the true, specified, or theoretically correct value. That is, error refers to the difference between the actual output of a software and the correct output. In this interpretation, error is essentially a measure of the difference between the actual and the ideal. Error is also used to refer to human action that results in software containing a defect or fault. This definition is quite general and encompasses all the phases.

Fault is a condition that causes a system to fail in performing its required function. A fault is the basic reason for software malfunction and is practically synonymous with the commonly used term *bug*, or the somewhat more general term *defect*. The term *error* is also often used to refer to defects (taking a variation of the second definition of error). In this book we will continue to use the terms in the manner commonly used, and no explicit distinction will be made between errors and faults, unless necessary.

Failure is the inability of a system or component to perform a required function according to its specifications. A software failure occurs if the behavior of the software is different from the specified behavior. Failures may be caused by functional or performance factors. Note that the definition does not imply that a failure must be *observed*. It is possible that a failure may occur but not be detected.

There are some implications of these definitions. Presence of an error (in the state) implies that a failure must have occurred, and the observance of a failure implies that a fault must be present in the system. However, the presence of a fault does not imply that a failure must occur. The presence of a fault in a system only implies that the fault has a *potential* to cause a failure. Whether a fault actually manifests itself in a certain time duration depends on how the software is executed.

There are direct consequences of this on testing. If during testing we do not observe any errors, we cannot say anything about the presence or absence of faults in the system. If, on the other hand, we observe some failure, we can say that there are some faults in the system. This relationship of fault and failure makes the task of selecting test cases for testing very challenging—an objective while selecting test cases is to select those that will reveal the defect, if it exists. Ideally we would like the set of test cases to be such that if there are any defects in the system, some test case in the set will reveal it—something impossible to achieve in most situations.

It should be noted that during the testing process, only failures are observed, by which the presence of faults is deduced. That is, testing only reveals the presence of faults. The actual faults are identified by separate activities, commonly referred to as "debugging." In other words, for identifying faults, after testing has revealed the presence of faults, the expensive task of debugging has to be performed. This is one of the reasons why testing is an expensive method for identification of faults.

8.1.2 Test Case, Test Suite, and Test Harness

So far we have used the terms *test case* or *set of test cases* informally. Let us define them more precisely. A *test case* (often called a *test*) can be considered as comprising a set of test inputs and execution conditions, which are designed to exercise the SUT in a particular manner [52]. Generally, a test case also specifies the expected outcome from executing the SUT under the specified execution conditions and test inputs. A group of related test cases that are generally executed together to test some specific behavior or aspect of the SUT is often referred to as a *test suite*.

Note that in a test case, test inputs and execution conditions are mentioned separately. Test inputs are the specific values of parameters or other inputs that

are given to the SUT either by the user or some other program. The execution
conditions, on the other hand, reflect the state of the system and environment
which also impact the behavior of the SUT. So, for example, while testing
a function to add a record in the database if it does not already exist, the
behavior of the function will depend both on the value of the input record as
well as the state of the database. And a test case needs to specify both. For
example, a test case for this function might specify a record r as input, and
might specify that the state of the database be such that r already exists in it.

Testing can be done manually with the tester executing the test cases in the
test suite and then checking if the behavior is as specified in the test cases. This
is a very cumbersome process, particularly when the test suite contains a large
number of test cases. It becomes even more cumbersome since the test suite
often has to be executed every time the SUT is changed. Hence, the current
trend is to automate testing.

With automated testing, a test case is typically a function call (or a method
invocation), which does all the activities of a test case—it sets the test data
and the test conditions, invokes the SUT as per the test case, compares the
results returned with expected results, and declares to the tester whether the
SUT failed or passed the test case. In other words, with automated testing,
executing a test case essentially means executing this function. A test suite
will then be a set of such functions, each representing a test case. To test a
SUT with the test suite, generally an automated test script will be written
which will invoke the test cases in the desired sequence.

To have a test suite executed automatically, we will need a framework in
which test inputs can be defined, defined inputs can be used by functions
representing test cases, the automated test script can be written, the SUT
can be executed by this script, and the result of entire testing reported to the
tester. Many *testing frameworks* now exist that permit all this to be done in a
simple manner. A testing framework is also sometimes called a *test harness*. A
test harness or a test framework makes the life of a tester simpler by providing
easy means of defining a test suite, executing it, and reporting the results.
With a test framework, a test suite is defined once, and then whenever needed,
complete testing can be done by the click of a button or giving a command.

8.1.3 Psychology of Testing

As mentioned, in testing, the software under test (SUT) is executed with a
set of test cases. As discussed, devising a set of test cases that will guarantee
that all errors will be detected is not feasible. Moreover, there are no formal
or precise methods for selecting test cases. Even though there are a number of

heuristics and rules of thumb for deciding the test cases, selecting test cases is still a creative activity that relies on the ingenuity of the tester. Because of this, the psychology of the person performing the testing becomes important.

A basic purpose of testing is to detect the errors that may be present in the program. Hence, one should not start testing with the intent of showing that a program works; rather the intent should be to show that a program does not work; to reveal any defect that may exist. Due to this, testing has also been defined as the process of executing a program with the intent of finding errors [68].

This emphasis on proper intent of testing is not a trivial matter because test cases are designed by human beings, and human beings have a tendency to perform actions to achieve the goal they have in mind. So, if the goal is to demonstrate that a program works, we may consciously or subconsciously select test cases that will try to demonstrate that goal and that will beat the basic purpose of testing. On the other hand, if the intent is to show that the program does not work, we will challenge our intellect to find test cases toward that end, and we are likely to detect more errors. Testing is essentially a destructive process, where the tester has to treat the program as an adversary that must be beaten by the tester by showing the presence of errors. This is one of the reasons why many organizations employ *independent testing* in which testing is done by a team that was not involved in building the system.

8.1.4 Levels of Testing

Testing is usually relied upon to detect the faults remaining from earlier stages, in addition to the faults introduced during coding itself. Due to this, different levels of testing are used in the testing process; each level of testing aims to test different aspects of the system.

The basic levels are unit testing, integration testing, system testing, and acceptance testing. These different levels of testing attempt to detect different types of faults. The relation of the faults introduced in different phases, and the different levels of testing are shown in Figure 8.1.

The first level of testing is called *unit testing*, which we discussed in the previous chapter. Unit testing is essentially for verification of the code produced by individual programmers, and is typically done by the programmer of the module. Generally, a module is offered by a programmer for integration and use by others only after it has been unit tested satisfactorily.

The next level of testing is often called *integration testing*. In this, many unit tested modules are combined into subsystems, which are then tested. The goal here is to see if the modules can be integrated properly. Hence, the emphasis is

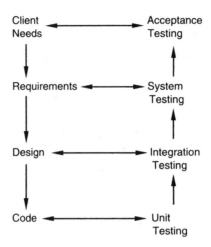

Figure 8.1: Levels of testing.

on testing interfaces between modules. This testing activity can be considered testing the design.

The next levels are *system testing* and *acceptance testing*. Here the entire software system is tested. The reference document for this process is the requirements document, and the goal is to see if the software meets its requirements. This is often a large exercise, which for large projects may last many weeks or months. This is essentially a validation exercise, and in many situations it is the only validation activity. Acceptance testing is often performed with realistic data of the client to demonstrate that the software is working satisfactorily. It may be done in the setting in which the software is to eventually function. Acceptance testing essentially tests if the system satisfactorily solves the problems for which it was commissioned.

These levels of testing are performed when a system is being built from the components that have been coded. There is another level of testing, called *regression testing*, that is performed when some changes are made to an existing system. We know that changes are fundamental to software; any software must undergo changes. However, when modifications are made to an existing system, testing also has to be done to make sure that the modification has not had any undesired side effect of making some of the earlier services faulty. That is, besides ensuring the desired behavior of the new services, testing has to ensure that the desired behavior of the old services is maintained. This is the task of regression testing.

For regression testing, some test cases that have been executed on the old system are maintained, along with the output produced by the old system. These test cases are executed again on the modified system and its output compared with the earlier output to make sure that the system is working as before on these test cases. This frequently is a major task when modifications are to be made to existing systems.

Complete regression testing of large systems can take a considerable amount of time, even if automation is used. If a small change is made to the system, often practical considerations require that the entire test suite not be executed, but regression testing be done with only a subset of test cases. This requires suitably selecting test cases from the suite which can test those parts of the system that could be affected by the change. Test case selection for regression testing is an active research area and many different approaches have been proposed in the literature for this. We will not discuss it any further.

8.2 Testing Process

The basic goal of the software development process is to produce software that has no errors or very few errors. Testing is a quality control activity which focuses on identifying defects (which are then removed). We have seen that different levels of testing are needed to detect the defects injected during the various tasks in the project. And at a level multiple SUTs may be tested. And for testing each SUT, test cases will have to be designed and then executed. Overall, testing in a project is a complex task which also consumes the maximum effort. Hence, testing has to be done properly in a project. The testing process for a project consists of three high-level tasks—test planning, test case design, and test execution. We will discuss these in the rest of this section.

8.2.1 Test Plan

In general, in a project, testing commences with a *test plan* and terminates with successful execution of acceptance testing. A test plan is a general document for the entire project that defines the scope, approach to be taken, and the schedule of testing, as well as identifies the test items for testing and the personnel responsible for the different activities of testing. The test planning can be done well before the actual testing commences and can be done in parallel with the coding and design activities. The inputs for forming the test plan are: (1) project plan, (2) requirements document, and (3) architecture or design document. The project plan is needed to make sure that the test plan is consistent with the overall quality plan for the project and the testing schedule matches that of the project plan. The requirements document and the design document are the basic documents used for selecting the test units and deciding the approaches to be used during testing. A test plan should contain the following:

— Test unit specification

— Features to be tested

— Approach for testing

— Test deliverables

— Schedule and task allocation

As seen earlier, different levels of testing have to be performed in a project. The levels are specified in the test plan by identifying the test units for the project. A test unit is a set of one or more modules that form a software under test (SUT). The identification of test units establishes the different levels of testing that will be performed in the project. Generally, a number of test units are formed during the testing, starting from the lower-level modules, which have to be unit-tested. That is, first the modules that have to be tested individually are specified as test units. Then the higher-level units are specified, which may be a combination of already tested units or may combine some already tested units with some untested modules. The basic idea behind forming test units is to make sure that testing is being performed incrementally, with each increment including only a few aspects that need to be tested.

An important factor while forming a unit is the "testability" of a unit. A unit should be such that it can be easily tested. In other words, it should be possible to form meaningful test cases and execute the unit without much effort with these test cases. For example, a module that manipulates the complex data structure formed from a file input by an input module might not be a suitable unit from the point of view of testability, as forming meaningful test cases for the unit will be hard, and driver routines will have to be written to convert inputs from files or terminals that are given by the tester into data structures suitable for the module. In this case, it might be better to form the unit by including the input module as well. Then the file input expected by the input module can contain the test cases.

Features to be tested include all software features and combinations of features that should be tested. A software feature is a software characteristic specified or implied by the requirements or design documents. These may include functionality, performance, design constraints, and attributes.

The *approach* for testing specifies the overall approach to be followed in the current project. The techniques that will be used to judge the testing effort should also be specified. This is sometimes called the *testing criterion* or the criterion for evaluating the set of test cases used in testing. In the previous sections we discussed many criteria for evaluating and selecting test cases.

Testing deliverables should be specified in the test plan before the actual testing begins. Deliverables could be a list of test cases that were used, detailed results of testing including the list of defects found, test summary report, and data about the code coverage.

The test plan typically also specifies the schedule and effort to be spent on different activities of testing, and the tools to be used. This schedule should be consistent with the overall project schedule. The detailed plan may list all the testing tasks and allocate them to *test resources* who are responsible for performing them. Many large products have separate testing teams and therefore a separate test plan. A smaller project may include the test plan as part of its quality plan in the project management plan.

8.2.2 Test Case Design

The test plan focuses on how the testing for the project will proceed, which units will be tested, and what approaches (and tools) are to be used during the various stages of testing. However, it does not deal with the details of testing a unit, nor does it specify which test cases are to be used.

Test case design has to be done separately for each unit. Based on the approach specified in the test plan, and the features to be tested, the test cases are designed and specified for testing the unit. Test case specification gives, for each unit to be tested, all test cases, inputs to be used in the test cases, conditions being tested by the test case, and outputs expected for those test cases. If test cases are specified in a document, the specifications look like a table of the form shown in Figure 8.2.

Requirement Number	Condition to be tested	Test data and settings	Expected output

Figure 8.2: Test case specifications.

Sometimes, a few columns are also provided for recording the outcome of different rounds of testing. That is, sometimes the test case specifications document is also used to record the result of testing. In a round of testing, the outcome of all the test cases is recorded (i.e., pass or fail). Hopefully, in a few rounds all test cases will pass.

With testing frameworks and automated testing, the testing scripts can be considered as test case specifications, as they clearly show what inputs are being given and what output to expect. With suitable comments, the intent of the test case can also be easily specified.

Test case design is a major activity in the testing process. Careful selection of test cases that satisfy the criterion and approach specified is essential for proper testing. We will later consider different techniques for designing good test cases.

There are some good reasons why test cases are specified before they are used for testing. It is known that testing has severe limitations and the effectiveness of testing depends very heavily on the exact nature of the test cases. It is therefore important to ensure that the set of test cases used is of high quality. Evaluation of test cases is often done through test case review. As for any review, a formal document or work product is needed, for review of test cases, the test case specification document is required. This is the primary reason for documenting the test cases. The test case specification document is reviewed, using a formal review process, to make sure that the test cases are consistent with the policy specified in the plan, satisfy the chosen criterion, and cover the various aspects of the unit to be tested. By reviewing the conditions being tested by the test cases, the reviewers can also check if all the important conditions are being tested.

Another reason for specifying the test cases in a document or a script is that by doing this, the tester can see the testing of the unit in totality and the effect of the total set of test cases. This type of evaluation is hard to do in on-the-fly testing where test cases are determined as testing proceeds. It also allows optimizing the number of test cases as evaluation of the test suite may show that some test cases are redundant.

8.2.3 Test Case Execution

With the specification of test cases, the next step in the testing process is to execute them. This step is also not straightforward. The test case specifications only specify the set of test cases for the unit to be tested. However, executing the test cases may require construction of driver modules or stubs. It may also require modules to set up the environment as stated in the test plan and test case specifications. Only after all these are ready can the test cases be executed.

If test frameworks are being used, then the setting of the environment as well as inputs for a test case is already done in the test scripts, and execution is straightforward.

During test case execution, defects are found. These defects are then fixed and tesing is done again to verify the fix. To facilitate reporting and tracking of defects found during testing (and other quality control activities), defects found are often logged. Defect logging is particularly important in a large software project which may have hundreds or thousands of defects that are found by different people at different stages of the project. Often the person who fixes a defect is not the person who finds or reports the defect. For example, a tester may find the defect while the developer of the code may actually fix it. In such a scenario, defect reporting and closing cannot be done informally. The use of informal mechanisms may easily lead to defects being found but later forgotten, resulting in defects not getting removed or in extra effort in finding the defect again. Hence, defects found must be properly logged in a system and their closure tracked. Defect logging and tracking is considered one of the best practices for managing a project [17], and is followed by most software organizations.

Let us understand the life cycle of a defect. A defect can be found by anyone at anytime. When a defect is found, it is logged in a defect control system, along with sufficient information about the defect. The defect is then in the state "submitted," essentially implying that it has been logged along with information about it. The job of fixing the defect is then assigned to some person, who is generally the author of the document or code in which the defect is found. The assigned person does the debugging and fixes the reported defect, and the defect then enters the "fixed" state. However, a defect that is fixed is still not considered as fully done. The successful fixing of the defect is verified. This verification may be done by another person (often the submitter), or by a test team, and typically involves running some tests. Once the defect fixing is verified, then the defect can be marked as "closed." In other words, the general life cycle of a defect has three states—submitted, fixed, and closed, as shown in Figure 8.3. A defect that is not closed is also called open.

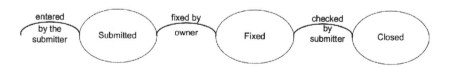

Figure 8.3: Life cycle of a defect.

This is a typical life cycle of a defect which is used in many organizations (e.g., [58]). Ideally, at the end of the project, no open defects should remain. However, this ideal situation is often not practical for most large systems. Besides using the log for tracking defects, the data in the log can also be used for analysis purposes. We will discuss some possible analysis later in the chapter.

8.3 Black-Box Testing

As we have seen, good test case design is the key to suitable testing of the SUT. The goal while testing a SUT is to detect most (hopefully all) of the defects, through as small a set of test cases as possible. Due to this basic goal, it is important to select test cases carefully—best are those test cases that have a high probability of detecting a defect, if it exists, and also whose execution will give a confidence that no failures during testing implies that there are few (hopefully none) defects in the software.

There are two basic approaches to designing the test cases to be used in testing: black-box and white-box. In black-box testing the structure of the program is not considered. Test cases are decided solely on the basis of the requirements or specifications of the program or module, and the internals of the module or the program are not considered for selection of test cases. In this section, we will present some techniques for generating test cases for black-box testing. White-box testing is discussed in the next section.

In black-box testing, the tester only knows the inputs that can be given to the system and what output the system should give. In other words, the basis for deciding test cases is the requirements or specifications of the system or module. This form of testing is also called functional or behavioral testing.

The most obvious functional testing procedure is exhaustive testing, which is impractical. One criterion for generating test cases is to generate them randomly. This strategy has little chance of resulting in a set of test cases that is close to optimal (i.e., that detects the maximum errors with minimum test cases). Hence, we need some other criterion or rule for selecting test cases. There are no formal rules for designing test cases for functional testing. However, there are a number of techniques or heuristics that can be used to select test cases that have been found to be very successful in detecting errors. Here we mention some of these techniques.

8.3.1 Equivalence Class Partitioning

Because we cannot do exhaustive testing, the next natural approach is to divide the input domain into a set of equivalence classes, so that if the program works correctly for a value, then it will work correctly for all the other values in that class. If we can indeed identify such classes, then testing the program with one value from each equivalence class is equivalent to doing an exhaustive test of the program.

However, without looking at the internal structure of the program, it is impossible to determine such ideal equivalence classes (even with the internal structure, it usually cannot be done). The equivalence class partitioning method [68] tries to approximate this ideal. An equivalence class is formed of the inputs for which the behavior of the system is specified or expected to be similar. Each group of inputs for which the behavior is expected to be different from others is considered a separate equivalence class. The rationale of forming equivalence classes like this is the assumption that if the specifications require the same behavior for each element in a class of values, then the program is likely to be constructed so that it either succeeds or fails for each of the values in that class. For example, the specifications of a module that determines the absolute value for integers specify one behavior for positive integers and another for negative integers. In this case, we will form two equivalence classes—one consisting of positive integers and the other consisting of negative integers.

For robust software, we must also consider invalid inputs. That is, we should define equivalence classes for invalid inputs also.

Equivalence classes are usually formed by considering each condition specified on an input as specifying a valid equivalence class and one or more invalid equivalence classes. For example, if an input condition specifies a range of values (say, $0 <$ count $<$ Max), then form a valid equivalence class with that range and two invalid equivalence classes, one with values less than the lower bound of the range (i.e., count < 0) and the other with values higher than the higher bound (count $>$ Max). If the input specifies a set of values and the requirements specify different behavior for different elements in the set, then a valid equivalence class is formed for each of the elements in the set and an invalid class for an entity not belonging to the set.

One common approach for determining equivalence classes is as follows. If there is reason to believe that the entire range of an input will not be treated in the same manner, then the range should be split into two or more equivalence classes, each consisting of values for which the behavior is expected to be similar. For example, for a character input, if we have reasons to believe that the program will perform different actions if the character is a letter, a number, or a special character, then we should split the input into three valid equivalence classes.

Another approach for forming equivalence classes is to consider any special value for which the behavior could be different as an equivalence class. For example, the value 0 could be a special value for an integer input.

Also, for each valid equivalence class, one or more invalid equivalence classes should be identified.

It is often useful to consider equivalence classes in the output. For an output equivalence class, the goal is to have inputs such that the output for that test case lies in the output equivalence class. As an example, consider a program for determining rate of return for some investment. There are three clear output equivalence classes—positive rate of return, negative rate of return, and zero rate of return. During testing, it is important to test for each of these, that is, give inputs such that each of these three outputs is generated. Determining test cases for output classes may be more difficult, but output classes have been found to reveal errors that are not revealed by just considering the input classes.

Once equivalence classes are selected for each of the inputs, then the issue is to select test cases suitably. There are different ways to select the test cases. One strategy is to select each test case covering as many valid equivalence classes as it can, and one separate test case for each invalid equivalence class. A somewhat better strategy which requires more test cases is to have a test case cover at most one valid equivalence class for each input, and have one separate test case for each invalid equivalence class. In the latter case, the number of test cases for valid equivalence classes is equal to the largest number of equivalence classes for any input, plus the total number of invalid equivalence classes.

As an example, consider a program that takes two inputs—a string s of length up to N and an integer n. The program is to determine the top n highest occurring characters in s. The tester believes that the programmer may deal with different types of characters separately. One set of valid and invalid equivalence classes for this is shown in Table 8.1.

Table 8.1: Valid and invalid equivalence classes.

Input	Valid Equivalence Classes	Invalid Equivalence Classes
s	EQ1: Contains numbers EQ2: Contains lowercase letters EQ3: Contains uppercase letters EQ4: Contains special characters EQ5: String length between 0-N	IEQ1: non-ASCII characters IEQ2: String length > N
n	EQ6: Integer in valid range	IEQ3: Integer out of range

With these as the equivalence classes, we have to select the test cases. A test case for this is a pair of values for s and n. With the first strategy for deciding test cases, one test case could be: s as a string of length less than N containing lowercase, uppercase, numbers, and special characters; and n as the number 5. This one test case covers all the valid equivalence classes (EQ1 through EQ6). Then we will have one test case each for covering IEQ1, IEQ2, and IEQ3. That is, a total of four test cases is needed.

With the second approach, in one test case we can cover one equivalence class for one input only. So, one test case could be: a string of numbers, and the number 5. This covers EQ1 and EQ6. Then we will need test cases for EQ2 through EQ5, and separate test cases for IEQ1 through IEQ3.

8.3.2 Boundary Value Analysis

It has been observed that programs that work correctly for a set of values in an equivalence class fail on some special values. These values often lie on the boundary of the equivalence class. Test cases that have values on the boundaries of equivalence classes are therefore likely to be "high-yield" test cases, and selecting such test cases is the aim of boundary value analysis. In boundary value analysis [68], we choose an input for a test case from an equivalence class, such that the input lies at the edge of the equivalence classes. Boundary values for each equivalence class, including the equivalence classes of the output, should be covered. Boundary value test cases are also called "extreme cases." Hence, we can say that a boundary value test case is a set of input data that lies on the edge or boundary of a class of input data or that generates output that lies at the boundary of a class of output data.

In case of ranges, for boundary value analysis it is useful to select the boundary elements of the range and an invalid value just beyond the two ends (for the two invalid equivalence classes). So, if the range is $0.0 \leq x \leq 1.0$, then the test cases are 0.0, 1.0 (valid inputs), and -0.1, and 1.1 (for invalid inputs). Similarly, if the input is a list, attention should be focused on the first and last elements of the list.

We should also consider the outputs for boundary value analysis. If an equivalence class can be identified in the output, we should try to generate test cases that will produce the output that lies at the boundaries of the equivalence classes. Furthermore, we should try to form test cases that will produce an output that does not lie in the equivalence class. (If we can produce an input case that produces the output outside the equivalence class, we have detected an error.)

Like in equivalence class partitioning, in boundary value analysis we first

determine values for each of the variables that should be exercised during testing. If there are multiple inputs, then how should the set of test cases be formed
covering the boundary values? Suppose each input variable has a defined range.
Then there are six boundary values—the extreme ends of the range, just beyond the ends, and just before the ends. If an integer range is min to max,
then the six values are $min-1, min, min+1, max-1, max, max+1$. Suppose
there are n such input variables. There are two strategies for combining the
boundary values for the different variables in test cases.

In the first strategy, we select the different boundary values for one variable,
and keep the other variables at some nominal value. And we select one test case
consisting of nominal values of all the variables. In this case, we will have $6n+1$
test cases. For two variables X and Y, the 13 test cases will be as shown in
Figure 8.4.

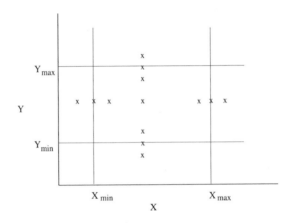

Figure 8.4: Test cases for boundary value analysis.

Another strategy would be to try all possible combinations for the values for
the different variables. As there are seven values for each variable (six boundary
values and one nominal value), if there are n variables, there will be a total of
7^n test cases—too large for practical testing.

8.3.3 Pairwise Testing

There are generally many parameters that determine the behavior of a software
system. These parameters could be direct input to the software or implicit
settings like those for devices. These parameters can take different values, and
for some of them the software may not work correctly. Many of the defects in
software generally involve one condition, that is, some special value of one of the

parameters. Such a defect is called a single-mode fault [70]. Simple examples of single-mode faults are a software not able to print for a particular type of printer, a software that cannot compute fare properly when the traveler is a minor, and a telephone billing software that does not compute the bill properly for a particular country.

Single-mode faults can be detected by testing for different values of different parameters. So, if there are n parameters for a system, and each one of them can take m different values (or m different classes of values, each class being considered as the same for purposes of testing as in equivalence class partitioning), then with each test case we can test one different value of each parameter. In other words, we can test for all the different values in m test cases.

However, all faults are not single-mode and there are combinations of inputs that reveal the presence of faults: for example, a telephone billing software that does not compute correctly for nighttime calling (one parameter) to a particular country (another parameter), or an airline ticketing system that has incorrect behavior when a minor (one parameter) is traveling business class (another parameter) and not staying over the weekend (third parameter). These multimode faults can be revealed during testing by trying different combinations of the parameter values—an approach called *combinatorial testing*.

Unfortunately, full combinatorial testing is often not feasible. For a system with n parameters, each having m values, the number of different combinations is n^m. For a simple system with 5 parameters, each having 5 different values, the total number of combinations is 3,125. And if testing each combination takes 5 minutes, it will take over 1 month to test all combinations. Clearly, for complex systems that have many parameters and each parameter may have many values, a full combinatorial testing is not feasible and practical techniques are needed to reduce the number of tests.

Some research has suggested that most software faults are revealed on some special single values or by interaction of a pair of values [25]. That it, most faults tend to be either single-mode or double-mode. For testing for double-mode faults, we need not test the system with all the combinations of parameter values, but need to test such that all combinations of values for each pair of parameters are exercised. This is called *pairwise testing*.

In pairwise testing, all pairs of values have to be exercised during testing. If there are n parameters, each with m values, then between each two parameter we have $m * m$ pairs. The first parameter will have these many pairs with each of the remaining $n - 1$ parameters, the second one will have new pairs with $n - 2$ parameters (as its pairs with the first are already included in the first parameter pairs), the third will have pairs with $n - 3$ parameters, and so on. That is, the total number of pairs is $m * m * n * (n - 1)/2$.

The objective of pairwise testing is to have a set of test cases that cover all the pairs. As there are n parameters, a test case is a combination of values of these parameters and will cover $(n-1)+(n-2)+... = n(n-1)/2$ pairs. In the best case when each pair is covered exactly once by one test case, m^2 different test cases will be needed to cover all the pairs.

As an example, consider a software product being developed for multiple platforms that uses the browser as its interface. Suppose the software is being designed to work for three different operating systems and three different browsers. In addition, as the product is memory intensive there is a desire to test its performance under different levels of memory. So, we have the following three parameters with their different values:

```
Operating System: Windows, Solaris, Linux
Memory Size: 128M, 256M, 512M
Browser: IE, Netscape, Mozilla
```

For discussion, we can say that the system has three parameters: A (operating system), B (memory size), and C (browser). Each of them can have three values which we will refer to as a_1, a_2, a_3, b_1, b_2, b_3, and c_1, c_2, c_3. The total number of pairwise combinations is $9 * 3 = 27$. The number of test cases, however, to cover all the pairs is much less. A test case consisting of values of the three parameters covers three combinations (of A-B, B-C, and A-C). Hence, in the best case, we can cover all 27 combinations by $27/3=9$ test cases. These test cases are shown in Table 8.2, along with the pairs they cover.

Table 8.2: Test cases for pairwise testing.

A	B	C	Pairs
a1	b1	c1	(a1,b1) (a1,c1) (b1,c1)
a1	b2	c2	(a1,b2) (a1,c2) (b2,c2)
a1	b3	c3	(a1,b3) (a1,c3) (b3,c3)
a2	b1	c2	(a2,b1) (a2,c2) (b1,c2)
a2	b2	c3	(a2,b2) (a2,c3) (b2,c3)
a2	b3	c1	(a2,b3) (a2,c1) (b3,c1)
a3	b1	c3	(a3,b1) (a3,c3) (b1,c3)
a3	b2	c1	(a3,b2) (a3,c1) (b2,c1)
a3	b3	c2	(a3,b3) (a3,c2) (b3,c2)

As should be clear, generating test cases to cover all the pairs is not a simple task. The minimum set of test cases is that in which each pair is covered by exactly one test case. Often, it will not be possible to generate the minimum set of test cases, particularly when the number of values for different parameters is different. Various algorithms have been proposed, and some programs are available online to generate the test cases to cover all the pairs.

For situations where manual generation is feasible, the following approach can be followed. Start with initial test cases formed by all combinations of values for the two parameters which have the largest number of values (as we must have at least this many test cases to test all the pairs for these two parameters). Then complete each of these test cases by adding value for other parameters such that they add pairs that have not yet been covered by any test case. When all are completed, form additional test cases by combining as many uncovered pairs as possible. Essentially we are generating test cases such that a test case covers as many new pairs as possible. By avoiding covering pairs multiple times, we can produce a small set of test cases that cover all pairs. Efficient algorithms of generating the smallest number of test cases for pairwise testing exist. In [25] an example is given in which for 13 parameters, each having three distinct values, all pairs are covered in merely 15 test cases, while the total number of combinations is over 1 million!

Pairwise testing is a practical way of testing large software systems that have many different parameters with distinct functioning expected for different values. An example would be a billing system (for telephone, hotel, airline, etc.) which has different rates for different parameter values. It is also a practical approach for testing general-purpose software products that are expected to run on different platforms and configurations, or a system that is expected to work with different types of systems.

8.3.4 Special Cases

It has been seen that programs often produce incorrect behavior when inputs form some special cases. The reason is that in programs, some combinations of inputs need special treatment, and providing proper handling for these special cases is easily overlooked. For example, in an arithmetic routine, if there is a division and the divisor is zero, some special action has to be taken, which could easily be forgotten by the programmer. These special cases form particularly good test cases, which can reveal errors that will usually not be detected by other test cases.

Special cases will often depend on the data structures and the function of the module. There are no rules to determine special cases, and the tester has to use his intuition and experience to identify such test cases. Consequently, determining special cases is also called *error guessing*.

Psychology is particularly important for error guessing. The tester should play the "devil's advocate" and try to guess the incorrect assumptions the programmer could have made and the situations the programmer could have overlooked or handled incorrectly. Essentially, the tester is trying to identify error-prone situations. Then test cases are written for these situations. For example, in the problem of finding the number of different words in a file (discussed in earlier chapters) some of the special cases can be: file is empty, only one word in the file, only one word in a line, some empty lines in the input file, presence of more than one blank between words, all words are the same, the words are already sorted, and blanks at the start and end of the file.

Incorrect assumptions are usually made because the specifications are not complete or the writer of specifications may not have stated some properties, assuming them to be obvious. Whenever there is reliance on tacit understanding rather than explicit statement of specifications, there is scope for making wrong assumptions. Frequently, wrong assumptions are made about the environments. However, it should be pointed out that special cases depend heavily on the problem, and the tester should really try to "get into the shoes" of the designer and coder to determine these cases.

8.3.5 State-Based Testing

There are some systems that are essentially stateless in that for the same inputs they always give the same outputs or exhibit the same behavior. Many batch processing systems, computational systems, and servers fall in this category. In hardware, combinatorial circuits fall in this category. At a smaller level, most functions are supposed to behave in this manner. There are, however, many systems whose behavior is state-based in that for identical inputs they behave differently at different times and may produce different outputs. The reason for different behavior is that the state of the system may be different. In other words, the behavior and outputs of the system depend not only on the inputs provided, but also on the state of the system. The state of the system depends on the past inputs the system has received. In other words, the state represents the cumulative impact of all the past inputs on the system. In hardware, the sequential systems fall in this category. In software, many large systems fall in this category as past state is captured in databases or files and used to control the behavior of the system. For such systems, another approach for selecting test cases is the state-based testing approach [22].

Theoretically, any software that saves state can be modeled as a state machine. However, the state space of any reasonable program is almost infinite, as it is a cross product of the domains of all the variables that form the state. For many systems the state space can be partitioned into a few states, each representing a logical combination of values of different state variables which share some property of interest [9]. If the set of states of a system is manageable, a state model of the system can be built. A state model for a system has four components:

– *States.* Represent the impact of the past inputs to the system.

– *Transitions.* Represent how the state of the system changes from one state to another in response to some events.

– *Events.* Inputs to the system.

– *Actions.* The outputs for the events.

The state model shows what state transitions occur and what actions are performed in a system in response to events. When a state model is built from the requirements of a system, we can only include the states, transitions, and actions that are stated in the requirements or can be inferred from them. If more information is available from the design specifications, then a richer state model can be built.

For example, consider the student survey example discussed in Chapter 5. According to the requirements, a system is to be created for taking a student survey. The student takes a survey and is returned the current result of the survey. The survey result can be up to five surveys old. We consider the architecture which had a cache between the server and the database, and in which the survey and results are cached and updated only after five surveys, on arrival of a request. The proposed architecture has a database at the back, which may go down.

To create a state machine model of this system, we notice that of a series of 6 requests, the first 5 may be treated differently. Hence, we divide into two states: one representing the the receiving of $1 - 4$ requests (state 1), and the other representing the receiving of request 5 (state 2). Next we see that the database can be up or down, and it can go down in any of these two states. However, the behavior of requests, if the database is down, may be different. Hence, we create another pair of states (states 3 and 4). Once the database has failed, then the first 5 requests are serviced using old data. When a request is received after receiving 5 requests, the system enters a failed state (state 5), in which it does not give any response. When the system recovers from the failed state, it must update its cache immediately, hence goes to state 2. The state model for this system is shown in Figure 8.5 (i represents an input from the user for taking the survey).

Note that we are assuming that the state model of the system can be created from its specifications or design. This is how most state modeling is done, and that is how the model was built in the example. Once the state model is built, we can use it to select test cases. When the design is implemented, these test

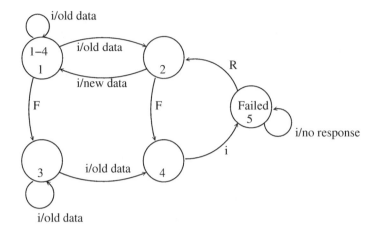

Figure 8.5: State model for the student survey system.

cases can be used for testing the code. It is because of this we treat state-based testing as a black box testing strategy.

However, the state model often requires information about the design of the system. In the example above, some knowledge of the architecture is utilized. Sometimes making the state model may require detailed information about the design of the system. For example, for a class, we have seen that the state modeling is done during design, and when a lot is already known about the class, its attributes, and its methods. Due to this, the state-based testing may be considered as somewhat between black-box and white-box testing. Such strategies are sometimes called *gray-box testing*.

Given a state model of a system, how should test cases be generated? Many coverage criteria have been proposed [69]. We discuss only a few here. Suppose the set of test cases is T. Some of the criteria are:

- **All transition coverage (AT).** T must ensure that every transition in the state graph is exercised.

- **All transitions pair coverage (ATP).** T must execute all pairs of adjacent transitions. (An adjacent transition pair comprises two transitions: an incoming transition to a state and an outgoing transition from that state.)

- **Transition tree coverage (TT).** T must execute all simple paths, where a simple path is one which starts from the start state and reaches a state that it has already visited in this path or a final state.

The first criterion states that during testing all transitions get fired. This will also ensure that all states are visited. The transition pair coverage is a stronger criterion requiring that all combinations of incoming and outgoing transitions for each state must be exercised by T. If a state has two incoming transitions t1 and t2, and two outgoing transitions t3 and t4, then a set of test cases T that executes t1;t3 and t2;t4 will satisfy AT. However, to satisfy ATP, T must also ensure execution of t1;t4 and t2;t3. The transition tree coverage is named in this manner as a transition tree can be constructed from the graph and then used to identify the paths. In ATP, we are going beyond transitions, and stating that different paths in the state diagram should be exercised during testing. ATP will generally include AT.

For the example above, the set of test cases for AT are given below in Table 8.3. Here req() means that a request for taking the survey should be given, fail() means that the database should be failed, and recover() means that the failed database should be recovered.

Table 8.3: Test cases for state-based testing criteria.

S.No.	Transition	Test case
1	$1 \to 2$	req()
2	$1 \to 2$	req();req();req();req();req();req()
3	$2 \to 1$	seq for 2; req()
4	$1 \to 3$	req();fail()
5	$3 \to 3$	req();fail();req()
6	$3 \to 4$	req();fail();req();req();req();req();req()
7	$4 \to 5$	seq for 6; req()
8	$5 \to 2$	seq for 6; req();recover()

As we can see, state-based testing draws attention to the states and transitions. Even in the above simple case, we can see different scenarios get tested (e.g., system behavior when the database fails, and system behavior when it fails and recovers thereafter). Many of these scenarios are easy to overlook if test cases are designed only by looking at the input domains. The set of test cases is richer if the other criteria are used. For this example, we leave it as an exercise to determine the test cases for other criteria.

8.4 White-Box Testing

In the previous section we discussed black-box testing, which is concerned with the function that the tested program is supposed to perform and does not deal with the internal structure of the program responsible for actually implementing that function. Thus, black-box testing is concerned with functionality rather than implementation of the program. White-box testing, on the other

hand, is concerned with testing the implementation of the program. The intent
of this testing is not to exercise all the different input or output conditions (although that may be a by-product) but to exercise the different programming
structures and data structures used in the program. White-box testing is also
called *structural testing*, and we will use the two terms interchangeably.

To test the structure of a program, structural testing aims to achieve test
cases that will force the desired coverage of different structures. Various criteria
have been proposed for this. Unlike the criteria for functional testing, which
are frequently imprecise, the criteria for structural testing are generally quite
precise as they are based on program structures, which are formal and precise.
Here we will discuss one approach to structural testing: control flow-based
testing, which is most commonly used in practice.

8.4.1 Control Flow-Based Criteria

Most common structure-based criteria are based on the control flow of the
program. In these criteria, the control flow graph of a program is considered
and coverage of various aspects of the graph are specified as criteria. Hence,
before we consider the criteria, let us precisely define a control flow graph for
a program.

Let the *control flow graph* (or simply *flow graph*) of a program P be G. A
node in this graph represents a block of statements that is always executed
together, i.e., whenever the first statement is executed, all other statements
are also executed. An edge (i, j) (from node i to node j) represents a possible
transfer of control after executing the last statement of the block represented
by node i to the first statement of the block represented by node j. A node
corresponding to a block whose first statement is the start statement of P is
called the *start* node of G, and a node corresponding to a block whose last
statement is an exit statement is called an *exit* node [73]. A *path* is a finite
sequence of nodes $(n_1, n_2, ..., n_k), k > 1$, such that there is an edge (n_i, n_{i+1})
for all nodes n_i in the sequence (except the last node n_k). A *complete path* is a
path whose first node is the start node and the last node is an exit node.

Now let us consider control flow-based criteria. Perhaps the simplest coverage criterion is *statement coverage*, which requires that each statement of the
program be executed at least once during testing. In other words, it requires
that the paths executed during testing include all the nodes in the graph. This
is also called the *all-nodes* criterion [73].

This coverage criterion is not very strong, and can leave errors undetected.
For example, if there is an `if` statement in the program without having an `else`
clause, the statement coverage criterion for this statement will be satisfied by a

test case that evaluates the condition to true. No test case is needed that ensures that the condition in the `if` statement evaluates to false. This is a serious shortcoming because decisions in programs are potential sources of errors. As an example, consider the following function to compute the absolute value of a number:

```
int abs (x)
int x;
{
        if (x >= 0) x = 0 - x;
        return (x)
}
```

This program is clearly wrong. Suppose we execute the function with the set of test cases { x=0 } (i.e., the set has only one test case). The statement coverage criterion will be satisfied by testing with this set, but the error will not be revealed.

A more general coverage criterion is *branch coverage*, which requires that each edge in the control flow graph be traversed at least once during testing. In other words, branch coverage requires that each decision in the program be evaluated to true and false values at least once during testing. Testing based on branch coverage is often called *branch testing*. The 100% branch coverage criterion is also called the *all-edges* criterion [73]. Branch coverage implies statement coverage, as each statement is a part of some branch. In the preceding example, a set of test cases satisfying this criterion will detect the error.

The trouble with branch coverage comes if a decision has many conditions in it (consisting of a Boolean expression with Boolean operators *and* and *or*). In such situations, a decision can evaluate to true and false without actually exercising all the conditions. For example, consider the following function that checks the validity of a data item. The data item is valid if it lies between 0 and 100.

```
int check(x)
int x;
{
        if ((x >= ) && (x <= 200))
                check = True;
        else check = False;
}
```

The module is incorrect, as it is checking for $x \leq 200$ instead of 100 (perhaps a typing error made by the programmer). Suppose the module is tested with the following set of test cases: { $x = 5$, $x = $ -5 }. The branch coverage criterion will be satisfied for this module by this set. However, the error will not be revealed, and the behavior of the module is consistent with its specifications for all test cases in this set. Thus, the coverage criterion is satisfied, but the error is not detected. This occurs because the decision is evaluating to true and false because of the condition ($x \geq 0$). The condition ($x \leq 200$) never evaluates to false during this test, hence the error in this condition is not revealed.

This problem can be resolved by requiring that all conditions evaluate to true and false. However, situations can occur where a decision may not get both true and false values even if each individual condition evaluates to true and false. An obvious solution to this problem is to require decision/condition coverage, where all the decisions and all the conditions in the decisions take both true and false values during the course of testing.

Studies have indicated that there are many errors whose presence is not detected by branch testing because some errors are related to some combinations of branches and their presence is revealed by an execution that follows the path that includes those branches. Hence, a more general coverage criterion is one that requires all possible paths in the control flow graph be executed during testing. This is called the *path coverage* criterion or the *all-paths* criterion, and the testing based on this criterion is often called *path testing*. The difficulty with this criterion is that programs that contain loops can have an infinite number of possible paths. Furthermore, not all paths in a graph may be "feasible" in the sense that there may not be any inputs for which the path can be executed.

As the path coverage criterion leads to a potentially infinite number of paths, some efforts have been made to suggest criteria between the branch coverage and path coverage. The basic aim of these approaches is to select a set of paths that ensure branch coverage criterion and try some other paths that may help reveal errors. One method to limit the number of paths is to consider two paths the same if they differ only in their subpaths that are caused due to the loops. Even with this restriction, the number of paths can be extremely large.

It should be pointed out that none of these criteria is sufficient to detect all kind of errors in programs. For example, if a program is missing some control flow paths that are needed to check for a special value (like pointer equals nil and divisor equals zero), then even executing all the paths will not necessarily detect the error. Similarly, if the set of paths is such that they satisfy the all-path criterion but exercise only one part of a compound condition, then the set will not reveal any error in the part of the condition that is not exercised.

Hence, even the path coverage criterion, which is the strongest of the criteria we have discussed, is not strong enough to guarantee detection of all the errors.

8.4.2 Test Case Generation and Tool Support

Once a coverage criterion is decided, two problems have to be solved to use the chosen criterion for testing. The first is to decide if a set of test cases satisfy the criterion, and the second is to generate a set of test cases for a given criterion. Deciding whether a set of test cases satisfy a criterion without the aid of any tools is a cumbersome task, though it is theoretically possible to do manually. For almost all the structural testing techniques, tools are used to determine whether the criterion has been satisfied. Generally, these tools will provide feedback regarding what needs to be tested to fully satisfy the criterion.

To generate the test cases, tools are not that easily available, and due to the nature of the problem (i.e., undecidability of "feasibility" of a path), a fully automated tool for selecting test cases to satisfy a criterion is generally not possible. Hence, tools can, at best, aid the tester. One method for generating test cases is to randomly select test data until the desired criterion is satisfied (which is determined by a tool). This can result in a lot of redundant test cases, as many test cases will exercise the same paths.

As test case generation cannot be fully automated, frequently the test case selection is done manually by the tester by performing structural testing in an iterative manner, starting with an initial test case set and selecting more test cases based on the feedback provided by the tool for test case evaluation. The test case evaluation tool can tell which paths need to be executed or which mutants need to be killed. This information can be used to select further test cases.

Even with the aid of tools, selecting test cases is not a simple process. Selecting test cases to execute some parts of as yet unexecuted code is often very difficult. Because of this, and for other reasons, the criteria are often weakened. For example, instead of requiring 100% coverage of statements and branches, the goal might be to achieve some acceptably high percentage (but less than 100%).

There are many tools available for statement and branch coverage, the criteria that are used most often. Both commercial and freeware tools are available for different source languages. These tools often also give higher-level coverage data like function coverage, method coverage, and class coverage. To get the coverage data, the execution of the program during testing has to be closely monitored. This requires that the program be instrumented so that required data can be collected. A common method of instrumenting is to insert some statements called *probes* in the program. The sole purpose of the probes is to generate data about program execution during testing that can be used to compute the coverage. With this, we can identify three phases in generating coverage data:

1. Instrument the program with probes

2. Execute the program with test cases

3. Analyze the results of the probe data

Probe insertion can be done automatically by a *preprocessor*. The execution of the program is done by the tester. After testing, the coverage data is displayed by the tool—sometimes graphical representations are also shown.

8.5 Metrics

We have seen that during testing the software under test is executed with a set of test cases. As the quality of delivered software depends substantially on the quality of testing, a few natural questions arise while testing:

− How good is the testing that has been done?

− What is the quality or reliability of software after testing is completed?

During testing, the primary purpose of metrics is to try to answer these and other related questions. We will discuss some metrics that may be used for this purpose.

8.5.1 Coverage Analysis

One of the most commonly used approaches for evaluating the thoroughness of testing is to use some coverage measures. We have discussed above some of the common coverage measures that are used in practice—statement coverage and branch coverage. To use these coverage measures for evaluating the quality of testing, proper coverage analysis tools will have to be employed which can inform not only the coverage achieved during testing but also which portions are not yet covered.

Often, organizations build guidelines for the level of coverage that must be achieved during testing. Generally, the coverage requirement will be higher for unit testing, but lower for system testing as it is much more difficult to ensure execution of identified blocks when the entire system is being executed. Often the coverage requirement at unit level can be 90% to 100% (keep in mind that 100% may not be always possible as there may be unreachable code).

Besides the coverage of program constructs, coverage of requirements is also often examined. It is for facilitating this evaluation that in test case specification the requirement or condition being tested is mentioned. This coverage is generally established by evaluating the set of test cases to ensure that sufficient number of test cases with suitable data are included for all the requirements. The coverage measure here is the percentage of requirements or their clauses/-conditions for which at least one test case exists. Often a full coverage may be required at requirement level before testing is considered as acceptable.

8.5.2 Reliability

After testing is done and the software is delivered, the development is considered over. It will clearly be desirable to know, in quantifiable terms, the reliability of the software being delivered. As reliability of software depends considerably on the quality of testing, by assessing reliability we can also judge the quality of testing. Alternatively, reliability estimation can be used to decide whether enough testing has been done. In other words, besides characterizing an important quality property of the product being delivered, reliability estimation has a direct role in project management—it can be used by the project manager to decide whether enough testing has been done and when to stop testing.

Reliability of a product specifies the probability of failure-free operation of that product for a given time duration. Most reliability models require that the occurrence of failure be a random phenomenon. In software even though failures occur due to preexisting bugs, this assumption will generally hold for larger systems, but may not hold for small programs that have bugs (in which case one might be able to predict the failures). Hence, reliability modeling is more meaningful for larger systems.

Let X be the random variable that represents the life of a system. Reliability of a system is the probability that the system has not failed by time t. In other words,

$$R(t) = P(X > t).$$

The reliability of a system can also be specified as the *mean time to failure* (MTTF). MTTF represents the expected lifetime of the system. From the reliability function, it can be obtained as [80]

$$MTTF = \int_0^\infty R(x)dx.$$

Reliability can also be defined in terms of failure intensity which is the failure rate (i.e., number of failures per unit time) of the software at time t.

From the measurement perspective, during testing, measuring failure rate is the easiest, if defects are being logged. A simple way to do this is to compute the number of failures every week or every day during the last stages of testing. And number of failures can be approximated by the number of defects logged. (Though failures and defects are different, in the last stages of testing it is assumed that defects that cause failures are fixed soon enough and therefore do not cause multiple failures.) Generally, this failure rate increases in the start of testing as more and more defects are found, peaks somewhere in the middle of testing, and then continues to drop as fewer defects are reported. For a given test suite, if all defects are fixed, then there should be almost no failures toward the end. And that could be considered as proper time for release of this software. That is, a release criterion could be that the failure rate at release time is zero failures in some time duration, or zero failures while executing a test suite.

Though failure rate tracking gives a rough sense of reliability in terms of failures per day or per week, for more accurate reliability estimation, better models have to be used. Software reliability modeling is a complex task, requiring rigorous models and sophisticated statistical analysis. Many models have been proposed for software reliability assessment, and a survey of many of the models is given in [33, 67].

It should be mentioned that as failure of software also depends critically on the environment in which it is executing, failure rates experienced in testing will reflect the ultimate reliability experienced by the user after software release only if testing closely mimics the user behavior. This may not be the case, particularly with lower levels of testing. However, often at higher levels, active effort is made to have the final test suite mimic the actual usage. If this is the case, then reliability estimation can be applied with a higher confidence.

8.5.3 Defect Removal Efficiency

Another analysis of interest is *defect removal efficiency*, though this can only be determined sometime after the software has been released. The purpose of this analysis is to evaluate the effectiveness of the testing process being employed, not the quality of testing for a project. This analysis is useful for improving the testing process in the future.

Usually, after the software has been released to the client, the client will find defects, which have to be fixed (generally by the original developer, as this is often part of the contract). This defect data is also generally logged. Within a few months, most of the defects would be uncovered by the client (often the "warranty" period is 3 to 6 months).

Once the total number of defects (or a close approximation to the total) is known, the *defect removal efficiency* (DRE) of testing can be computed. The defect removal efficiency of a quality control activity is defined as the percentage reduction in the number of defects by executing that activity [61]. As an example, suppose the total number of defects logged is 500, out of which 20 were found after delivery, and 200 were found during the system testing. The defect removal efficiency of system testing is 200/220 (just about 90%), as the total number of defects present in the system when testing started was 220. The defect removal efficiency of the overall quality process is 480/500, which is 96%. Incidentally, this level of DRE is decent and is what many commercial organizations achieve.

It should be clear that DRE is a general concept which can be applied to any defect removal activity. For example, we can compute the DRE of design review, or unit testing. This can be done if for each defect, besides logging when and where the defect is found, the phase in which the defect was introduced is also analyzed and logged. With this information, when all the defects are logged, the DRE of the main quality control tasks can be determined. This information is extremely useful in improving the overall quality process.

8.6 Summary

– Testing is a dynamic method for verification and validation, where the software to be tested is executed with carefully designed test cases and the behavior of the software system is observed. A test case is a set of inputs and test conditions along with the expected outcome of testing. A test suite is a set of test cases that are generally executed together to test some specific behavior. During testing only the failures of the system are observed, from which the presence of faults is deduced; separate activities have to be performed to identify the faults and remove them.

– The intent of testing is to increase confidence in the correctness of the software. For this, the set of test cases used for testing should be such that for any defect in the system, there is likely to be a test case that will reveal it. To ensure this, it is important that the test cases are carefully designed with the intent of revealing defects.

– Due to the limitations of the verification methods for early phases, design and requirement faults also appear in the code. Testing is used to detect these errors also, in addition to the errors introduced during the coding phase. Hence, different levels of testing are often used for detecting defects injected during different stages. The commonly employed testing levels are unit testing, integration testing, system testing, and acceptance testing.

- For testing a software product, overall testing should be planned, and for testing each unit identified in the plan, test cases should be carefully designed to reveal errors and specified in a document or a test script.

- There are two approaches for designing test cases: black-box and white-box. In black-box testing, the internal logic of the system under testing is not considered and the test cases are decided from the specifications or the requirements. Equivalence class partitioning, boundary value analysis, and cause-effect graphing are examples of methods for selecting test cases for black-box testing. State-based testing is another approach in which the system is modeled as a state machine and then this model is used to select test cases using some transition or path-based coverage criteria. State-based testing can also be viewed as gray-box testing in that it often requires more information than just the requirements.

- In white-box testing, the test cases are decided based on the internal logic of the program being tested. Often a criterion is specified, but the procedure for selecting test cases to satisfy the criteria is left to the tester. The most common criteria are statement coverage and branch coverage.

- The main metric of interest during testing is the reliability of the software under testing. If defects are being logged, reliability can be assessed in terms of failure rate per week or day, though better models for estimation exist. Coverage achieved during testing, and defect removal efficiency, are other metrics of interest.

Self-Assessment Exercises

1. Define fault, error, and failure.
2. Suppose you have to test a procedure that takes two input parameters, does some computation with them, and then manipulates a global table, the manipulation itself depending on the state of the table. What will the complete specification of a test case for this procedure contain?
3. What are the different levels of testing and the goals of the different levels?
4. Suppose for logging defects, each defect will be treated as an object of a class Defect. Give the definition of this class.
5. Suppose a software has three inputs, each having a defined valid range. How many test cases will you need to test all the boundary values?

6. For boundary value analysis, if the strategy for generating test cases is to consider all possible combinations for the different values, what will be the set of test cases for a software that has three inputs X, Y, and Z?

7. Suppose a software has five different configuration variables that are set independently. If three of them are binary (have two possible values), and the rest have three values, how many test cases will be needed if pairwise testing method is used?

8. Consider a vending machine that takes quarters and when it has received two quarters, gives a can of soda. Develop a state model of this system, and then generate sets of test cases for the various criteria.

9. Consider a simple text formatter problem. Given a text consisting of words separated by blanks (BL) or newline (NL) characters, the text formatter has to covert it into lines, so that no line has more than MAXPOS characters, breaks between lines occur at BL or NL, and the maximum possible number of words are in each line. The following program has been written for this text formatter [41]:

```
alarm := false;
bufpos := 0;
fill := 0;
repeat
    inchar(c);
    if (c = BL) or (c = NL) or (c = EOF)
    then
        if bufpos != 0
        then begin
            if (fill + bufpos < MAXPOS) and (fill != 0)
            then begin
                outchar(BL);
                fill := fill + 1; end
            else begin
                outchar(NL);
                fill := 0; end;
            for k:=1 to bufpos do
                outchar(buffer[k]);
            fill := fill + bufpos;
            bufpos := 0; end
        else
            if bufpos = MAXPOS
            then alarm := true
            else begin
                bufpos := bufpos + 1;
                buffer[bufpos] := c; end
until alarm or (c = EOF);
```

For this program, do the following:

a) Select a set of test cases using the black-box testing approach. Use as many techniques as possible and select test cases for special cases using the "error guessing" method.

b) Select a set of test cases that will provide 100% branch coverage.

10. Suppose that the last round of testing, in which all the test suites were executed but no faults were fixed, took 7 full days (24 hours each). And in this testing, the number of failures that were logged every day were: 2, 0, 1, 2, 1, 1, 0. If it is expected that an average user will use the software for two hours each day in a manner that is similar to what was done in testing, what is the expected reliability of this software for the user?

Bibliography

[1] F. B. Abreu and R. Carapuca. Candidate metrics for object-oriented software wihin a taxonomy framework. *Journal of Systems and Software*, 26(1):87–96, Jan. 1994.

[2] V. R. Basili. *Tutorial on models and metrics for software management and engineering*. IEEE Press, 1980.

[3] V. R. Basili, L. Briand, and W. L. Melo. A validation of object-oriented design metrics as quality indicators. *IEEE Transactions on Software Engineering*, 22(10):751–761, Oct. 1996.

[4] V. R. Basili and A. Turner. Iterative enhancement, a practical technique for software development. *IEEE Transactions on Software Engineering*, SE-1(4), Dec. 1975.

[5] V. R. Basili and D. M. Weiss. Evaluation of a software requirements document by analysis of change data. In *5th Int. Conf. on Software Engineering*, pages 314–323. IEEE, 1981.

[6] L. Bass, P. Clements, and Rick Kazman. *Software Architecture in Practice, Second Edition*. Addison-Wesley Professional, 2003.

[7] K. Beck. *Extreme Programming Explained*. Addison-Wesley, 2000.

[8] K. Beck. *Test Driven Development: by Example*. Addison-Wesley Professional, 2002.

[9] R.V. Binder. *Testing Object-Oriented Systems—Model, Patterns, and Tools*. Addison-Wesley, 1999.

[10] B. Boehm. Software engineering. *IEEE Transactions on Computers*, 25(12), Dec. 1976.

[11] B. Boehm. *Tutorial: software risk management*. IEEE Computer Society, 1989.

[12] B. W. Boehm. *Software Engineering Economics*. Prentice Hall, Englewood Cliffs, NJ, 1981.

[13] B. W. Boehm. Software engineering economics. *IEEE Transactions on Software Engineering*, 10(1):135–152, Jan. 1984.

[14] B. W. Boehm. Improving software productivity. *IEEE Computer*, pages 43–57, Sept. 1987.

[15] G. Booch. *Object-Oriented Analysis and Design*. The Benjamin/Cummings Publishing Company, 1994.

[16] F. Brooks. *The Mytical Man Month*. Addison-Wesley, 1975.

[17] N. Brown. Industrial-strength management strategies. *IEEE Software*, July 1996.

[18] R.N. Charette. *Software Engineering Risk Analysis and Management*. McGraw Hill, 1989.

[19] R.N. Charette. Large-scale project management is risk management. *IEEE Software*, July 1996.

[20] E. Chen. Program complexity and programmer productivity. *IEEE Transactions on Software Engineering*, SE-4:187–194, May 1978.

[21] S. R. Chidamber and C. F. Kemerer. A metrics suite for object-oriented design. *IEEE Transactions on Software Engineering*, 20(6):476–493, June 1994.

[22] T.S. Chow. Testing software design modeled by finite state machines. *IEEE Transactions on Software Engineering*, SE-4(3):178–187, 1978.

[23] P. Clements, F. Bachmann, L. Bass, D. Garlan, J. Ivers, R. Little, R. Nord, and J. Stafford. *Documenting Software Architectures: Views and Beyond*. Addison-Wesley, 2003.

[24] A. Cockburn. *Writing Effective Use Cases*. Addison-Wesley, 2001.

[25] D.M. Cohen, S.R. Dalal, M.L. Fredman, and G.C. Patton. The AETG system: An approach to testing based on combinatorial design. *IEEE Transactions on Software Engineering*, 23(7):437–443, 1997.

[26] S. D. Conte, H. E. Dunsmore, and V. Y. Shen. *Software Engineering Metrics and Models*. The Benjamin/Cummings Publishing Company, 1986.

[27] J. S. Davis. Identification of errors in software requirements through use of automated requirements tools. *Information and Software Technology*, 31(9):472–476, Nov. 1989.

[28] T. DeMarco. *Structured Analysis and System Specification.* Yourdon Press, 1979.

[29] L. Dobrica and E. Niemela. A survey on software architecture analysis methods. *IEEE Transactions on Software Engineering*, 28(7):638–653, 2002.

[30] J. Eder, G. Kappel, and M. Schrefl. Coupling and cohesion in object-oriented systems. Technical report, University of Klagenfurt, 1994.

[31] M. E. Fagan. Design and code inspections to reduce errors in program development. *IBM System Journal*, (3):182–211, 1976.

[32] M. E. Fagan. Advances in software inspections. *IEEE Transactions on Software Engineering*, 12(7):744–751, July 1986.

[33] W. Farr. Software reliability modeling survey. In M. R. Lyu, editor, *Software Reliability Engineering*, pages 71–117. McGraw Hill and IEEE Computer Society, 1996.

[34] S. I. Feldman. Make—a program for maintaining computer programs. *Software Practice and Experience*, 9(3):255–265, March 1979.

[35] M. Fowler. *UML Distilled—A Brief Guide to the Standard Object Modeling Language.* Addison-Wesley Professional, 2003.

[36] M. Fowler, K. Beck, J. Brant, W. Opdyke, and D. Roberts. *Refactoring: Improving the Design of Existing Code.* Addison-Wesley, 1999.

[37] D. P. Freedman and G. M. Weinberg. *Handbook of Walkthroughs, Inspections, and Technical Reviews—Evaluating Programs, Projects, and Products.* Dorset House, 1990.

[38] E. Gamma, R. Helm, R. Johnson, and J. Vlissides. *Design Patterns—Elements of Reusable Object-Oriented Software.* Addison-Wesley Professional, 1995.

[39] T. Gilb and D. Graham. *Software Inspection.* Addison-Wesley, 1993.

[40] H. Gomma and D. B. H. Scott. Prototyping as a tool in the specification of user requirements. In *Fifth Int. Conf. on Software Engineering*, pages 333–341, 1981.

[41] J. Goodenough and S. L. Gerhart. Towards a theory of test data selection. *IEEE Transactions on Software Engineering*, SE-1:156–173, 1975.

[42] S. E. Goodman and S. T. Hedetniemi. *Introduction to the Design and Analysis of Algorithms.* McGraw-Hill, 1977.

[43] R. Grady and D. Caswell. *Software Metrics: Establishing a Company-wide Program.* Prentice Hall, 1987.

[44] R. B. Grady and T. V. Slack. Key lessons learned in achieving widespread inspection use. *IEEE Software*, pages 48–57, July 1994.

[45] E.M. Hall. *Managing Risk: Methods for Software Development and Enhancement.* Addison-Wesley, 1998.

[46] M. Halstead. *Elements of Software Science.* Elsevier North-Holland, 1977.

[47] W. Harrison, K. Magel, R. Kluczny, and A. DeKock. Applying software complexity metrics to program maintenance. *IEEE Computer*, pages 65–79, Sept. 1982.

[48] S. Henry and D. Kafura. Software structure metrics based on information flow. *IEEE Transactions on Software Engineering*, 7(5):510–518, 1981.

[49] S. Henry and D. Kafura. The evaluation of software systems' structures using quantitative software metrics. *Software Practice and Experience*, 14(6):561–573, June 1984.

[50] C. A. R. Hoare. An axiomatic basis for computer programming. *Communications of the ACM*, 12(3):335–355, 1969.

[51] IBM-Rational. Rational unified process best practices for software development teams. Technical report, IBMwebsite, 1993.

[52] IEEE. IEEE standard glossary of software engineering terminology. Technical report, 1990.

[53] IEEE. IEEE recommended practice for software requirements specifications. Technical report, 1998.

[54] IEEE. IEEE recommended practice for architectural description of software-intensive systems. Technical Report 1471-2000, 2000.

[55] International Standards Organization. Software engineering—product quality. part 1: Quality model. Technical Report ISO9126-1, 2001.

[56] I. Jacobson. *Object-oriented Software Engineering—A Use Case Driven Approach.* Addison-Wesley, 1992.

[57] P. Jalote. *CMM in Practice—Processes for Executing Software Projects at Infosys.* Addison-Wesley, 1999.

[58] P. Jalote. *Software Project Management in Practice.* Addison-Wesley, 2002.

[59] P. Jalote, A. Palit, and P. Kurien. The timeboxing process model for iterative software development. In *Advances in Computers, Vol. 62*, pages 67–103. Academic Press, 2004.

[60] P. Jalote, A. Palit, P. Kurien, and V. T. Peethamber. Timeboxing: A process model for iterative software development. *The Journal of Systems and Software*, 70:117–127.

[61] S.H. Kan. *Metrics and Models in Software Quality Engineering*. Addison-Wesley, 1995.

[62] T. Korson and J. D. Gregor. Understanding object-oriented: A unifying paradigm. *Communications of the ACM*, 33(9):40–60, Sept. 1990.

[63] P. Kruchten. *The Rational Unified Process*. Addison-Wesley, 1999.

[64] W. Lie and S. Henry. Object-oriented metrics that predict maintainability. *Journal of Systems and Software*, 23(2):111–122, 1993.

[65] B. Liskov. Data abstraction and hierarchy. *SIGPLAN Notices*, 23(5), May 1988.

[66] B. Meyer. *Object Oriented Software Construction*. Prentice Hall, 1988.

[67] J. D. Musa, A. Iannino, and K. Okumoto. *Software Reliability—Measurement, Prediction, Application*. McGraw Hill, 1987.

[68] G. Myers. *The Art of Software Testing*. Wiley-Interscience, New York, 1979.

[69] J. Offutt, S. Liu, A. Abdurazik, and P. Ammann. Generating test data from state-based specifications. *The Journal of Software Testing, Verification, and Reliability*, 13(1):25–53, March 2003.

[70] M.S. Phadke. Planning efficient software tests. *Crosstalk*, Oct 1997.

[71] L. H. Putnam. A general empirical solution to the macro software sizing and estimation problem. *IEEE Transactions on Software Engineering*, SE-4:345–361, July 1978.

[72] L. H. Putnam and W. Myers. *Industrial Strength Software: Effective Management Using Measurement*. IEEE Computer Society, 1997.

[73] S. Rapps and E. J. Weyuker. Selecting software test data using data flow information. *IEEE Transactions on Software Engineering*, 11(4):367–375, Apr. 1985.

[74] W. W. Royce. Managing the development of large software systems. In *Proc. 9th Int. Conf. on Software Engineering (ICSE-9); originally in IEEE Wescon, Aug 1970*, pages 328–338. IEEE, 1987.

[75] SEI (Software Engineering Institute). *The Capability Maturity Model: Guidelines for Improving the Software Process.* Addison-Wesley, 1995.

[76] M. Shaw and D. Garlan. *Software Architecture: Perspectives on an Emerging Discipline.* Prentice Hall, 1996.

[77] M. D. Smith and D. J. Robson. Object oriented programming: The problems of validation. *Proc. of 6th Int. IEEE Conference on Software Maintenance*, pages 272–282, Nov. 1990.

[78] M. D. Smith and D. J. Robson. A framework for testing object-oriented programs. *Journal of Object-Oriented Programming*, pages 45–53, June 1992.

[79] W. P. Stevens, G. J. Myers, and L. Constantine. Structured design. *IBM Systems Journal*, 13(2), 1974.

[80] K. S. Trivedi. *Probability and Statistics with Reliability, Queuing, and Computer Science Applications, Second Edition.* Wiley-Interscience, 2002.

[81] C. Watson and C. Felix. A method of programming measurement and estimation. *IBM Systems Journal*, 16(1), Jan. 1977.

[82] G. M. Weinberg and E. L. Schulman. Goals and performance in computer programming. *Human Factors*, 16(1):70–77, 1974.

[83] E. F. Weller. Lessons learned from three years of inspection data. *IEEE Software*, pages 38–53, Sept. 1993.

[84] N. Wirth. Program development by stepwise refinement. *Communications of the ACM*, 14(4):221–227, April 1971.

[85] M. Woodward, M. Hennell, and D. Hedley. A measure of control flow complexity in program text. *IEEE Transactions on Software Engineering*, SE-5:45–50, Jan. 1979.

[86] R. T. Yeh and P. Zave. Specifying software requirements. *Proceedings of the IEEE*, 68(9):1077–1088, Sept. 1980.

[87] B. H. Yin and J. W. Winchester. The establishment and use of measures to evaluate the quality of designs. *Software Engineering Notes*, 3:45–52, 1978.

[88] E. Yourdon and L. Constantine. *Structured Design.* Prentice Hall, 1979.

[89] W. M. Zage and D. M. Zage. Evaluating design metrics on large-scale software. *IEEE Software*, pages 75–81, July 1993.

Index

PrintedintheUnitedStates